Acclaim for *Does the Soul Survive?*

"Rabbi Spitz has taken a fascinating journey from skepticism to hope. No matter our ultimate conclusion, this record of that journey is certain to tantalize, intrigue and uplift the questing spirit."

—**Rabbi David Wolpe,** Sinai Temple, Los Angeles; author of *Making Loss Matter: Creating Meaning in Difficult Times*

"Beautiful.... Intelligent, deeply grounded in the classical sources and, most importantly, tinged with the kind of warmth and wisdom that make a great book. This book can change the way you understand your place in the universe."

—**Rabbi Marc Gafni,** philosopher; author of *Soul Prints, Certainty, Uncertainty*; Fellow, Hartman Institute, Jerusalem

"Elie Spitz provides a map for some very tricky territory. With admirable candor and real openness of heart, he leads his readers through contemporary and traditional views of the soul, its nature and purposes.... He is clear without being simplistic, inspiring without beating a drum for his views. I know of no book on the soul which so seamlessly blends the personal and the scholarly. Rabbi Spitz brings to this subject a passion and clarity which will engage and enlighten his readers."

—**Peter Pitzele, Ph.D.,** author of *Our Fathers' Wells: A Personal Encounter with the Myths of Genesis*

"In *Does the Soul Survive?* Rabbi Spitz allows all of us to take that same journey of soul: to be able to look without fear through the healing lens of faith at what it means to be alive, what it means to be human, what it means to be God's child. Anyone who reads this book will find it, as I did, uplifting, insightful and profoundly true. It transforms all our lives for the better."

—**Rabbi Bradley Shavit Artson,** Dean, Ziegler School of Rabbinic Studies, University of Judaism; author of *It's a Mitzvah! Step-by-Step to Jewish Learning*

"Whether or not we believe, having the conversation about the continued existence of the soul contributes to the healing. Opening to the possibility that there is more than a rigid and unpenetrable curtain between the worlds allows us to approach loss with questions. These call forth creative possibilities for continuing our connection with those we have lost."

> —**Anne Brener,** internationally recognized bereavement therapist; author of *Mourning & Mitzvah: A Guided Journey to Walking the Mourner's Path Through Grief to Healing* (Jewish Lights)

"A path-breaking book. When Elie Spitz writes about Judaism and reincarnation, he not only examines relevant texts drawn from two thousand years of teaching, he integrates them with his own remarkable experiences. This is a book that has the capacity to expand your soul."

> —**Joseph Telushkin,** author of *Jewish Literacy* and other works

"Elie Spitz's personal quest for an understanding of the soul and afterlife benefits all who read this remarkable book. In the tradition of Dr. Brian Weiss, he brings credibility and a religious context to belief in reincarnation. Even the skeptic will be swayed by Rabbi Spitz's personal experiences."

> —**Rabbi Stewart Vogel,** co-author of the *New York Times* bestseller *The Ten Commandments*

"Rabbi Elie Spitz masterfully blends scholarship, inspiration and information.... His courageous, heartfelt journey into unknown territory will most assuredly survive with his soul."

> —**Nancy Rosanoff,** author of *Knowing When It's Right*

DOES THE SOUL SURVIVE?

DOES THE SOUL SURVIVE?

A Jewish Journey to Belief in

Afterlife, Past Lives & Living with Purpose

RABBI ELIE KAPLAN SPITZ

foreword by
BRIAN L. WEISS, M.D.

For People of All Faiths, All Backgrounds
JEWISH LIGHTS Publishing
Woodstock, Vermont

Does the Soul Survive?
A Jewish Journey to Belief in Afterlife, Past Lives & Living with Purpose

2001 First Quality Paperback Edition
2001 Second Hardcover Printing
© 2000 by Elie Kaplan Spitz

Grateful acknowledgment is given for permission to use material from the following sources: From *Jewish Views of the Afterlife* by Simcha Paull Raphael, © 1994 and *Spiritual Intimacy: A Study of Counseling in Hasidism* by Zalman Meshullam Schachter-Shalomi, © 1991, used by permission of the publisher, Jason Aronson, Inc., Northvale, N.J. From *Many Lives, Many Masters* by Brian L. Weiss, M.D., reprinted with the permission of Simon & Schuster. Copyright © 1988 by Brian L. Weiss, M.D.

Library of Congress Cataloging-in-Publication Data

Spitz, Elie Kaplan, 1954–
Does the soul survive? : a Jewish journey to belief in afterlife, past lives and living with purpose / Elie Kaplan Spitz.
    p. cm.
Includes bibliographical references.
ISBN 1-58023-094-6 (hc.)
1. Transmigration—Judaism. 2. Soul (Judaism). I. Title.
BM635.7 .S65 2000
296.3'3-dc21   00-009624

ISBN 1-58023-165-9 (pbk.)

10   9   8   7   6   5   4   3   2   1

Manufactured in the United States of America

For People of All Faiths, All Backgrounds
Published by Jewish Lights Publishing
A Division of LongHill Partners, Inc.
Sunset Farm Offices, Route 4, P.O. Box 237
Woodstock, VT 05091
Tel: (802) 457-4000   Fax: (802) 457-4004
www.jewishlights.com

This book is indebted to the source of Creation, with gratitude for the many blessings of life, including the following of God's partners:

שהחינו—"That enlivened me"—To my parents, Heddy and Arthur Spitz, who gave me an abiding feeling of love and modeled affirmation of life.

וקימנו—"That grounded me"—To my wife, Linda Kaplan Spitz, my beloved companion who supports and guides my life journey, and to our children, Joseph Ephraim, Jonathan Tamir, and Anna Rose Miriam, who nurture us, keep us humble, and provide deep joy.

והגיענו לזמן הזה—"And that enabled me to reach this moment"—To my many mentors, including Professor Ze'ev Falk, a model of piety who encouraged me to write; and Marielle Fuller, an artist of the imagination who enables me to trustingly go inward.

Contents

Foreword

Brian L. Weiss, M.D.

I am, on the one hand, a well-known psychiatrist who has studied more than 2,000 patients over the past twenty years, patients who have remembered details of prior lifetimes and whose clinical symptoms have often dramatically resolved because of these memories. I have written four best-selling books based on my patients' experiences, and these books have been translated into more than thirty languages, including Hebrew.

I am, on the other hand, a Jew, taught in a Conservative synagogue in New Jersey. In my Jewish training, I was never introduced to the doctrines of reincarnation and soul survival after physical death. The vast majority of Jews in the United States knows nothing about the existence of these doctrines in mystical Jewish literature, or they are just now beginning to suspect that there is far more to Judaism than meets the eye.

Recently, I took part in a live video conference via satellite that linked up me, alone in a studio in Miami, to very large audiences in Jewish Community Centers in Detroit and Philadelphia. Two Orthodox rabbis hosted the events in the other cities, and we engaged in a spiritual dialogue about reincarnation in Judaism, the clinical and religious perspectives.

The rabbis and I agreed. We were on the same page. The rich tradition of *gilgul,* or reincarnation, in Judaism was presented and was in general harmony with my detailed clinical investigations.

Many Jews in the two audiences had their private beliefs in soul survival and reincarnation validated. At the least, they understood that the concepts were acceptable and open to serious discussion.

My secret wish was that everyone in the audience had a copy of this new and wonderful book by Rabbi Elie Spitz. *Does the Soul Survive?* is at once authoritative, accessible, and inspiring. It is for lay Jews and for Jewish scholars. It is the missing link, because until now we have been lacking a book that ties these concepts together and presents them in such a clean and understandable way to the twenty-first-century Jew.

I cannot tell you how many times other Jews have come up to me at seminars or conferences and have told me how comforting and valuable my work and books have been to them, but they had one problem: their religion did not accept these beliefs.

Finally I have a simple, yet complete response. Go read Rabbi Spitz's book, you will find a whole new world. And it's a most enjoyable book at that.

Acknowledgments

The first draft of this book was written during a sabbatical in Jerusalem. I thank the board and members of Congregation B'nai Israel of Tustin, California, who with generosity and wisdom enabled my family and me to spend the academic year of 1997–1998 in Israel. The staff of Beit Sefer Keshet provided a creative, caring school environment for our sons. I am also indebted to the Shalom Hartman Institute for opening its doors to me for engaging seminars and a comfortable library.

My sabbatical also offered fine friends who encouraged and guided my writing. I am grateful to:

Ari Goldman, the first to read my unfolding manuscript and assure me that it had potential;

Shira Dicker, who actively edited and showed me how to bring greater immediacy to my stories;

Winston Pickett, who taught me that writing and editing are separate tasks;

Menachem Kallus, who tutored me in the texts of Chaim Vital;

And the following readers who each added direction: Ray Lederman; Jeffrey Kamins; Levi Kelman; Stuart Kelman; and Rolinda Schonwald.

Upon my return to California, the revisions of the manuscript continued with the help of the following friends and mentors: Peter Pitzele; Bradley Shavit Artson; Mike Lefkowitz; Kerry (Shia) Olitzky; and Neil Gillman. A special thank you to Erica Taylor, my

writing coach, who edited the manuscript to a new level of co-
herence and fluidity.

Neil Widerman and Seguti Gutierrez-Nolasco patiently solved
my computer problems.

Bob Markel, my agent, kept me hopeful.

Stuart Matlins, the publisher of Jewish Lights, was the publisher I sought. He has led me with enthusiasm and wisdom. I am
grateful for the competence and partnership of the staff of Jewish
Lights, particularly my editors, Sandra Korinchak and Bryna S.
Fischer.

I wish to thank my synagogue, Congregation B'nai Israel,
which for the past twelve years has offered me a community of
teachers and friends and a laboratory of life experiences out of
which this book emerged. I thank the following congregants who
gave me permission to tell their stories: Ching-Lan Shane St. John;
Pearl and Zane Gerber; Edward, Jordana, and Ben Heyman; and
Jackie Wolf. Johanna Rose was the first of my congregants to en-
courage me to turn my sermons into a book. In addition, I thank
my colleagues, Joseph Telushkin, Allen Krause, and his wife, Sherri,
for their stories.

My wife's experiences are woven throughout this book. Linda
consistently enables me to grow. She does so by offering her love,
support, and curiosity. Together we are blessed with three children—Joey, Jonathan, and Anna Rose—who bring much joy to our
lives. The writing of this book was a lengthy process during which
I was all too often preoccupied. I thank my family for their pa-
tience and encouragement.

Thank you, God, for allowing me to reach this moment.

Introduction

I wish to share with you a journey, my own journey, from denial to acceptance. I begin my story in August 1996 at the annual Sermon Seminar for Rabbis held in Los Angeles. My overwhelming sense as I prepare to address this audience of more than eighty rabbis is apprehension. Although I deliver more than 100 sermons each year and I have presented to this audience before, today is different. Today I worry that this assembly will find me gullible, label me foolish, and question my credibility. Why? My sermon for today is titled "Why I Now Believe in Survival of the Soul."

For years I squirmed when listening to testimonials of the supernatural. People confided in me, shared remarkable stories surrounding death and dying, and as their rabbi I listened sympathetically. At the same time, I assumed that the described events were either coincidences or hallucinations to which mourners ascribed special meaning as a balm to the pain of loss.

The sermon I was about to deliver emerged from a shift in my own attitude. I had begun to consider these stories of the supernatural more seriously. This shift occurred a few years earlier, when a series of events drew me to reconsider whether my reflexive rejection of the supernatural was largely a means of self-protection from the fear of the unknown. When I began to view these accounts as real, the many stories fit together like jigsaw puzzle pieces to form a picture of an otherwise hidden realm of reality. The stories I found most compelling were those that I heard from people whom I knew and trusted. In addition, my careful survey of traditional Jewish sources affirmed a faith in survival of the soul that forced me to reconsider my "scientific" assumptions.

As I rise from my seat and walk to the podium I scan the room. Present are some of my favorite teachers and colleagues from Southern California, representing all the major Jewish denominations. We are meeting at Stephen S. Wise Temple, one of Los Angeles's largest and most prestigious congregations, to prepare for our upcoming High Holy Days, Rosh Hashanah and Yom Kippur, the best attended of all the Jewish holidays. My colleagues are seated in the synagogue social hall at long tables behind cups of coffee, danish, and papers covered with notes and doodles.

"Rabbi Yaakov said," I begin while maintaining eye contact with my colleagues, "'this world is like a passageway before the world to come. Prepare yourself so that you might enter into the main banquet room.'[1] These words of the *Ethics of the Fathers*," I emphasize, "are to be taken literally. The passageway is this world and before us is another realm of reality, the world to come."

I describe to my colleagues how over the years I have begun to believe that we possess a soul and that the soul survives this life. As I continue to speak, I gain my stride and relate in an increasingly calm, personal tone stories of graveside mysteries and near-death experiences, describing my sense of discovery. As the emotion in my voice rises, so do my colleagues' heads. They are listening intently as I draw my fifteen-minute talk to a close. I conclude by emphasizing that a belief in survival of the soul only roots us more deeply in living this life each day as a precious gift.

When I finish, hands in the audience shoot up, a rare post-sermon occurrence in a synagogue or even at a sermon seminar. Among them is the hand of a senior colleague whom I deeply admire and who is looked to by many of us in the room as a rabbinic role model. I call on him first.

"Isn't such a faith in survival of the soul dangerous?" he asks coolly, with a trace of annoyance in his voice.

The room is still as my colleagues await my reply. I am aware of how rapidly my heart is beating and how adrenaline flows through my system. I take a deep breath and pause.

"Yes," I say. "Faith in the survival of the soul might lead to magical thinking, the belief in an ability to defy reality, and an unrealistic holding on to departed loved ones. But when responsibly approached, faith in the survival of the soul can also be an important source of affirmation and comfort. Like love, such faith is dangerous but no less real."

As I call on other colleagues, their reactions range from first-hand testimonials to uneasiness and skepticism. One rabbi from Orange County, California, who identifies himself as an ardent rationalist, shares the following:

> About ten years ago my wife went into the hospital for routine surgery. Due to a surgical error she developed a life-threatening blood infection, coupled with pneumonia and other complications. The doctors gave her less than a ten percent chance of survival. She had a tube inserted in her throat to aid her with breathing, which prevented her from speaking. When they finally removed her breathing tube, she said, "While I was declining in strength and my pain was increasing, I became aware of all the prayers that people were saying for me. I could actually hear their voices. The prayers formed a cocoonlike structure around me. Each prayer added to the enveloping support. Why is it," she asked, "that our friends the Weisses weren't praying for me?"
>
> What she could not have known was that the Weisses were in Europe around the time that she went in for routine surgery. They did not know she had been gravely ill. I still have no way to explain her uncanny knowledge and the sense that words of prayer had kept her alive.[2]

Another colleague from a large Reform congregation stands up and reports that the previous year he sent a written survey to his congregants asking them to comment on their faith in the supernatural. The responses included many personal anecdotes. He was amazed first by how many people had stories to share and second by his inability to predict based on economic or social background which congregants would offer such accounts.

The feeling in the room is highly charged. I sense that for many participants it is the first time they have publicly shared their stories of the supernatural. An Orthodox rabbi in his sixties approaches the podium and comments that he has never before heard rabbis publicly discuss the supernatural. With a smile, he shares that when he was a psychology major at a leading university many years ago, a prominent teacher announced in the first class, "There are three things you must remember: There is no God, no mind, and no breast-feeding in my class." The rabbi continues, "I am glad that we live in a time of greater openness."

Even after the formal sermon seminar concluded, some of the rabbis continued their discussion. The following day the religion writer for the *Los Angeles Times,* John Dart, called the director of the Board of Rabbis to ask about the seminar. The organizer of the meeting told him that my sermon prompted an animated discussion on survival of the soul. Just as bookstores had begun to place books on the topic of soul and the supernatural on their display tables, Jewish religious leaders were openly discussing a topic that had previously been pushed aside. John Dart interviewed me, and the newspaper story on rabbis debating the supernatural appeared later that week.

September 13, 1996, is Rosh Hashanah, and I prepare to deliver my "Survival of the Soul" sermon to my congregation. The Jewish New Year is a time of contemplation, both of turning inward to renew our spirituality and of turning outward to strengthen our ties to the community. From the pulpit I face my congregants—more than 1,000 individuals, mostly conventional professionals raising their families in Orange County, California, a community gradually shifting away from its right-wing tradition. Despite my eight-year record of teaching in the community, despite my experience of presenting the same topic at the sermon seminar only one month earlier, and despite the fact that my congregants have come to know and to trust me, I am still filled with anxiety.

As I begin to speak, I seek out the eyes of individuals, searching for a sign of their response. I closely observe the congregation's mood—focused, still. I pace the pulpit, my voice taking on intensity as I strive to convey the central drama: my own awakening to the mysteries of the soul.

When I complete the sermon there are audible sighs in the room. One particularly loud sigh emanates from a key leader in the community. I am unsure if his reaction reflects disbelief or a release from the taut tension of the sermon. Only when the service ends close to two hours later do I receive more specific input. Congregants, including the man with the big sigh, gather around the podium and tell me how appreciative they are of my talk. "Rabbi," one congregant says, "your presentation should be a book. Too many Jews don't know that Judaism believes in the afterlife." Others ask if they can meet me to offer their own stories of soul survival.

This book is a personal memoir of how I have moved from skeptic to believer in the reality of the soul. My understanding of the soul's journeys is a product of firsthand experience and reading. My initial sermon before my congregation on survival of the soul dealt largely with experiences of telepathy and near-death accounts. In this book I share those transformative stories and go beyond them into other realms of soul survival, including communication with the dead and reincarnation. These latter topics admittedly require a greater stretch of credulity. Consequently, I only began to explore the work of mediums and past-life regression after I had a foundation of faith in survival of the soul itself. I will share why I have grown to believe that not only does the soul survive, but it also returns and is reembodied in this realm.

This book is actually two books in one: personal experiences coupled with the insights of contemporary investigators, and an examination of Judaism's traditional perspectives on the soul and its survival. I am a rabbi, a committed Jew, and it was important for me to know what my tradition had to teach about the soul. Reading the literature of an ongoing, ancient spiritual tradition confirmed my own experiences, offered nuanced insights of past thinkers, and affirmed a reality that is intangible and unsuited to controlled, scientific testing.

My teacher, Rabbi Simon Greenberg, said, "If you are saying something that has never been said before, it is probably wrong." On the topic of the soul's journeys, however, the Jewish mystical tradition is rich in teachings. I hope that in sharing Judaism's perspectives, you, the reader, will gain both a richer understanding of Judaism and a more grounded context for evaluating my stories, those of other contemporaries, and incidents in your own life.

Although others can offer more dramatic tales and greater experience with past-life regression and mediums, I hope you will identify with my journey. Perhaps through my story you will open yourself to consider the reality of the supernatural. It is my hope that you will review remarkable events in your own life, which, unless consciously examined, are as potentially fleeting and elusive as a dream. Supernatural events in your own life may prompt you to recognize a reality that does not meet the eye.

In recent years there has been an increased level of interest in survival of the soul. Among the presenters of the supernatural are accomplished physicians and thinkers. Claims of survival of the soul are cross-cultural, span history, and are integrated into most traditional faiths. The increasing interest and faith in survival of the soul may grow into a cultural wave that is as potentially transformative for society as the civil rights movement and feminism. A renewed faith in "the soul's journeys" will call for a reassessment of priorities and enable traditional religions to renew and thereby transform their adherents. Those finding wisdom in Judaism may be encouraged to consider Judaism as the soil on which to nurture spirituality and to thereby elevate their souls.

The increased attention to soul will also change how religious leaders understand and present their own faiths. For most of this century, rabbis ignored the supernatural or denied it. We were skeptical of anything that could not be seen, controlled, or measured. A soul eludes scientific testing. For years on the pulpit, I also categorized accounts of the paranormal as "twilight zone stories," which I assumed were simply products of wish-fulfilling illusion, superstition, and the movies. I suspected that charlatans who offered easy and false answers to people in pain promoted these phenomena.

In funeral eulogies many rabbis speak of immortality only as the perpetuation of the memory of the departed among the living. Even some of our best rabbis avoid talk about God or reduce God to the best expression of natural processes. There is, however, a growing trend of pausing to reflect on seeming coincidence and the possibility of other realms of human awareness. As a result, there is an increasing faith in the existence of a soul, of an essential part of us that endures. This soul, divinely based yet unique, contains the possibility of transsensory levels of consciousness.

Soul work moves in stages, often unanticipated. In that light, my own awakening to the mystery of soul emerged from unexpected events. Once I became more curious about survival of the soul, the stories of others continued to come to me as if drawn by a magnet.

1

Telepathy: A Window on
the Soul's Survival

In my own life I have ignored many experiences that would have provided-evidence for survival of the soul. Although I was raised to value an open mind, like many in my generation I was blind to the supernatural, which was defined as anything that could not be scientifically proven or seen. On most levels I was a predictable product of middle-class, Jewish-American values, with the most unusual aspect of my upbringing being that I was the child of Holocaust survivors.

Allow me to digress to share with you my roots, which offer greater context for my story. When I was six years old my father, a businessman, saw the chance to make a good real estate investment, which led my parents to raise their four children on the outskirts of Phoenix, Arizona. My parents were from Czechoslovakia, and the family business revolved around wigs. My father was the son of the wig maker with whom my mother had apprenticed, making wigs for religious Jewish women, who by tradition cover their hair after getting married.

Although my parents had minimal formal education, they strongly encouraged each of us to excel in school. As they said, "No one can ever take an education away from you." In college in the 1970s I majored in psychology and Jewish philosophy, completing most of my studies at Hebrew University in Jerusalem. Although I had a strong inclination toward the rabbinate, I chose not to pursue that course because I felt too young and ambivalent about key religious beliefs. Instead I opted for law school at Boston University. My legal training furthered my ability to look at problems dispassionately and analytically. I practiced law in Boston for several years, first in the criminal sector and later as legal counsel for Brigham and Women's Hospital, part of the collective of Harvard teaching hospitals. The task of writing medical-legal protocols allowed me to pursue my philosophic interests.

After three years of practice I became very ill with encephalitis, which in the throes of the illness left me delirious. My recovery was slow, and I was unable to continue my work. I had always loved to travel and decided to explore some new countries while recuperating. I sold my possessions and traveled backpack-style for close to a year to Hawaii, French Polynesia, mainland China, Hong Kong, and Southeast Asia. At the end of my trip I needed to decide whether to resume my career in law. My college roommate invited me to join him on a trip to Los Angeles, where he had scheduled several medical residency interviews. In Los Angeles I decided to visit the University of Judaism. The dean of the rabbinical school agreed to meet me, so I borrowed my friend's blazer and told him that I would be back in a half hour. When the half hour was up he knocked on the door because he needed his blazer back to proceed to his own appointment. I returned the coat and continued my meeting with the dean, who invited me to begin studies in the winter session and to apply to rabbinical school in the spring.

From the day I began I loved rabbinical school. My passion had always been toward understanding people and the world, along with a desire to express my strong attachment to the Jewish people. I studied eagerly and received a superb rabbinical school education at the University of Judaism and the Jewish Theological

Seminary in New York. My course of study enabled me to adeptly read sacred Jewish texts, skillfully perform traditional rituals, and describe Jewish history, values, and philosophy. Yet, in the course of my studies I never heard a discussion on survival of the soul. I did learn about Jewish concepts of messiah, resurrection, and the world to come, but they were never brought down to the level of the real world. The concepts were presented as traditional theoretical constructs rather than as communal "maps" that describe reality.

In my work as a rabbi my concerns regarding the soul grew less abstract and more practical. I had to help people make decisions about shutting off ventilators and discontinuing dialysis. When people died I needed to offer solace and meaning. These dilemmas challenged me to contemplate the nature of life and death. At the outset my speculation remained largely legal and psychological, which matched my training. My first dramatic encounter with the paranormal shifted my attention to what happens after we die, a topic I had never really addressed in my years of education.

One Sunday morning, Ching-Lan, the wife of a congregant, called to tell me that her husband, Al, had died the previous day. I arranged to meet with her on Monday. They had been married nearly twenty-five years when he died of a chronic wasting illness. They had met when he worked for an athletic club and she was the beautiful, gentle rebel of a formerly aristocratic Chinese family, and had fallen in love and eloped. Now they had two nearly grown children.

Soon after Ching-Lan welcomed me to her apartment on Monday I encountered the first twist to this story when Ching-Lan shared the following experience:

Rabbi, something amazing occurred yesterday. I received a phone call from my son's former karate teacher with whom I had not spoken in about two years. He's an older Japanese man whom we call Sensei.

"Sensei," I said. "I was thinking of you because I wanted to let you know that Al died yesterday."

"That's precisely why I am calling," he replied. "During the night I awoke and I saw a lit figure in the corner of the room. It was Al. He seemed to indicate a concern for Kubbi [their son]. I reassured him that I would serve as a father figure for your son. And I want you to know that I will do so."

When she told me this story I listened respectfully, but I didn't know what to make of it. I had no mental category in which to place stories of the supernatural and instead proceeded to my "standard intake" to prepare for the eulogy. The family made only one request. Al suffered from a progressive kyphosis, a curvature of the spine. It gave him the appearance of a deformed, clumsy person. He said that when he returned in another life he hoped to come back as something more beautiful. He said he would like to return as a butterfly. His daughter asked that I conclude the eulogy with that image.

The second twist happened at graveside. Many congregants were present to support the bereaved widow, who was a much beloved part of the community and active as a volunteer at the synagogue. I was very fond of her, too. In the course of my eulogy I verbally slipped and called Ching-Lan "Lingchau." I had no clue where this Chineselike word had come from.

As soon as I pronounced the wrong name I realized my mistake. Although Ching-Lan just smiled, I was struck by the enormity of my error, calling a family member at graveside by the wrong name! I paused briefly to regain my focus and then concluded with how Al imagined himself returning as a butterfly. As I shared the image I noticed that many of the people were distracted, seemingly looking past me.

After the eulogy I immediately approached Ching-Lan and begged her forgiveness for having called her by the wrong name. "Don't worry," she said with a smile. "It's okay. That was Al's private pet name for me."

Twist three followed immediately after Ching-Lan's words. Congregants approached me and several remarked, "Rabbi, did you know that just as you were talking about Al wanting to become a butterfly, a white butterfly passed over your right shoulder and hovered there?"[1]

These three incidents were not immediately transformative for me. Although they seemed dramatic, I still lacked a way to integrate them into my experience or even to acknowledge them. However, soon after I was drawn to consider the possibility of survival of the soul by an incident that occurred closer to home.

My wife, Linda, is a professor of neurology. Hers is a world of intellectual analysis and empirical data. By nature and training she is quite skeptical of supernatural phenomena. One Friday afternoon Linda was driving on a California freeway, merging into traffic. She was preoccupied with the mundane details of her day: picking up the kids from school, making final preparations for Shabbat, ticking off her shopping list, figuring out how to get all the errands and cooking done before Shabbat candlelighting, when all work must cease. In the midst of all these considerations and the resultant stress as another driver cut her off, she suddenly experienced the powerful sensation of her Uncle Shaika's presence.

The episode happened very fast. Linda felt as if her awareness was drawn to her Israeli uncle's presence in the upper right corner of her field of vision. She perceived her uncle somehow present, expressing his love for her. It was a riveting and unusual experience. Because Linda was running late to prepare for Shabbat, she did not have a chance to call Israel before sundown that Friday, so she called the next day as soon as Shabbat ended.

Her Aunt Sarah answered and said, "Linda, I am glad you are calling. Your Uncle Shaika died yesterday." When Linda asked when he died, she learned that it was almost the exact moment when she had experienced the powerful impression of his presence in the car. She had not spoken with her aunt or uncle in

several weeks. Years before, when Linda was in college, she had
spent a summer in Israel getting to know her Uncle Shaika. Ever
since then, she regularly wrote to her aunt and uncle and visited
them whenever she was in Israel. Uncle Shaika considered Linda
as a daughter. When she told me the story, I thought back to
Ching-Lan and to the surprising knowledge of Sensei that Al
had died.

Prompted by Linda's experience, I began to recall similar stories people had shared with me as their rabbi, which I had failed
to consider seriously. I was surprised by how many comparable
experiences I had stashed away in my mental miscellaneous file,
the place in which I put stories I did not know what to do with
and that left me feeling uncomfortable. Viewed collectively, they
suggested a pattern of "knowing," a demonstration of the power of
telepathy, the ability of minds to communicate. As a rabbi I assume
that people tell me these stories because they identify me with
the realm of the spirit and seek an outlet of understanding when
remarkable, mysterious experiences occur. The following are
some of those stories:

A woman in her fifties working on her doctorate in a literary
field called to make an appointment to discuss her studies. She
is a serious student, a particularly organized woman who is self-
described as very rational. In the course of our conversation she
said, "Rabbi, I had an experience that I want to tell you about.
One night I had a very vivid dream in which my brother, who
died several years before, appeared to me and said that something important was going to happen. I was so startled by the intensity and vividness of the dream and the message that I awoke
and sat on the edge of my bed. Soon the phone rang. It was my
family thousands of miles of away. They told me that my father
had just died of a sudden heart attack. Neither I nor they had
any indication that he had even been sick."

Another woman, a principal of a neighboring Jewish school,
attended a presentation on Jewish mourning given by a
nationally acclaimed author at my synagogue. I mentioned to

the author over lunch that I had become aware of the importance of the supernatural in and around death, a topic he had excluded from his book. The principal overheard me and said, "I have a great story to tell you in that regard. My husband and I were beginning to drive the hour and a half from Palm Springs to our home when my otherwise healthy husband suddenly felt a severe pain over his heart. The pain was so severe that I had to take over at the wheel. When we listened to the messages on the answering machine at home, we learned that his father had had a sudden heart attack at almost the precise moment that my husband had that pain."

A female physician told my wife that while in medical school her roommate awakened her one night at 3:00 A.M., saying, "You are shouting 'Daddy, Daddy' and something about drooping eyelids." The next day the roommate learned that her father had suddenly been hospitalized thousands of miles away with a severe muscle disease that affected his breathing and was difficult to diagnose. When she asked about his eyelids, which were indeed drooping, the doctors were able to make the diagnosis and save his life.

Years later, when this same man was in a coma, the daughter flew cross-country, repeating over and over to herself in her mind, "Dad, wait for me, I'm coming. Don't die." When she reached his hospital room he suddenly opened his eyes and awoke from the coma. He said, "I heard you say 'Wait for me, I'm coming. Don't die,' and I waited." Soon after, he died.

I had read similar stories of telepathy, particularly surrounding death, in Jewish sources. But I had previously relegated the phenomena to the exaggeration of folklore. The following tales are examples from the world of Hasidism (the Jewish folk piety movement begun in the early eighteenth century) of the telepathic awareness of a loved one's death.

On a day of the Festival of Simchat Torah [when the annual cycle of reading from the Five Books of Moses begins anew], the Ropshitzer [Rabbi Naftali Zevi, Galicia, 1760–1827] stood at the window, and saw how the Hasidim celebrated and danced in the courtyard. He was in an exalted mood and his countenance was illumined with great joy. Suddenly he moved his hand as a signal that they should cease. They saw that his face had become pale and they were stricken with great fright. Gradually he recovered himself and cried out with great enthusiasm: "And, if a commanding officer of the army falls, is the battle broken off? Friends, continue your dance."

At that very moment his friend, Rabbi Abraham, had breathed forth his soul in Ulanov.[2]

Rabbi Pinchas of Koretz [Ukraine, 1726–1791] passed away suddenly while in Spitovka on a journey to the Holy Land. On the same day, the 10th of Elul 5551 [1791], Rabbi Jacob Samson of Spitovka, who already resided in the Holy Land, saw a vision: The *Shekhina,* God's Majesty, appeared to him in the form of a woman in lamentation; he perceived that her lamentation was for a friend of her youth who had died. Thereupon he awoke and cried with grief: "Rabbi Pinchas of Koretz has died!"

He was asked how he knew this.

"Outside of him," he replied, "there exists in this day no *tzaddik* [saintly person] for whom the *Shekhina* would lament." He stood up, made the rent in his garment according to tradition as a sign of his grief, and spoke the blessing of God's righteousness. For many days he mourned his passing.

After a long time the news came to the Holy Land: Rabbi Pinchas is no more.[3]

Since my transformation from skeptic to believer I have learned how many people have similar tales. You don't need to be a rabbinic master, I learned, to mysteriously perceive a friend's death many miles away.[4] Most people, on a less dramatic level, have experienced thinking about an old friend only to have that friend call, send a letter, or arrive in town. Our minds are potential receptors for information in ways we can't always analytically explain. A German-Jewish psychiatrist told me that although he remained unsure about survival of the soul, he was convinced of the human capacity for telepathic communication. He could consistently think of a song, he said, which his wife would then spontaneously begin to sing, or he and his wife could intuit what the other was thinking.

An awareness of telepathic communication may also have a great influence on a person's life. The following is a story of Hans Berger, the discoverer of the electroencephalogram (the EEG):

> As a nineteen-year-old [German] student, I had a serious accident during a military exercise near Wurzburg and barely escaped certain death. Riding on the narrow edge of a steep ravine through which a road led, I fell with my rearing and tumbling horse down into the path of a mounted battery and came to lie almost beneath the wheel of one of the guns. The latter, pulled by six horses, came to a stop just in time and I escaped, having suffered no more than fright. This accident happened in the morning hours of a beautiful spring day. In the evening of the same day, I received a telegram from my father who enquired about my well-being. It was the first and only time in my life that I received such a query. My oldest sister, to whom I had always been particularly close, had occasioned this telegraphic enquiry, because she had suddenly told my parents that she knew with certainty that I had suffered an accident. My family lived in Cologne at the time. This is a case of spontaneous telepathy in which at a time of mortal danger, and as I contemplated certain death, I transmitted my thoughts, while my sister, who was particularly close to me, acted as the receiver.[5]

The experience so deeply affected Berger that he left his study of astronomy to devote his life to inquiry of the mind's relationship to the physical world. His achievement, the invention of the electroencephalogram, endures as a key tool in the exploration and diagnosis of brain activity.

Not all stories of soul survival demonstrate telepathy or are to be taken at face value. Hope and expectation may explain many cases in which a widow, widower, or loved one believes that he or she has seen an apparition or has received a message. There is the possibility of coincidence, too. Yet, among the large number of telepathic stories there is a consistent pattern of love, death, and knowledge that transcends the five senses. The apparent ability of a person who has died or is dying to send a message demonstrates that there are means of communication that we cannot explain scientifically. Moreover, telepathy makes more plausible the existence of a part of us—a soul—that transcends our physical body and survives death.

My curiosity about survival of the soul was reinforced by a near-death experience account I recalled having heard toward the beginning of my rabbinate. In 1989 an out-of-town visitor to my synagogue approached me on a Friday night after services. "Rabbi," he said. "Do you have a moment? I'd like to tell you of something that changed my life." We moved to a corner away from other people so we could speak privately. He related the following incident:

> A few years ago I was in a very serious car accident. My car was totaled, and I was lying unconscious on the side of the road. It was as if I was no longer in my body. I looked down and could see myself bleeding. Paramedics gathered around me, and I was drawn toward a light along with a feeling of great calm. At a certain point I was given a choice to return to my body and did so. All of a sudden I became aware of my bodily pain, but my life was changed. Somehow in that moment I both lost the fear of death and began to appreciate that each day is a gift.

The visitor told me his story a few years before Linda's experience with telepathy; as such it was toward the bottom of my mental miscellaneous file. In the months leading up to my 1996 Rosh Hashanah sermon, as my curiosity grew about survival of the soul, I asked myself: How do these kinds of telepathic communications occur? In what sense is the ability of a person to communicate upon death related to survival of the soul? These stories and questions drew me deeper into the literature of near-death experiences.

ᔕᐞ

2

Near-Death Experiences (NDEs):
The Literature

In recent years a variety of physicians have written books on near-death experiences that emerged from their medical work. Among the best known is Elisabeth Kübler-Ross, a Swiss-born psychiatrist famous for her groundbreaking work with the dying. In her seminal book, *On Death and Dying,*[1] Kübler-Ross described five psychological stages through which a person passes in dying. She wrote during an era when physicians routinely avoided discussing death with their patients. Cancer was referred to as the "big C," and family members rarely discussed it with the ill patient. Kübler-Ross's work helped bring discussion of approaches to death out into the open and paved the way for the hospice movement, which assists people who wish to die outside a hospital.

In the course of her work with dying adults and children, Kübler-Ross recorded firsthand accounts of near-death experiences, also referred to as NDEs. She encountered people who were able to predict the moment of their death, and she listened to stories about signs from and meetings with the deceased. Initially skeptical about the reality behind the paranormal, Kübler-Ross collected 20,000 anecdotes of near-death experience from around the world while she served on the faculty of the University of Chicago.

Among the elements of the anecdotes that forced her to reassess her initial skepticism are the following examples:

- Tales of out-of-body experiences that provided inexplicable capacities of awareness, such as a blind man who described the color and pattern of the operating physician's tie.
- Startling similarities in near-death experiences, both cross-culturally and across a range of ages. These accounts consistently included tales of being greeted into a light by deceased loved ones.
- In the context of car accidents, in some instances the beloved greeter had died only moments before, unbeknownst to the child who later described the encounter that had occurred while he or she lay unconscious in a separate room.[2]

Kübler-Ross, a recipient of more than twenty honorary doctorates, spoke and wrote of how she had grown to believe in the survival of the soul. Within the medical community her conclusions were characterized as unscientific, and some asserted that she had "lost her marbles" after her many years of work with the dying.

Other physicians provided their patient experience as evidence of the universality of near-death experiences. Dr. Raymond Moody, Jr., of the University of Virginia wrote *Life After Life* in 1975, with an introduction by Kübler-Ross. This landmark book, which has sold more than ten million copies, is based on a survey of about 150 patients who survived life-threatening accidents or extreme danger or who were pronounced clinically dead. Moody, who coined the term *near-death experience*, found common elements that consistently appeared in these accounts, which he summarized in the following composite vignette:

A man is dying, and as he reaches the point of greatest physical distress, he hears himself pronounced dead by his doctor. He begins to hear an uncomfortable noise, a loud ringing or buzzing, and at the same time feels himself moving very rapidly through a long dark tunnel. After this, he suddenly finds himself outside his own physical body, but still in the immediate physical environment, and he sees his own body from a distance, as though he is a spectator. He watches the resuscitation attempt from this unusual vantage point and is in a state of emotional upheaval.

After a while he collects himself and becomes more accustomed to his odd condition. He notices that he still has a "body," but one of a very different nature and with very different powers from the physical body he has left behind. Soon other things begin to happen. Others come to meet and to help him. He glimpses the spirits of relatives and friends who have already died, and a loving, warm spirit of a kind he has never encountered before—a being of light appears before him. This being asks him a question, nonverbally, to make him evaluate his life and helps him along by showing him a panoramic instantaneous playback of the major events of his life. At some point he finds himself approaching some sort of barrier or border, apparently representing the limit between earthly life and the next life. Yet he finds that he must go back to the earth, that the time for his death has not yet come. At this point he resists, for by now he is taken up with his experience in the afterlife and does not want to return. He is overwhelmed by intense feelings of joy, love, and peace. Despite his attitude, though, he somehow reunites with his physical body and lives.

Later he tries to tell others, but he has trouble doing so. In the first place, he can find no human words adequate to describe these unearthly episodes. He also finds that others scoff, so he stops telling other people. Still, the experience affects his life profoundly, especially his views about death and its relationship to life.[3]

Moody surmised that one person among thirty has had or knows someone who has had a near-death experience. Most of these people, Moody said, don't share their stories because they have difficulty finding words to describe the surreal nature of an NDE. They may also find that people are uncomfortable with their story and therefore readily dismiss it. Nonetheless, the experiences are vividly remembered and profoundly affect their lives, especially their views about death. Moody withheld making any conclusions as to the underlying mechanism of these reports and encouraged greater study of the operative biochemistry and physiology.

Dr. Melvin Morse, a pediatrician in Seattle, took up the challenge and further explored what did not cause these experiences. Morse was drawn into research on near-death experiences through a nine-year-old patient, Kate, who nearly drowned. When she was revived, she described physical details of the hospital scene that took place while she was unconscious. She also spoke of a guide taking her through a tunnel where she met her grandfather and several other people. A figure of light appeared and asked if she wanted to return to her mother. She replied "yes" and then awoke.

Kate also told of how she had traveled out-of-body to her home during her NDE. She shocked her parents with the accuracy of her vivid account. She told them that she had observed her brother playing with a G.I. Joe in a jeep and her sister with her Barbie doll. She described the clothes her parents were wearing, that her dad sat in the living room, and what her mother was cooking.[4]

Her story motivated Morse, who was primarily a research physician, to examine the phenomenon of near-death experiences more thoroughly. He visited the Children's Hospital in Seattle and identified twelve children who suffered cardiac arrests and had survived. Upon interviewing them, he found that eight recounted vivid memories that contained several elements of a near-death experience. He also interviewed 121 children who were critically ill, on medication, but not near death. None of these children experienced NDE-like encounters. This led Morse to believe that near-death experiences were not drug induced or the psychological product of fear.

Morse published his groundbreaking findings in 1986 in a mainstream juried medical journal, the *American Journal of Diseases of Children.* The responses were widely divergent. First, his funding dried up for more research in this field. The paranormal was and is still taboo in most Western medical circles and in much of society at large. Second, physicians from around the country began to send him related anecdotes. Among the insights Morse gained was that children did not describe being greeted into the light by a living parent, who he would have assumed would be the greatest source of psychological comfort in a trauma. The "greeters" were always people who had already died.

Fascinated by the accumulating evidence of the universal nature of near-death experiences, Morse wondered what the long-term impact was on the children. Ten years after he had conducted his initial interviews, he spoke with the eight children again. In his book, *Closer to the Light,* Morse wrote that each of the young adults vividly recalled his or her near-death experience. Remarkably, all had finished school, not one had a substance abuse problem, and the young people, who ranged from seventeen to twenty-seven, appeared more mature and happier than their peers. Each stated a lack of fear of death because of the blissful feelings associated with the NDE. Each articulated a purpose for his or her return from death, which for one child was as simple as being kinder to his parents; for another it was what led him to become a research scientist. The near-death experiences, Morse said, had transformed the children into people who saw life as purposeful and precious.

Elisabeth Kübler-Ross, twenty-two years after completing *On Death and Dying,* published *On Life After Death*[5] in 1991 as a summary of her many speeches and articles on the topic. She wrote that initially there were several observations that had motivated her to learn more about survival of the soul:

- Even the angriest patients were able to relax deeply before approaching death and spoke of encounters with loved ones.

- Immediately after death, the patient's face changed to an expression of serenity, even though the throes of death were
  hard.
- Immediately after a patient's death, she found that as a caring
  physician, she experienced dissociation from the patient, as
  if the beloved patient was no longer in the "shell."
- Barriers of time and space could be overcome in death. "If,
  for example, a young American dies in Asia and thinks of his
  mother in Washington, he will bridge the thousands of miles
  through the power of thought in a split second and be with
  her."[6]

In the 1980s Kübler-Ross largely dedicated herself to working with dying children. She said that in her experience not a
single child saw her mother or father during a near-death experience unless the parent had already died. In reference to the
variety of religious figures perceived in NDEs she wrote, "The
factors determining who you see are that the person must have
passed on before you, even if only by one minute, and you must
have genuinely loved them. A Jewish boy would not see Jesus, because a Jewish boy doesn't love Jesus. But these are only religious
differences."[7]

Near-death experiences alone are not a proof for the existence
or survival of the soul. They are simply accounts of people who
survived death. Furthermore, there are biological explanations of
these sensory experiences, which are presented below. Nonetheless, the accumulated anecdotes, when examined closely and coupled with the common elements of the stories, support the
concept of a realm of life beyond this one.

The concept of another plane of reality, a standard belief in
most traditional religions and cultures, has only in the last 100 years
been rejected by the collective wisdom of Western culture. In the
past century, a time of dramatic leaps in scientific knowledge, there
developed a profound distrust of that which could not be materially
identified. Ironically, we who live in an age of skepticism are most

aware that there is more to reality than what we see. All around us are radio-, television-, and computer-generated waves. With the right receiver we convert the unseen into a fax, a segment of classical music, or an e-mail message. Near-death experiences offer clues to the possibility that with the right kind of receiver we may access glimpses of the soul in a realm that transcends our visible world.

Some leading physicians, such as Dr. Sherwin Nuland of Yale Medical School, have proposed biological explanations of near-death experiences. They describe the NDE as simply a product of oxygen deprivation (anoxia), which triggers endorphins (morphinelike painkillers naturally occurring in the brain) that produce euphoria and the appearance of light and, in combination with the imagination, foster the vision of deceased loved ones.[8] Other scientists, including the late Dr. Carl Sagan, have asserted that the experience of light in trauma is derived from a deeply imbedded memory of passing through the birth canal.[9]

Both of these popular suggestions prove problematic upon close inspection.[10] Neither artificial nor natural opiates have been shown to effectively induce the NDE state. Oxygen deprivation may cause fuzzy thinking and prolonged stupor, unlike the vivid memories and intense pain described in accounts of a near-death experience.[11] The birth canal thesis became less plausible with the publication of evidence that the eyesight of babies is too poor to perceive the birth canal. In sum, there is currently no widely accepted physiological explanation for near-death experiences.[12]

Although natural physiology may play a part in the near-death experience phenomenon, the common elements of the accounts suggest there is more involved. There is, for instance, the element of being greeted into the light by only those who have already died, an element that holds true for accounts of children as well as for people who could not have known that the greeter had died. In regard to out-of-body experiences attendant to NDEs, there are vivid descriptions by the then-unconscious patients of events in the hospital and in the patients' homes that are corroborated in specific detail by witnesses. Furthermore, detailed visual accounts by blind people of hospital or home situations exist that have been verified by physicians.

It is also intriguing that hypnotized people undergoing past-life regression consistently provide elements of near-death experience accounts in descriptions of their former deaths. Many of these subjects are unaware of the near-death experience phenomenon. During past-life hypnosis (which I will explore more thoroughly later), there is no oxygen deprivation taking place to account for the experience of perceiving light, emerging from the body, and being greeted by loved ones.

The accumulated data of NDEs are massive. In the specificity of detail, the data suggest that another level of consciousness is at work that is not subject to scientific testing. Near-death experiences point to another realm of awareness that transcends the body and the five senses, a dimension of existence that we identify with soul.

As I reconsidered personal stories of telepathy and studied writings on near-death experiences, I reread the familiar stories of the Bible.[13] I playfully considered: How did Ishmael know of his father Abraham's death so as to participate in his burial (Genesis 25:9)? Did Isaac send him a messenger? Or did Abraham's spirit come to his son and inform him of his physical demise? Moreover, when Moses at the burning bush expressed his doubts to God that he could be God's spokesman, God responded: "There is your brother Aaron the Levite. He, I know, speaks readily. Even now he is setting out to meet you, and he will be happy to see you . . . and he shall speak for you to the people" (Exodus 4:14, 4:16). How did this precision of timing work? How did Aaron know that he needed to find Moses at that very moment? The Bible is silent on how these communications worked or God's direct role in providence.

My exploration of contemporary literature on near-death

experience also led me to investigate Judaism's positions on the nature of the soul and what happens after we die. To know my tradition's views, I felt, would help ground me in this spiritual journey. I began my exploration of Jewish text knowing that Judaism is not monolithic. Although the law on how to eat and how to observe the Sabbath is well defined, the rabbis permitted great latitude in interpreting the narratives of the Bible and in forging an understanding of the nature of soul and its survival. To enter into Jewish literature was to gain entry into a family discussion that spanned generations and millennia and provided the insight that the mysteries of life and death are both unfolding and yet familiar.

3

What Is Soul?

Soul is a popular term in current American culture. Recent titles of best-selling books offer the soul chicken soup and care and claim descriptions of the soul's fire, seat, and code.[1] At the same time, these works offer scant definition of soul. *Soul* is commonly used as the term for an inner component that survives the physical plane. It is also used to describe an inner force that serves as "the font of who we are"[2] or "a quality or dimension of experiencing life or ourselves . . . with depth, value, relatedness, heart, and personal substance."[3] *Soul*'s definitions are multifaceted and elusive because it is not an object. I hoped to find in Jewish texts a more nuanced analysis of the nature of soul.

Although there are a variety of understandings of soul in the Jewish tradition, the common starting point is that soul is no less than an extension of God. In the crafting of Adam, the Torah says, "God formed Adam out of the dust of the ground, and breathed into his nostrils the *neshamah* of life; and Adam thus became a living creature" (Genesis 2:7). In Hebrew there are three terms used for breath—*nefesh*, *ruach*, and *neshamah*—words that in the Jewish mystical tradition are also used to describe facets of soul. The image of breath conveys the idea that soul is intangible, animates life, and links us to the source of creation.

The rabbis of the Babylonian Talmud (largely completed by the fifth century C.E.) elaborated on the link between soul and its source as follows:

> As God fills the whole world, so also the soul fills the whole body. As God sees, but cannot be seen, so also the soul sees, but cannot be seen. As God nourishes the whole world, so also the soul nourishes the whole body. As God is pure, so also the soul is pure. As God dwells in the innermost part of the Universe, so also the soul dwells in the innermost part of the body.[4]

Characterizing soul as an extension of God helps me appreciate why soul is so hard to define. God is *other,* neither object nor person. To experience God and soul entails some detachment from our own self-involvement, our "I." The image of soul as breath helps convey a paradox. Although we don't normally see our breath, if we take a mirror, breathe in deeply, and exhale, we can see our breath as film on the mirror. The more breath we see, the less reflection we see of ourselves. To define objects is to grasp them with our senses, which requires an awareness of ourselves. The more fully we encounter soul, the more our "I" of self-awareness and attachment recedes.

We engage soul with the aid of our imagination. Imagination is also the vehicle for finding the metaphors to describe our soul experiences. In that light, Dr. Peter Pitzele, a master psychodramatist and author of *Our Father's Wells,*[5] points out that even before God created Adam, God said, "Let us make Adam in our image and in our likeness" (Genesis 1:26). On this phrase Pitzele comments:

> Here we see the Poet at work. Elohim, the image-maker, creates through Imagination. Adam, this first creation, resembles the Creator, for the human creature is endowed with the divine spark, made in the "image" of the Imaginer, an emanation.[6]

Imagination enables us to enter the realm between understanding and the unconscious, where tradition teaches that our soul is accessed.[7]

The flame is an image that the *Zohar*, the classic mystical commentary on the Torah composed by the end of the thirteenth century, uses to express the multifaceted nature of soul. I find this image particularly helpful. Soul as divine spark possesses qualities of light. It is pure, dynamic, and the tool of awareness, which enables enlightenment. In addition, the bands of color in a flame, ranging from blue to orange to yellow, convey that the soul, too, is composed of nestled, complementary qualities. The *Zohar* describes three dimensions of soul—*nefesh, ruach,* and *neshamah* (the same three words for breath)—and correlates them with facets of inner human existence.[8] On a more cosmic level it describes them as separate realms of creation.[9] Understanding Judaism's approach to soul requires an examination of these three dimensions of soul as described in the *Zohar*.

Soul on the most primary level of human existence is called *nefesh,* representing the realm of action and physical pleasure. Our bodies are the foundation of our lives and we are fundamentally physical beings. With our bodies we act in the world. At the next level, *nefesh* supports and connects with *ruach,* the realm of feelings, which enables personality and the expression of love. Animals, too, have a body and feelings and thus have soul, but one that is limited to the lower dimensions of soul possibility.

With *neshamah,* the third level of soul, we evidence uniquely human capacities. The *neshamah* is identified with analytic thought, the quest for meaning, and transcendence. Only humans ask (so we surmise), "What is the significance of my life?" This capacity for self-reflection and awareness is our link to God and is identified as the breath of life *(nishmat chayim)* that God uniquely breathed into Adam (Genesis 2:7). In traditional mystical writings, soul is often called by the term *neshamah* because it is that part of the personality most identified with self-identity and transpersonal relationships. As we will see later, *neshamah* is also that dimension of soul most identified with soul survival and reincarnation.

Isaac Luria (Egypt-Israel, 1534–1572) was the most influential teacher of Jewish mysticism, with the possible exception of the author of the *Zohar,* Moses de Leon (Spain, d. 1305).[10] He identified two more realms of soul—*chayah* and *yechidah*, which are often grouped together as a fourth dimension of creation.[11] These two higher spheres are accessed by intuition or disciplined imagination and might be called "spirit," as distinguished from soul, because of their intrinsic link to the Divine. Luria returned to the image of breath to describe the five interrelated but distinct units of soul, using a metaphor of God as glassblower:

> To blow glass requires the glassblower to blow in deeply to get a breath, and then exhale through the glass tube. As the breath moves through the glass it expands and shapes it. When the work is completed the breath rests on the glass. In reverse order, the breath on the glass is *nefesh,* the most basic level of life force present in all living things. The *ruach,* which means wind, is the force that blows through the glass giving it shape. The *neshamah* is the outward breath of the glass blower. The *chayah* is the inward breath of the glassblower and *yehidah* is the soul of the glassblower. These dimensions of soul are intertwined and continuous.[12]

For Luria the three lower facets of soul were identified with the personality of the individual, the upper two (spirit) were extensions of God and hence universal.

In Hasidism the three lower levels of soul were given a more psychospiritual, developmental emphasis. The *Maggid* of Mezeritch (Rabbi Dov Baer, d. 1772), the chief disciple of the founder of Hasidism, the Ba'al Shem Tov (1698–1760), taught in the eighteenth century that the levels of soul were acquired in stages:[13]

> When a man is born he has only an animal soul, the *nefesh.* When he overcomes the Evil Urge [physical compulsions such

as the craving for food or sex] the person is given a *ruach.* The entire world of angels is then in his domain. If the person is even more worthy [and he learns to master his emotions, such as anger] he is given a *neshamah,* corresponding to the Divine throne. This means that his every intent and thought creates a throne for God. When a person of this level thinks about his love of God, he is placed in the Universe of Love. . . . Such a person must never remove his thoughts from God, even for an instant, for God Himself rests in his thoughts.[14]

In this Hasidic description soul development moves in stages and is a lifelong pursuit. How we live our lives and our level of awareness determine which rungs of soul are most profoundly engaged.

In the Jewish mystical tradition, therefore, soul is identified with more than the spiritual dimension. Soul encompasses all aspects of our inner lives as manifest in our daily human activities. When our deeds are linked to an inner core we are acting in a way that we would call soulful or authentic.

A helpful way to conceive of these multiple levels of soul is to equate them with the four levels of human pleasure.[15] This approach enables us to concretize what are otherwise abstract concepts. The first level, physical pleasure, includes the pursuits of comfort, security, sports, sex, and listening to music. We naturally long to rest on a hammock in Hawaii, smelling the fragrant breeze, relaxing, and sipping a tall, cool drink. We may acquire physical pleasures for money, yet we have learned that money alone and physical pleasure do not assure fulfillment. Likewise, if our children were to tell us that all they want to do is swing on the hammock in the backyard we would have concerns, because as parents we want them to experience more profound pleasures than the physical, identified with that lowest level of soul called *nefesh.* As parents we want our children to also have the pleasures of relationship.

The next level of pleasure and soul is that of emotional

satisfaction. Among the purest examples of positive and satisfying emotions is love. Our love of our children, spouse, or best friend is among our greatest sources of pleasure (and pain!). Our children are literally "priceless." The capacity to engage in the range of emotions and attachments is identified with *ruach*. There is no currency of exchange from one category of pleasure to another. As the Beatles sang, "Money can't buy me love."

The third category of pleasure is that of meaning. I understand why veterans cling to memories of wartime service. While risking their lives for a higher calling, they were engaged in the consummate act of meaning, which helped define who they are and provided a sense of purpose, a high level of pleasure. The category of meaning includes all craft and service that enable us to better the physical and emotional lives of those around us. Where wealth and family are insufficient to produce a feeling of completeness, charitable acts provide a purpose and the pleasure of making a difference in the world. This third realm of pleasure emerges from thought, identified with the uniquely human capacities of *neshamah*. Through the gift of mind we discern our place in the world, creating and identifying causes in which we believe and to which we may contribute.

The final level of pleasure is accessed through the intuitive faculty with imagination as its instrument. In this realm the inspiration for musical composition and scientific discovery is found, often marked by a "Eureka!" insight. It is understandable that artists and musicians are driven by their art rather than by money (and, in some cases, at the expense of family); there is great pleasure in the act of creation.

This final realm is also the sphere in which we may experience profound connection with the world, manifest as an intuition of "oneness." Such experiences engage the *chayah* and *yechidah* dimensions of soul, dimensions that transcend our ego-identity and link us with the universal "One." There are many possible settings for such "peak moments," including watching a sunset, holding a newborn, praying at a site of historical significance, or observing an act of unconditional love. In such moments time is suspended and there is a sense of letting go of self-involvement. In religious terms these are holy moments, moments in which we feel close to God.

Holy moments are seared into memory. Although years pass we can still vividly conjure up the sensual elements of the place, the memory of who was with us, and feelings of love. While in the midst of such experiences, we were not analyzing but simply *being.* It is hard to put such moments, which generate awe, into words. From hindsight we appreciate that at those times (which exist on a continuum of intensity) when we felt oneness, we were profoundly alive and all levels of our being were engaged. All the major religions have at their core a quest for connection to the source of oneness, also referred to as the Divine or God. Religious rituals serve to cultivate memory of encounter with the Divine, to educate us to the presence of oneness, and to provide induction devices that foster holy moments.

The experience of contact with the source of life and love provides great meaning and intense pleasure. In that regard the great codifier of Jewish law, Moses Maimonides (Spain-Egypt, 1135–1204), a sober rationalist, wrote of relationship with God:

> What is the love of God that is befitting? It is to love the Eternal with a great and exceeding love, so strong that one's soul shall be knit up with the love of God, and one should be continually en-raptured by it, like a lovesick individual, whose mind is at no time free from his passion for a particular woman, the thought of her filling his heart at all times, when sitting down or rising up, when he is eating or drinking. Even intenser should be the love of God in the hearts of those who love the Divine. And this love should continually possess them, even as God commanded us in the phrase, "[And you shall love the Lord, your God] with all your heart and with all your soul" (Deuteronomy 6:5).[16]

As we move up the chain of pleasure (or soul) in the course of our spiritual development, we become correspondingly less self-involved and more aware of inner qualities that link us to the Divine, which brings us back to the image of soul as a flame composed of multiple bands of color. Each of our faculties—the physical, the emotional, the intellectual, and the intuitive—derives from the source of creation and is nestled one in the other as a chain of soul. We can't engage our emotions fully when we are worried about putting food on the table, and we can't develop a constancy of religious practice without thought. At the same time, the inner flame (the blue) enables the outer bands of color to flourish. When we perform a deed in a way that involves all elements of soul (or pleasure), we are acting "soulfully." To achieve such alignment requires being fully present in the moment.

In this life our challenge is to cultivate our inner flame so that it burns brightly. We do so by nurturing a balance of the realms of pleasure and cultivating the awareness that all facets of life are linked and derive from the source of life. The more we fan our intuitive spirit (the inner flame) the more we cultivate the entire flame of soul. Judaism in rabbinic and mystical texts emphasizes that we shape, cultivate, and elevate soul by both our compassionate and ritual acts. We engage the entire chain of soul when we perform deeds with focused, unself-conscious action coupled with an awareness of the ultimate import of our deeds.

Judaism's description of a multifaceted and integrated soul evolved over the millennia. In the Five Books of Moses there is no overt distinction drawn between body and soul. For some of the early rabbis, body and soul were viewed as separate but interdependent components. In that regard the following parable is told about God's judgment at the end of days:

> An orchard owner appointed a lame man and a blind man to guard his orchard, thinking that because of their defects each one would be incapable of any mischief. However, the two guards conspired to steal and eat the fruit by means of the lame man sitting on the shoulders of the blind one. When accused of

wrongdoing each pleaded innocent—one pointing to his inability to see and the other to his inability to walk. The orchard owner put the lame man on the blind man's shoulders and then passed judgment on them as one.[17]

The rabbis of the Talmud voiced different opinions as to the ability of the soul to survive without the body. According to some, neither body nor soul could survive without the other.[18] An apparently more widely held rabbinic view was that the soul may have a fully conscious life when disembodied,[19] which became the dominant view in post-talmudic writings (sixth century and onward). This view is the basic concept underlying belief in a medium's ability to confer with the deceased.

The medieval Jewish philosophers debated the nature of soul and the degree to which individual identity was attached to soul in the afterlife.[20] Drawing on views expressed earlier in the Talmud, mystics of the medieval period shaped an understanding of soul that would later permeate and dominate communal self-understanding. In this articulation, the soul was multifaceted, unique, and immortal, and it entered the body to fulfill a particular task for that life. Soul, it was emphasized, derived from God and thereby provided the ability to imitate (although not impersonate) the creator.

Body and soul, medieval Jewish philosophers and mystics concurred, were interdependent. Just as the wine stains the flask and the flask influences the taste of the wine, so body and soul interpenetrate and yet are distinctive. Moreover, the soul is cultivated in stages while encased in the body. Soul is grown in this life through the struggle between opposing forces: animal-like lusts on one side and discernment and will on the other. This inner wrestling potentially leads to self-awareness, higher aspirations, and inner integration. In the words of Saadiah Gaon (Egypt-Babylonia, 882–942 C.E.): "Soul requires the good acts of the body to perfect its peculiarly immaterial, celestial-like substance, even as the body needs the faculties of sensation and reason that the soul provides."[21]

My reading of contemporary authors and Jewish sacred texts left me humbled in trying to define soul. Any attempt to define soul in clear, unequivocal terms resulted either in distortion or glibness. Yet my exploration left me more keenly aware that there is a unique part of each of us, a divine spark that enlivens all facets of our lives and unites us with the source of oneness. This life provides difficult choices through which we may elevate and refine our soul. At the same time, as a reader of the Bible I was aware that the Torah, the Five Books of Moses, does not discuss a world to come or the survival of the soul. This left me perplexed and curious. What happens to our soul upon the demise of our bodies?

∽

4

Survival of the Soul: Judaism's Views

As a Jew and a rabbi I naturally turned to the Torah, the Five Books of Moses, for insight and affirmation regarding survival of the soul. After an initial reading I was disappointed. I could not find an explicit statement on the afterlife in the Five Books of Moses. A closer reading made me aware that the Bible is subtle and complex (see appendix for a fuller analysis of immortality of the soul and Torah). The concept of soul in the Torah is found through a subtle reoccurring phrase used in the descriptions of the deaths of leading biblical figures.[1]

When Abraham, Ishmael, Isaac, Jacob, Aaron, and Moses die, the Torah says of each that he expired and "was gathered to his people (ונאסף אל עמיו)."[2] The expression "gathered to his people" cannot refer to death itself, for the phrase already acknowledges that they died. It cannot refer to burial for it is often followed by a description of burial. Nor is the phrase a reference to an ancestral grave, because Abraham, Ishmael, and Moses were each buried apart from their ancestors.

Classic Jewish commentators understand the expression "and he was gathered to his people" as a reference to survival of the soul. The following are a couple of examples:

- Ralbag (Levi ben Gershon, Provence, 1288–1344): "The expression is connected with the soul, for while it is in the body it is, as it were, in isolation; when the soul leaves the body, it rejoins its Source and is gathered back to its glory."[3]
- Sforno (Ovadia ben Yaakov, Italy, 1470–1550): "He was gathered into the bond of eternal life with the righteous of all generations, who are his people because they are similar to him. The plural, "his people," implies that there are many nations in the World to Come. . . . Everyone's share in the World to Come is a product of his own unique accomplishments during life. Therefore, no two portions in the Hereafter are alike."[4]

The Torah's reticence on the afterlife is understandable within its historical context. The Torah rejected the class-based, afterlife-obsessed Egyptian culture in which the Israelites suffered.[5] The Egyptian pharaohs treated tens of thousands of their subjects as pawns, forcing slave laborers to build their pyramids. Exhibits of the royal Egyptian tombs bear witness to the gold, art, and wardrobes that were placed alongside the mummies to provide comfort and as bribes to assist the pharaohs in the afterlife. In contrast to the Egyptian's emphasis on the rewards of afterlife for the elite, the Israelite religion focused on a national reward or punishment in this earthly realm. The final outcome of the Israelites' fate depended on their collective obedience to God's covenant.

The Torah's strong reaction against death-based culture is also evidenced by the strict laws of ritual taint by virtue of any contact with death.[6] An example of such a Torah directive is found in Numbers 19:11–14, which states that any contact with death or the corpse of a human being, even being under the same roof with a corpse, renders a person ritually impure. These taboos applied even more strictly to *kohanim*, the priests, who, when in a state of impurity, were forbidden to serve in any role in the Temple ritual (Leviticus 21:1–4).

We do see in the later biblical writings of the prophets and the Latter Writings *(Ketuvim)* suggestions of an afterlife and survival of spirit.[7] The most unequivocal example is the story of King Saul, who successfully uses a medium—the Witch of En-Dor—to call on Samuel, the deceased prophet (this story will get more attention in the discussion of mediums in chapter 11).[8] There is also the image of the immortality of body and soul of the prophet Elijah, who is carried heavenward in a chariot of fire that appears in the first book of Samuel (28:11-15).

There are also comments made in the prophetic narrative that allude to consciousness beyond the grave. Jeremiah speaks of the matriarch Rachel, who long after her death weeps for her children—the exiled Israelite nation—and refuses to be comforted (Jeremiah 31:15). Abigail, who was to become King David's wife, says, "If any man sets out to pursue you and take your life, your life shall be bound up in the bond of life with the Lord your God; but God will fling away the lives of your enemies as from the hollow of a sling" (1 Samuel 25:29). Although these descriptions may be understood as metaphors, their repeated and complementary use suggests a belief in soul survival.

In the early years of the Common Era in Palestine, the rabbis preached that the reward for a life well lived in this world *(olam hazeh)* was a place in "the world to come" *(olam haba).* In the words of the *Mishnah* (the authoritative code of Jewish law edited in Palestine by the beginning of the third century C.E.), "all of Israel has a place in the world to come."[9] The phrase "the world to come" was used imprecisely among the rabbis in their discussions. Often a rabbi used the phrase to refer to the messianic era, a future time of harmony and peace in which the righteous will be brought back to their bodies (resurrection). Others used "world to come" to refer to the immediate spiritual reward, upon death, of an individual's soul being gathered into a realm of other righteous souls. These two divergent ideas are often fused and confused in rabbinic writing.

The world to come was conceived as both a reward of the community and for the individual righteous.[10] In the words of

Rabbi Joshua ben Levi, "Whoever utters songs of praise to God in this world *[olam hazeh]* will be privileged to do so in the world to come *[olam haba]*."[11] In an ethical vein, Rabbi Eliezer told his fellow rabbis:

> Be careful of the honor of your colleagues; restrain your children from [rote] recitation; and seat them between the knees of the disciples of the Sages; and when you pray, know before whom you stand; and on that account you will be worthy of the life of the world to come.[12]

Righteous gentiles, the rabbis held, also had a place in the world to come.[13] There are several stories in the Talmud of a voice from heaven *(bat kol)* announcing to a gentile in the aftermath of a kind act, "You are invited to an existence in the world to come."[14] God's openness to all peoples, alongside a special relationship with the Jewish people, is presented in the following talmudic image:

> In the world to come, the Holy Blessed One will take a scroll of Torah in His embrace and say, "Let the person who has occupied himself herewith come and take a reward." Immediately the nations of the world will gather together in disarray. . . . The Holy Blessed One will say to them, "Do not enter before Me in disorder, but let each nation present itself together with its teachers."[15]

The Talmud defined the standard by which a gentile nation or individual would be judged as pious. This standard was composed of seven basic moral duties, referred to as the "laws of Noah."[16] According to the Talmud, upon death each person—Jew and non-Jew—will engage in a life review that will clarify his or her achievements and failings.[17] To remind us to live responsibly, Akaviah ben Mahalalel, a leading early rabbi (first century, Palestine) said: "Ponder three things and you will avoid falling into sin. Know your origin, your destination, and before Whom you will be required to give an accounting."[18]

Judaism as a religion was and is primarily focused on living in relationship with God *now*. Ongoing legal debate from the earliest rabbis onward, beginning in the first century before the Common Era, strove to clarify "God's expectations" of the Jewish people. Salvation was of secondary importance. Yet, Jewish literature was and is far more than legal discourse; it contains an extensive literature of both philosophic and mystical speculation. Many opinions emerged on the nature of the world to come, with no one theory becoming dogma. The intergenerational debate between sages, while varying in time and place, shared a consensus that the soul survives this plane of existence.

My growing faith in survival of the soul, buttressed by my examination of traditional Jewish sources, led me to speak on the topic to laypeople in a variety of rabbinic settings. At the end of my talks, members of the audience repeatedly came forward with their firsthand accounts, some of which included apparitions of the deceased. I was among the first with whom some of these people shared their stories because they were afraid that others would not understand and would label them as weird or unstable. My simple act of listening with acceptance offered them much appreciated affirmation. A sampling of the first-person stories include these:

> One night I came to the home of a nationally accomplished lawyer to conduct an evening prayer service in honor of his wife, whom we had buried earlier that day. "Rabbi," he said. "I have to tell you what happened yesterday, because I still can't get it out of my mind. As you know I am nearly deaf. When my wife became ill she said that she did not want to die because she was my 'ears.' After she died our son stayed with me until the funeral. He only left once to go home to get a fresh change of clothes. While he was gone I sat in my chair in the living room. I was fully awake. Suddenly I became aware of a lit figure that had my wife's face. She seemed to be reassuring me that she was okay. She then pointed toward the sliding door. When I

looked up I saw my son entering the room. He had forgotten his key. He said that he had been ringing the door with no response. He gained entry by the sliding door, which was usually locked."

A mother in my community lost her twenty-five-year-old daughter in a tragic car accident. In a phone conversation with me she shared this experience: "The night before the funeral while falling asleep but not yet asleep, I was aware of a woman's face that came toward me from a bright light and conveyed, 'Don't worry, she is with us and she is all right.' Next a man's face came forward and conveyed the same. Although the faces were unknown to me, their shape struck me as familial. The experience was totally new for me," she added. "But I found it profoundly real, and it provided me with comfort."

After I delivered a sermon on survival of the soul before an affluent Los Angeles congregation, many people came forward to speak with me. A middle-aged Persian male physician told me, "Ten years ago I sat in the hospital by my father, who was dying of congestive heart failure. His lungs were filling up with fluid, and he lay in bed for days almost motionless. At five in the morning my father suddenly sprang up in his bed. He looked toward the curtain around his bed as if listening and then pointed to himself, nodded, lay back down, and was dead within three minutes. I replay this scene regularly in my mind and believe that it was the moment that the angel of death came to take my father."

I also heard claims that struck me as farfetched. A man at the same Los Angeles synagogue told me that the day after his mother-in-law died, a dark rain cloud appeared over his house and his wife told him that the cloud was a sign from her mother. He spoke in a cynical tone, designed either to make fun of his wife or to disguise his own desire to believe. Other stories reminded me of my experience with the butterfly at Al's funeral. A young Persian engineer, for instance, said that on the final day of formal mourning, a hummingbird appeared, which felt like a sign from his father. It is admittedly hard to judge which "signs" result from coincidence and which point to another level of reality.

I found enough credible anecdotes to form a critical mass that strengthened my faith in survival of the soul. This faith, enhanced by my Jewish study, provided me with greater calm in dealing with severe illness and death. When I learned of individuals' illnesses, I was able to more honestly discuss their initial fears and offer them hope for the probability of successful treatment. At the same time, I was more accepting and open with people who could not be cured. I could share with them my experiences and faith that their physical deterioration did not mean that they would cease to exist.

My Rosh Hashanah sermon to my congregation focused largely on telepathy and near-death experiences, culminating with the assertion that I had grown to believe in survival of the soul. After I delivered the sermon, I believed that I had brought personal closure to the topic. But more unexpected experiences awaited me, and further reading would pose other questions. Now that I had come to accept survival of the soul, I faced the associated issue: What happens with the soul in the other realm? As far as I knew, it was not a question that people could really answer. After all, even those who experience a near death have not experienced death. They return to their bodies alive and tell us their stories. For sources, I turned to the extensive Judaic literature, particularly among the mystics, on soul and its stages of passage, as well as to the writings of Tibetan Buddhism. The similarities between these two ancient cultures left me even more intrigued.

5

What Happens After I Die?

We now step into cloudy, complex waters. We may gather glimpses of soul survival, but we do not find a clear picture of the afterlife. Whether listening to accounts of near-death experiences, observing past-life regressions, or watching a medium at work, we view only occasional frames from a larger film of the soul's story. These images are filtered through the imagination, and the imagination is a curved lens that may distort the picture. Imagination may supply material that is fantasy and even psychosis, ideas that are disconnected from reality. At the same time, imagination may bring into sharper focus fleeting events and maps of both inner and outer reality.

Traditional cultures have evolved images of the soul and afterlife, products of lifetimes of inspired thought and popular belief. Portraits of soul vary from culture to culture in the descriptive vocabulary used and in the interpretive emphasis based on cultural values. Upon close reading of the literature on soul from traditional cultures, remarkable similarities emerge despite the diversity of geographic and cultural settings. A starting point for this deeper and more winding journey is with my own people's wisdom.

Judaism's early rabbis offer relatively little discussion on the nature of the world to come. In fact, their tone is one of distinct humility in describing what awaits us. In an early *midrash* (a rabbinic tale from the Palestinian rabbis of the first centuries C.E.) the rabbis describe even Moses as refusing to provide details:

> The children of Israel are gathered in front of Moses and he is asked; "Tell us what goodness the Holy Blessed One will give us in the World to Come?" Moses responds, "I do not know what I can tell you. Happy are you for what is prepared for you."[1]

The rabbis explain that their reticence is rooted in genuine ignorance. In their words:

> All our prophets foretell only what will happen in the days of the Messiah, but as for *olam haba* [the world to come] 'no eye has seen and no ear has heard, O God, beside You' [Isaiah 650:3], but God alone knows what He prepared for him that waits for them.[2]

When the ancient rabbis do offer a description of the world to come, it sounds very different than our current lives, as in the following quote from the Babylonian Talmud (edited by the sixth century C.E.):

> In the World to Come there is no eating or drinking, nor procreation or commerce, nor jealousy or enmity, or rivalry—but the righteous sit with crowns on their head and enjoy the radiance of the *Shekhina* [Divine Presence].[3]

Rabbi Harold Kushner, a leading contemporary rabbi and author of the best-selling *When Bad Things Happen to Good People*, was asked if he believed in the world to come. He said, "Yes, but I can't really comprehend a disembodied world. I know myself as the man that I see in the mirror. My personality is intertwined with my body. I know 'me' by the sound of my voice and my physical appearance. Hence, I can't really describe who 'I' will be in the world to come."[4]

Nonetheless, it is natural to contemplate what awaits us and how we will arrive there.[5] A comprehensive description of the steps through which the soul passes after death is interspersed throughout the *Zohar,* the classic mystical commentary to the Torah. After its appearance in the thirteenth century,[6] the *Zohar* was almost universally accepted among Jews as an important sacred text.[7]

The *Zohar*'s views are fully explored and placed into a larger context by Simcha Paull Raphael in his book, *Jewish Views of the Afterlife.* The author sifts through Jewish texts on this subject by literary period, from the Bible onward. Jewish sacred texts, particularly the Talmud and *Zohar,* are not written as systematic philosophy. To develop a clear picture of afterlife from the texts requires extracting and compiling comments that were originally imbedded in legal discussion and biblical commentary. Raphael also draws parallels between Jewish descriptions of the afterlife, those contained in the *Tibetan Book of the Dead,* and contemporary accounts of near-death experiences.[8]

Raphael dedicated fifteen years to the research of his book. He summarizes his findings in a seven-step description of the soul's journey from death through rebirth. Each step is based on quotes drawn primarily from the Talmud or the *Zohar.* The following distillation offers a Jewish map of survival of the soul.

1. The Dying Process

During the dying process the person may have intuitions of imminent demise and even ethereal visitors. The Talmud records that the dying Rabbi Yohanan ben Zakkai proclaimed that King Hezekiah of Judah (a particularly righteous king) was coming to greet him.[9] The moment of death is painless. The Talmud tells of Rav Nahman appearing in a dream, soon after his death, to his friend Raba. Rav Nahman described the moment of death as "like pulling a hair out of milk."[10]

As the soul leaves the body it is met by a radiant light, which is termed *Shekhinah,* or divine-feminine presence, in mystical writings. Hence, the *Zohar* explains, "When a man is on the point of leaving this world . . . the *Shekhinah* shows herself to him, and then the soul goes out in joy and love to meet the *Shekhinah.* If he is righteous, he cleaves and attaches himself to her. But if not, then the *Shekhinah* departs, and the soul is left behind, mourning for its separation from the body."[11]

Just as the biblical patriarchs were "gathered to their people," so the *Zohar* describes, "At the hour of a man's departure from the world, his father and his relatives gather around him . . . and they accompany his soul to the place where it is to abide."[12] But before the soul can move, the individual must look back to review his or her life. The Talmud records: "When a man departs to his eternal home all his deeds are enumerated before him and he is told: Such and such a thing have you done, in such and such a place on that day."[13] The *Zohar* elaborates:

> R. Eleazar said: "On the day when man's time arrives to depart from the world . . . three messengers stand over him and take an account of his life and of all that he has done in this world, and he admits all with his mouth and signs the account with his hand . . . so that he should be judged in the next world for all his actions, former and later, old and new, not one of them is forgotten."[14]

The description of the final severance of the soul from the body is strikingly similar in disparate sources. The *Tibetan Book of the Dead* describes the soul departing the body as the "rending of the silver cord," as if the soul were connected by an umbilical cord of energy links to the body. Jewish commentators have found the same image in the metaphor of the dying process in the Book of Ecclesiastes (12:6): ". . . the man goes to his eternal home and the mourners go about the streets, before the silver cord is loosed." In accounts of near-death experiences there is a recurring description of descending a passageway or passing through a door, which is matched in the *Zohar* by the statement that as the soul leaves the world, it enters the Cave of Makhpelah,[15] which functions as a passageway to *Gan Eden* (the Garden of Eden).[16]

2. Separation from the Physical Body

The separation from the physical body creates confusion for the soul. Rabbi Levi (Palestine, third century) in the Jerusalem Talmud depicts the soul as hovering over the body for three days, hoping to return to the body and departing only when there is no more hope of return.[17] In a related vein the *Zohar* states, "For seven days the soul *[nefesh]* goes to and from the house to the grave and from the grave to the house, mourning for the body."[18] This transition phase, the Talmud asserts, may entail suffering— "Like a needle in living flesh, so does the corpse feel the worms,"[19] a surprisingly graphic description. Hasidic masters defined this anguish as psychological, an unsatisfied yearning for the "worms of his wants,"[20] the longing for the physical identified with the *nefesh* level of soul.

3. Emotional Purification

Upon death there occurs an intense encounter with the consequences of the dark and dishonorable, representing unresolved negative emotions. The torments of *Gehenna* [Hebrew for "hell"] described by mystics, Raphael writes, are symbolic rather than literal, a state of mind rather than a place. The encounter with *Gehenna,* the *Zohar* accounts, enables the cleansing through abreaction, discharge, and catharsis of the *ruach,* the second tier of soul, which contains the emotional energy fields.[21]

4. Final Completion of the Personality

Once the consciousness of the departed one is cleansed of negative emotion, the soul simultaneously undergoes two transformations. First, the soul experiences emotional bliss, and second, all the accumulated learning of the *ruach,* the personal self, is passed on to the *neshamah,* the higher self, which provides insight that completes the personality. This passage to a higher level of *neshamah* awareness (the third level of soul) and personality wholeness is symbolically called, in the *Zohar,* the journey through the realms of the lower levels of *Gan Eden.* In this idyllic setting, identified with God's original earthly creation and its corresponding ethereal mirror, the postmortem being enters into the world of the infinite, the Divine.

5. Heavenly Repose of the Soul

In the upper *Gan Eden* the soul finds heavenly repose. It is preceded by the *neshamah*'s dip into the River of Light and another life review, from the perspective of many lifetimes. "The meaning of all that has been experienced in the most recent life becomes instantly apparent from the vantage point of the *neshamah,* the eternal, transpersonal self."[22] It would appear that the experience in *Gan Eden* is dependent on the level of consciousness achieved in this life. Further evolution occurs in that realm, which allows for movement among "the seven heavens," representing escalating planes of closeness to the Divine referred to in the *midrash.*[23] Eventually the *neshamah*'s repose is completed and it begins another transit stage.

6. Return to the Source

In upper *Gan Eden* the highest levels of the soul, the *chayah* or *yechidah* (the universal dimensions of soul that are direct extensions of God), are unfettered by the lower aspects of soul and are able to experience the joy of God's presence. The *Zohar* speaks of how the lower levels of soul return to their source, *tzror hachayim,* the "storehouse of life."[24] Raphael surmises, based on the *Zohar*'s emphasis on reincarnation, that in *tzror hachayim* the soul returns to receive its message for the next incarnation.

7. Preparation for Rebirth

Judaism speaks of reincarnation—in Hebrew *gilgulei neshamot,* which translates as "the rolling of souls" (from body to body). A medieval text titled *Seder Yetzirat Ha-Vlad,* "The Creation of the Embryo," offers the image of a life preview as a preparation for rebirth, which has become popular Jewish legend. An excerpt:

> Between morning and evening the angel carries the soul around and shows her where she will live and where she will die, and the place where she will be buried, and he takes her through the whole world, and points out the just and the sinners and all things. In the evening he replaces her in the womb of the mother, and there she remains for nine months. . . .
>
> Finally, the time comes for the soul to enter the world. It is reluctant to leave; but the angel touches the baby on the nose, extinguishes the light above the head, and sends it forth into the world. Instantly, the soul forgets all that it has seen and learned and enters the world, crying, having just lost a place of shelter, rest, and security.[25]

Beyond the Jewish mystics' seven stages of soul journey, as described by Raphael, Judaism provides an alternative form of rebirth—resurrection of the dead. While reincarnation represents the soul's return to a new body, resurrection is defined as the return of the soul to the original body. I encountered firsthand faith in resurrection most graphically in a monastery. Situated at the base of Jabal Mussa in Egypt's Sinai desert, which is believed by Christians to be the biblical Mount Sinai, is Saint Catherine's Monastery. The monastery's lower level contains piles of bones sorted largely by type,[26] the remains of centuries of monks. The bones of former heads of the monastery are preserved intact as skeletons wearing their formal garb under an arch of femurs. The monk who showed me around had a giddy look, as if he were anticipating that one day he, too, would find his place among the heaps. The bones were stored in anticipation that God would breathe the breath of life back into the bones, bringing the monks back to life.

Resurrection of the dead is so central a Jewish concept that Maimonides counted it among his thirteen articles of faith.[27] I sought a fuller understanding of this remarkable image of renewal in order to compose as complete a picture as possible of what happens after we die. What is resurrection of the dead, and do I believe it will happen to me?

৶

6

Traditional Judaism
on Resurrection of the Dead

Earlier I cited a text from *Mishnah Sanhedrin* that promises, "All of Israel has a place in the world to come." That quote continues, "and the following have no portion in the world to come: one who says, 'There is no resurrection of the dead. . . . '" This tenet is so fundamental that the rabbis placed it as the second blessing in the *Amidah,* a unit of nineteen blessings recited three times a day as a central Jewish prayer. The blessing identified with resurrection reads, "Praised are you, Lord our God, who gives life to the dead."

Although the Bible does not present as a basic tenet the belief that the dead will ultimately be revived in their own bodies and live again on the earth, the idea emerges suggestively in Hebrew scripture. The most direct source is found in the following statement of Daniel (12: 2–3, 12:13):

> Many of those who sleep in the dusty earth shall awake, some to the everlasting life, others to eternal reproach and contempt. Then the knowledgeable shall shine like the brightness of the sky; those who led the many to righteousness will be like the stars, forever and ever. . . . As for you, go on to the

end; you shall rest, and arise to your destiny at the end of days.

Josephus, the Jewish historian of first-century Palestine, wrote that faith in resurrection was a key point of contention between the two vying parties for leadership of the Jewish people. The early rabbis, also known as the Pharisees, believed in resurrection. The Sadducees, identified with the priesthood and political power prior to the destruction of the Temple, believed that death was final.[1] Political tension may have prompted the early rabbis to place this religious concept at the center of their system of beliefs.

There were three elements that made the notion of resurrection compelling to the rabbinic mind. First, it offered a concrete promise of reward and punishment. For instance, in the time of Daniel (dated by modern scholars to the second century B.C.E.), Syrian ruler Antiochus IV—the ruler made famous by the Hanukkah story—persecuted and murdered the righteous, while apostates thrived. Resurrection held the promise that events would continue in the land of the living, with the righteous victorious. Second, resurrection promised a revival of the Jewish people as a community. It was insufficient that individuals would receive their reward alone, particularly in the context of a religion that saw its relationship with God as communal and therefore demanded national reward. Third, body and soul were viewed as an integrated whole in this lifetime and hence in the future, too.

Once resurrection of the dead became a rabbinic doctrine (by the second century), the rabbis identified key passages as prooftexts in addition to the lines from Daniel. For instance, there is Ezekiel's description of the Valley of Bones (37:1–14) in which the dead were revived with the breath of life:

The hand of the Lord came upon me. He took me out by the spirit of the Lord and set me down in the valley and it was full of bones. . . . I prophesied, as I had been commanded, and while I was prophesying, suddenly there was a rattling sound and the bones came together, bone to matching bone. . . . I prophesied as God commanded me and spirit entered them and they came to life and stood up on their feet, a vast force. . . . You shall know, My people, [God said], that I am the Lord, when I have opened your graves and lifted you out of your graves. I will put my breath into you and you shall live again, and I will set you upon your own land.

Some Jewish commentators pointed to this image as a description of the resurrection of the dead in the future.[2] Likewise, some rabbis cited the following statement of Isaiah (26:19): "Your dead shall live, my dead bodies shall arise—awake and sing, you who dwell in the earth!—For your dew is as the dew of light, and the earth shall bring to life the shades."[3]

Already in the Babylonian Talmud (edited by the sixth century C.E.), the rabbis debated physical concerns relating to resurrection, which they failed to resolve.[4] Some of the conundrums were: Will bodies be imperfect as in this world or perfected? How will the bodies travel to the land of Israel? Will the bodies be clothed or naked? When will judgment occur? And who will be chosen?[5] Aware that the body decomposes, the rabbis posited an "almond-shaped" bone, called the *luz,* located at the end of the spine, which will serve as the nucleus of the new body at the time of the resurrection.[6]

The discussion of resurrection of the dead continued after the talmudic era. The concept maintained a place of great importance despite drastically differing opinions as to its definition. The example of Moses Maimonides, whose authority on religious matters derived from his expertise in Jewish law, provides an illuminating illustration of the resurrection debate.

Maimonides composed both a commentary on the *Mishnah* and the *Mishneh Torah,* a fourteen-volume encyclopedic work on Jewish law. In his writings, Maimonides offered a list of thirteen articles of faith.[7] Although not unanimously accepted by all Jews, his list, which comes as close as Judaism gets to a catechism, included a statement of faith in resurrection of the dead.[8] Yet, the influential author gave this pivotal belief scant description in his writing. Moreover, in his classic book of philosophy, *Guide for the Perplexed (Moreh Nevukhim)*, written in his fifties, he failed to mention resurrection of the dead. Instead, he wrote repeatedly of the final reward as the disembodied soul basking in the spiritual presence of God, which he calls *olam haba*, "the world to come."

The debate on resurrection continued during Maimonides' lifetime. Some contemporaries accused Maimonides of heresy, asserting that he failed to personally affirm a belief in resurrection of the dead. Among Maimonides' last writings was a response to his critics, "The Epistle on Resurrection of the Dead."[9] In this work, Maimonides reiterated that the ultimate reward is disembodied, a spiritual bliss in which there is no eating or drinking.[10] Yet, he affirmed that God, who wrought the miracle of creation, has the power to bring back the dead into their bodies.[11] He asserted that this miracle will occur in the messianic era in order to allow souls another opportunity to mature. Once embodied, a person will face moral choices and gain intellectual understandings that will allow a soul to attain a higher level of love of God. This improved soul will persist and return to the realm of souls after the demise of the resurrected body. In sum, resurrection is only a stop, a repeat performance, on the path to the final destination, the disembodied realm of God's presence.

Despite Maimonides' authoritative legal standing, his philosophic viewpoints were bitterly attacked.[12] Maimonides, who was influenced by Aristotle, had emphasized the transience of the body and the eternity of the soul. Critics of Maimonides, who included some of the leading rabbis of Europe, challenged his limited description of resurrection of the soul as a radical departure from the traditional faith in resurrection as the final reward.

Nahmanides (Spain-Israel, 1194–1270) presented the more popular perspective of resurrection of the body. Nahmanides was a renowned scholar of Jewish law as well as a mystic. In a long essay, "The Gate of Reward," Nahmanides directly challenged Maimonides and wrote that the final reward entails reunification of soul and body.[13] In this reembodied state, Nahmanides asserted, humanity will endure eternally. Yet, a close reading of his essay reveals that his understanding of "body" was not the same as the body we now inhabit. In the messianic era, which Nahmanides called *olam haba*, "the world to come," the body will not necessarily need food or water. Just as Moses during his forty days and nights on Mount Sinai endured by basking in God's light, so in this future time we will be embraced by God's sustaining light. Nonetheless, he maintains that "God did not create [the body] for naught" and that our united body and soul is a microcosm of the universe and an essential part of God's plan.

Over time, the concept of resurrection lost its importance for many Jewish thinkers. Already in the fifteenth century such prominent rabbis as Hasdai Crescas[14] and Joseph Albo[15] relegated resurrection to a "specific doctrine" rather than a fundamental tenet of faith. In modern times, the whole topic of resurrection has been largely ignored. Within the Reform movement by the nineteenth century, resurrection was rejected as a supernatural superstition.[16] In both the Reform and the twentieth-century American Reconstructionist movements, the second blessing of the *Amidah* was changed to eliminate the reference to this traditional concept. Dr. Neil Gillman, a leading thinker in the Conservative movement, recently wrote *The Death of Death*,[17] in which he reviewed the literature on the afterlife and concluded that resurrection of the dead is an important Jewish myth because it affirms the integration of body and soul and God's supreme power to conquer even death.

As for my own view, I find it hard to believe that all those bones in St. Catherine's Monastery will rise back to life or that graves will open up and people will roll out. I appreciate the value of concrete, national reward. I understand the purpose of reconstituting a physical community. I acknowledge the interdependence of body and soul. Yet, I lack any evidence to support the belief that my soul will return to my decomposed body and I will arise again.

I don't deny the possibility of a miracle, which by definition is outside the boundaries of our natural experience. I am also on notice of the *Zohar*'s condemnation of the person who denies resurrection:

> Curse on those who say that the Holy One will not raise the dead, because it seems to them an impossibility! Let those fools who are far from Torah and from the Holy One think a little. Aaron had in his hand a rod made of dry wood, the Holy One turned it into a living creature for a short time, with spirit and body; can He not also, then at the time when He will gladden the world, turn into a new creation those bodies which once had spirits and holy souls in them, who kept the command-ments and studied the Law day and night, and which He had hidden for a time in the earth?[18]

Frankly, the idea of returning to my present body just doesn't appeal to me as a future vision, nor does it strike me as true. I am much more identified with Maimonides' spiritual description of soul survival as the ultimate goal.[19]

At this point in my life journey, I relate to resurrection metaphorically as a description of a future time in which the world will be renewed and reordered. In that light, the end of days will not mark the resurrection of individuals but global whole-ness. The great mystic Isaac Luria conveyed a related image when he taught that the messianic era, the end of days, would see the re-constituting of the body of Adam to the original high spiritual plane that he inhabited prior to his fall. Holy acts by individuals in this life, Luria taught, elevate our respective holy sparks, which de-rive from and reconstitute the body parts of the original Adam. I identify more with the individual empowerment and global aspi-rations of this mythic image of the resurrection of the ethereal Adam than with the hope of returning after my death to my re-constituted body.

Rather than gaining faith in resurrection of the body, I have come to believe that each soul returns to a new body, which is called reincarnation. The concepts of resurrection and reincarnation are mutually exclusive. If we have existed in many bodies, which one would we come back in?[20] I am more drawn to the possibility of coming back into a new body (reincarnation) than returning to my current body (resurrection).

The emphasis on reincarnation over resurrection as our soul's intended journey has traditional Jewish roots, too. Although great Jewish thinkers like Maimonides never mentioned the concept of reincarnation, it gained in popular acceptance after the thirteenth century. Isaac Luria, for instance, ignored the concept of resurrection and instead spoke at length about reincarnation.[21] Some *siddur* (the traditional prayer book) commentators in the post-Maimonides era reinterpreted the *Amidah's* blessing, "Praised are you . . . who revives the dead," to refer to the promise of reincarnation.

Jewish ideas about the afterlife have never been static. Reincarnation for Jewish mystics evolved as an important explanation of "why bad things happen to good people" and as a relevant variable in rabbinic counseling. My own interest in rabbinic ideas on reincarnation—a return of our soul to a new body—stemmed from experiences with the contemporary use of hypnosis to access "memories" of previous lives.

෴

7

Past-Life Regression:
An Introduction

Six months before my talk at the Sermon Seminar for Rabbis, my secretary, Dorothy Waldie, who knew I was developing an interest in tales of the paranormal, gave me a book by Dr. Brian Weiss titled *Many Lives, Many Masters*.[1] I read the book jacket, which described the book as being about a psychiatrist's work with past-life regression. The notion that I possessed memories of previous lives struck me as too strange to warrant an investment of my time. I promptly put the book aside.

A few months later, I was on the phone with Pearl, the congregant whose twenty-five-year-old daughter had died in a tragic car accident. She told me of her encounters with ethereal figures who had assured her that her daughter was fine in the other world. I said, "Pearl, I don't know what to do with such unusual stories." She replied, "Just listen respectfully. When you do, it offers me affirmation and comfort." Then she asked if I had read Brian Weiss's book. I told her that it was on my bookshelf and that I would look at it.

When I began to read the book I was quickly drawn in by the author's fine writing and his impressive credentials. Weiss, I learned, is a graduate of Columbia University and Yale Medical School, where he served as chief resident in psychiatry. Afterwards, he became chairman of the psychiatry department at Mount Sinai Hospital in Miami. He achieved a national reputation for his conventional research projects on biological psychiatry and substance abuse. Prior to a firsthand experience in 1980, Weiss had so little interest in the supernatural that when his wife suggested that they visit a psychic with another couple, he squelched the idea, saying he would rather spend the time and money on a movie.

Weiss's therapeutic work with Catherine, a twenty-seven-year-old Catholic lab technician at his hospital, led to a change in his methodology and eventually in his entire worldview. Catherine came to him in 1980 complaining of anxiety, panic attacks, and phobias that had been with her since childhood and had grown worse in her adult years. As a result, she suffered from depression and insomnia. Weiss worked with her using the standard psychiatric tools of medication and talk therapy, which sought to uncover through conversation the underlying sources of her problem. They met once or twice a week for eighteen months, during which she showed little improvement.

In their work together, Dr. Weiss encouraged Catherine to consider the use of hypnosis to gain greater access to pivotal memories. The basic Freudian notion is that when a child undergoes an emotional trauma, he or she will often suppress the memory. The memory lies away from consciousness and is surrounded by defense mechanisms, such as denial, forming a kind of memory capsule. The capsule protects against the pain of the memory and also produces psychological "toxins" that seep out and cause emotional distress and anxiety. When an adult is able to revisit the traumatic memory, he or she reopens the capsule and thereby drains it of its emotional power. The memory, viewed from an adult perspective, can be reintegrated in a healthy, nonthreatening way. Improvement in mental health is often dramatic, and even instantaneous, when the memory ceases to fester.

When Catherine finally agreed to use hypnosis, Weiss first explored her early childhood memories. Although he uncovered some early traumas, Catherine still failed to improve. During the second session of hypnosis Weiss said to her, "Go back to the time from which your symptoms arise." She then referred to herself as Aronda and placed herself in the year 1863 B.C.E. and said that her daughter was Clestra, who in this life is her niece Rachel.

Weiss was puzzled but continued to interview Catherine as if she were describing a current life. He then had her move forward in time and she described herself as a Spanish prostitute in 1756 C.E. During the session her expressions, which matched her descriptions of events, were remarkably different from her expressions in a conscious state. Catherine spoke in English while hypnotized but described in great detail events of another time and place.

In subsequent sessions, Weiss continued to regress Catherine and to explore traumas in her "previous lives." He remained unsure as to the actual source of Catherine's vivid descriptions. At the end of each account of a past life, she presented a near-death experience even though she stated in her fully conscious state that she had never read anything about this phenomenon. On one occasion in describing events "between lives," she spoke in a husky voice, which she had done before in describing this in-between phase. Catherine's words transformed Weiss's understanding of past-life regression and of life itself. She spoke to Weiss of his own family:

> Your father is here and your son, who is a small child. Your father says you will know him because his name is Avrom, and your daughter is named for him. Also his death was due to his heart. Your son's heart was also important, for it was backward, like a chicken's. He made a great sacrifice for you out of his love. His soul is very advanced. . . . His death satisfied his

parents' debts. Also he wanted to show you that medicine could only go so far, that its scope is very limited.[2]

Weiss was shocked. He had no explanation for Catherine's knowledge. As a traditional psychiatrist, he shared nothing of his personal life with his patients. None of his Miami friends knew his father's Yiddish name. It was true that his daughter was born four months after his father died and, in accord with Eastern European Jewish custom, she was named for her deceased grandfather. Weiss's son, Adam, had died when he was twenty-three days old from a congenital heart defect. The pulmonary vein had entered on the wrong side, as if his heart was turned backward, a genetic defect that occurs in one out of every ten million births. The loss of Adam, his first son, took place while Weiss still lived in New Haven, and he rarely spoke about the trauma.

Moved and confused, Weiss said to Catherine, "Who tells you these things?"

"The Masters," she whispered. "The Master Spirits tell me. They tell me I have lived eighty-six times in physical state."[3]

Weiss found that he had no explanation for Catherine's knowledge of his private life. Just as remarkable, she began to make dramatic progress in dealing with her emotional problems. During the ensuing sessions she described many previous lives in great detail, including names, dates, scenery, and descriptions of moments in these lives and sometimes of someone who in the current life was with her in that particular life. She described traumas that he tried to help her to accept and integrate. After a few months of regression work, her symptoms disappeared and she resumed a happier life. During this treatment period she also began to manifest psychic capacities, such as accurately anticipating his questions before he asked them. She also spent time under hypnosis not in a past life but rather as a conduit of highly evolved "spirit-entities" who existed in a realm between lives.

Weiss began to use past-life regression with other patients and found it quite effective, particularly for phobias. Nonetheless, he shared in his writing that he waited close to four years to write a book about his experiences because he feared the medical community would find his work farfetched. Weiss's book fascinated me, particularly his transcriptlike accounts of his sessions with Catherine, but I remained unconvinced. I still needed to know if Brian Weiss was trustworthy, which I could only determine by meeting him in person.

During this period of intense study on the afterlife I wrote a letter to Elisabeth Kübler-Ross through her publisher. I shared my gratitude for her courageous work and said that I would like to meet her. The same day that I gave that Rosh Hashanah sermon on "Survival of the Soul," I received a postcard from her inviting me to her home in Scottsdale, Arizona. My mother lived in Phoenix, which made it convenient to see Kübler-Ross a few weeks later. When I first met the famous doctor I told her of the coincidence that her card arrived the same day that I had given a sermon about her. She smiled and said, "Of course, there is no coincidence!"[4]

Kübler-Ross had suffered a major stroke a couple of years before, which severely limited her physical mobility. Fortunately it left her probing, witty mind intact. Kübler-Ross said she distrusted the many "new age healers" who visited her. She dismissed them as "phony-baloneys." Although skeptical by nature she also spoke of her faith in "spooks" and the survival of the soul, which at that time she was eager to experience firsthand. I asked her opinion of Brian Weiss. She said she knew him and believed that he was a man of integrity. She encouraged me to meet him, though she had little interest in past-life work herself, saying "there is enough psychological work to do in this life."

Upon my return to California I registered for a one-day seminar in Los Angeles with Weiss.[5] I sat in the front row to get a good close look at him. I was quickly impressed by Weiss's self-effacing wit and knowledge. There were several hundred people present, and he led us in two group past-life regressions, which failed to produce any remarkable results for me.

Toward the end of the day he selected volunteers for one-on-one past-life regressions. He demonstrated a style of rapid induction that was stunning. First, Weiss had a female volunteer describe an early childhood memory from this life. Then, Weiss told her that he was going to take her even further back in time to a previous life. He led her, using guided imagery, over a bridge while counting backwards. Once on the other side the woman described the color, pattern, and feel of the clothing she was wearing and said she was about eight years old. She went on to provide vivid details of her parents' home and the surrounding scenery. When asked when and where she lived, she replied, "I think, eighteenth-century France." The interview was brief, less than fifteen minutes. It was only a glimpse into the kinds of memories identified as "past-life." Afterwards, Weiss induced an older woman who recounted the joy of being in the light between lives.

As soon as the session ended I approached the first regression subject to assess her credibility. She was in her mid-forties. She said this was her first regression and that she was motivated to attend the seminar by a chance meeting with Weiss a few weeks before at a bookstore in San Diego prior to a book signing. She struck me as sincere. My curiosity was piqued, but I still needed more data to help me decide whether reincarnation could be real.

As my interest in reincarnation grew, I learned of a new resource. A friend in New York, Rabbi Joseph Telushkin, had a videotape of a past-life regression that he had conducted with a young Jewish woman from the San Fernando Valley in California. I arranged a meeting with Telushkin, who trained as an Orthodox rabbi and currently makes his living as a successful writer of Jewish books, novels, and filmscripts.[6] Rabbi Telushkin had studied hypnosis years before and had used his skill mostly to help relieve friends of pain. However, a filmmaker friend encouraged Rabbi Telushkin to hypnotize a subject so that they might explore together if past-life regression could be documented. The filmmaker offered to film the encounter.

Telushkin approached a friend to serve as the subject. The woman, in her mid-thirties, had proven to be a deep hypnotic/trance subject in the past. The woman agreed to participate as a favor but said that she was not interested in knowing the results. She said to Telushkin that it struck her as weird to think that she had lived before.

Rabbi Telushkin invited me to his home to view the videotape, which began with the woman already under hypnosis. In an interview format, responding to Telushkin's questions, she stated that she had just completed travel on the Oregon Trail. During her account, she spoke with a different cadence than her normal speech and used some unusual idioms. For example, she explained that she was having trouble finding a suitable spouse because the men she met were so "refractory." She told Telushkin her name and described herself as a twenty-three-year-old schoolteacher originally from Ithaca, New York. She explained that she was motivated to go to Oregon because of a pamphlet she had read, which she cited by name. She named the organizer of the wagon train, the man who led it, and the point of origin, Independence, Missouri. She also reported that she had kept a diary of her travels.

After the session, Telushkin, researched the Oregon Trail, finding resources at the New York Public Library and used bookstores. He was able to corroborate most of the names the subject had mentioned. He acquired a copy of the pamphlet she had named, and even found corroboration of numerous details she had mentioned. It was clear that outside of hypnosis the subject knew nothing about the Oregon Trail and little of early American history. Telushkin was amazed by the results of this, his first past-life regression, and was glad to have a filmed record of the session.

I trusted Rabbi Telushkin, and he trusted that this woman knew little about the Oregon Trail. The subject's entire manner, her change in tone of voice, and the use of unusual idioms riveted my attention. I was impressed by the specificity of her account. In

the end, I was most struck by Telushkin's corroboration of the
woman's story through his research. When I had observed past-life
regressions before, I wondered if the "memories" were not solely
products of the imagination. However, if the details of this story,
including specific names, were historically accurate, and if the subject knew little if anything about the Oregon Trail, then the "memories" might really be memories and not products of the
imagination. I wanted to see more.

8

Training with Dr. Brian Weiss

When my wife and I learned of a weeklong training seminar offered by Brian Weiss, we decided to attend. The timing was right: we needed a vacation and we were curious. The workshop was held at the Omega Institute, a retreat center in New York's Catskill Mountains. We joined 120 participants, most of them therapists who had come from all over the country and from abroad. My initial impetus was philosophical. I wanted to evaluate whether reincarnation could exist by watching Weiss in action.

The mornings were dedicated to teaching hypnosis skills and the afternoons to practicing on each other. Prior to this event I had never been hypnotized, nor had I hypnotized anyone else. My only exposure to hypnosis was in college, when a medical student hypnotized other students on stage and had them do odd things, such as bark like a dog or make faces as if eating an onion. Needless to say, this brief exposure to stage hypnotism—more theatrics than serious trance work—left me a bit distrustful about the value of hypnotism.

Hypnosis technique, as taught by Brian and his wife, Carole, was remarkably similar to self-guided meditation, which I had practiced for many years. The hypnotist guided the subject to breathe out slowly and then gradually (in stages) to relax all the muscles of his or her body. Next, the subject was to imagine a light above his or her head that entered the skull and flowed through the body, allowing for even greater relaxation.

The subject entered into even deeper states of calm by following as the hypnotist counted backwards or by imagining him- or herself walking down a set of stairs. At the outset, the subject was asked to imagine entering a garden to more fully use the senses and to experience profound calm. From there, the subject could be encouraged to recollect an early childhood memory. The whole induction process took about twenty minutes.

When relaxed, I learned, we are able to access memories and images that are otherwise unavailable to our busy minds. This phenomenon is most familiar to us in the state that occurs just before we fall asleep or when we first awake. When deeply relaxed and not asleep, our unconscious is able to scan our memory and select relevant material that is not too jarring. Our unconscious serves as a filter sifting memories that we are prepared to revisit.

At first I was hesitant to be induced. I was willing only when I learned to trust the person performing the induction and when I realized that I would always remain in control. All I had to do was open my eyes to end the hypnosis session. I learned that just as when I am asleep and the mind protects me from falling out of bed and distinguishes between familiar and threatening sounds, so the mind's inner eye determines what material is safe enough for us to examine.

In observing others under hypnosis, I came to understand that memories exist along a continuum. On the most accessible level, the subjects were aware of a broad category of experience, comparable to chapter headings. On a deeper level, subjects could provide specific details of a detached experience, as if watching a television screen or an event from a distance. Deeper yet, subjects were able to re-create a scene, including expressing their feelings as if they had reentered the moment. Yet, each of these descriptions remained a memory, an account filtered by the mind of the adult before me.

Each day Weiss demonstrated how he used hypnosis in past-life recall. The memories were reached most commonly by asking a person in a state of deep hypnosis to imagine walking across a bridge. Upon reaching the other side, he or she would remember a previous life. For the first two days of the seminar, I sat on the edge of my chair observing the hypnosis sessions, wondering whether the person would indeed recount an "earlier life." By the third day the suspense was gone. Each subject presented memories of previous lives as assuredly as he or she recalled early childhood memories from this life.

One afternoon Weiss accepted volunteers who had been unsuccessful in accessing such memories in our practice sessions. One middle-aged woman under hypnosis identified herself as a soldier in the First World War. She described in vivid detail the battle scene and an attack that took place on his (her) position.

Weiss then said, "Move forward in time. Where are you?"

"I don't know," she replied with anxiety in her voice. "I can't see myself."

"Where are you?" Weiss asked. She was silent for a few minutes, seeming to struggle with the fruitless search. Finally she spoke.

"I'm floating at about tree level. Wait, now I see myself. I am being put into an ambulance. I think I'm dead."

Weiss explained how subjects sometimes described, just after death scenarios, the soul as in a state of confusion. Hers was not the first out-of-body experience I had witnessed that week, but the drama of her account impressed me greatly.

One afternoon, as part of the student practice sessions, I watched one of Weiss's New York colleagues perform a past-life regression with an obese woman in her early forties. The hypnotist was a therapist who had his own distinctive hypnosis style and a Boris Karloff cadence. The woman had complained of sexual abuse in a previous life. He took her through some of the earlier traumas and enabled her to see those events from a distance and to gain a greater sense of control and understanding. He then brought her to the womb of this life. "What is there to remember from the womb?" I thought. "Who can have thoughts before they are born?" Yet, from the perspective of the womb she described her future parents and her ambivalence about being born.

The therapist gave her hope that this life would be better than the past, and she agreed to be born. In graphic detail he slowly led her through the birth canal and welcomed her into this world. It was breathtaking to watch and a bit intimidating. It seemed that working with a person in the womb and bringing him or her to birth was a high level of achievement because of the lack of concrete description.

I was so impressed with the apparent skill of this therapist that I asked him to regress me next. He agreed to do so on a porch outside. First he interviewed me, including the question "Did you have any heroes in your childhood?" I told him that as a child growing up in Phoenix, Arizona, I felt very drawn to Geronimo, the great Apache leader.

He led me into a state of deep relaxation and guided me to a safe, lovely garden. When he told me to see myself relaxing beside a cool, flowing stream, he turned on a water fountain for effect, which I later appreciated as a pretty clever move. While I was in a deep state of relaxation he told me that I would remember an early childhood memory. Remarkably, I then saw myself at the age of one and a half in my first home. I could see the wooden floor, the large black phone atop a small wooden table, and I could feel myself crawling and pulling myself up to the phone. The memory was quite sensually vivid, which surprised me because I didn't think I could remember back that far. Next, the hypnotist told me that I would go even further back in time and that I would remember a previous life. He also advised me not to categorize the images as either memory or imagination, but just to share whatever came up.

At first the image was a little vague. I saw myself in a cave with the first rays of dawn coming through the entrance. I was twenty-five years old and a hunter. I was getting ready to meet several other Native Americans for the day's hunt. Upon emerging from the cave I saw the wild grain. It was the early 1700s in Montana (the number and place just popped up in my mind). The weather was cool, and I was in a leather kilt. I saw myself riding on a horse. I could feel my physical strength, particularly in my arms and chest, and that of the horse.

When asked to picture the next significant event, I felt myself enter into the scene. I see people preparing for an evening campfire in the village. The occasion is the celebration of the fall harvest. My wife, who is eighteen, stands to my left. We have a newborn and a three-year-old boy who is very dear to me. I have given him a miniature decorated tomahawk.

Once evening falls, I am seated in the circle with the shaman, my uncle, at the head. My uncle has gray hair and great dignity and is widely respected. I am closely identified with him. I feel both my inward strength and my biceps. I feel strong and great joy. Although I'm only an observer of the celebratory dance, I am excited. My wife is not present around the campfire, but I am aware of my fondness for her.

Told to proceed to the next phase of my life, I see myself as an older man, about forty-five. I feel my inner strength and dignity. The strength that was formerly in my biceps has moved to my chest. I feel that I am admired and part of the inner council. The younger men are deferential, and I am a bit aloof. I have been through many battles with other Native American tribes. I have fought for my people. I survived but feel anger and toughness over the loss of friends. The only one who penetrates my toughness is my wife, toward whom I feel tenderness. We have five children. My eldest is now in his twenties. His biceps bulge the way

mine once did. I am not close to my other children due to the
wars that separated me from them in their early years.

Asked to proceed to the last day of my life, I am in a cave lying
down. It is dark except for a small fire. My wife is lovingly tending
to me. I am fifty-six. With my wife is our two-year-old granddaugh-
ter, our anchor for the future. I feel ready to die. My life is full. I am
a little softer but still sense my inner strength.

Told to experience my death, I feel shortness of breath. I am
calm as my heart stops. I'm drawn upward. My wife's head lies on
my chest. She loved me much. The infant wants her attention, but
she is focused on me. I'm in a gray area but am headed toward
light. I want to give my wife a hug and I do, but not physically. I
move upward. Above me is a whitish light, but I am still enveloped
in a gentle dark cloud.

"See if there is a guide," the hypnotist says. I am calm. An ethereal figure that I do not recognize joins me on my right, then another on my left. I move upward into a full gentle light and feel
immense calm.

When I opened my eyes, I was a little dazed, as if emerging
from a trance. Upon regaining my sense of alertness, I marveled
over the vivid detail and the multiple senses engaged during the
regression. At the outset the images that arose had the arms-length
feeling of being presented on a movie screen. As I entered deeper
into the "memory," it grew more and more immediate and three-
dimensional. In a regression mode I felt that I was not observing
from a distance but involved in a vivid and engaging moment.

Reflecting on the experience, it felt a little bizarre to think that
I was formerly a Native American of the Plains. Yet at the same
time, it felt somehow logical. I have a lifelong attachment to Native
American cultures. I grew up in Phoenix, an area in which Native
American history and lore are important. My hero as a child was
Geronimo. I admired his strength, independence, and determina-
tion. My older brother sent me a postcard of Geronimo a few years
ago that is perched on a bookshelf in my office until this day.

My affinity for Native Americans could be viewed as the source of these images or, on the other hand, my childhood identification could be rooted in a past life. There exists the possibility that the therapist's intake question about my childhood heroes led me to think of myself as a Native American. In fact, I can only know what I experienced. I was surprised to find myself in a cold climate, because Geronimo and the Native Americans I had studied were the desert Natives of the American Southwest. In addition, I was touched by the experience of my "death," which felt profoundly real.

I asked my guide how I could determine the authenticity of the memory. He said, "Try and conjure up being in Tokyo, Japan— a place you have read about. Now, compare the quality of that image with the experience during your Native American account." By that criterion, the Native American account was far more "real." I was still left unsure whether the difference in vividness was due to hypnosis, the use of Native American imagery as psychological projection, or because the past-life recollection was a genuine account of my past. I learned that in the realm of past-life regression there exists a continuum of possible experience, ranging from fantasy to actual memory.

In a practice session in our room, I explored my ability to bring my wife, Linda, back to an earlier life. When I induced Linda, she described herself as a man in nineteenth-century Paris, France. I recently asked her to review her diary entries, written immediately after the regression, and to retell her experience. Linda related the following to me.

> You started by asking me to look at my feet and I saw the feet of a soldier. I did not have a sense of time, though I could describe the way the uniform looked. I was a young man walking across a huge green area like a large public park. I was able to describe his conversation with a young woman and how she looked. I wrote the man's name—LeFleur—his address, his captain's name, and the word *Algiers*. He was on a boat for two

days at one point. I don't remember that but I [Linda] found it in my notes. The man married and became a father and at one point I wrote the ages of his children: twenty-five (Marie), eighteen, and twelve. I made sketches in my diary of a uniform and an old-fashioned typewriter. I knew he worked for a newspaper and it didn't seem so very long ago. I mentioned to you *Le Monde*, but somehow I also knew the word *Allemagne,* which I think means "Germany" in French.

I remember his office at the newspaper and how it was tiny, crowded, and near many other people working. I remember how it felt to sit and write there. Also I remember a scene of walking upstairs to his apartment and the wife having supper ready. Their daughter, a redhead, could play the violin. Looking back now I think she was the twelve-year-old. The eighteen-year-old was a quiet boy. This man reviewed plays and art. I know he liked being able to attend the openings of exhibitions.

There were no ordeals, traumas, or even a particular connection to this French man. Afterwards she described the experience as sort of like looking at photos of someone else's grandchildren.

On the last full day of the conference Brian Weiss asked for a volunteer to serve as a therapist. I raised my hand and he chose me. A bubbly female therapist in her forties was chosen as the subject. Brian Weiss met us at the side of the stage. I asked the other volunteer what issue she would like to explore. She said that she often had a constriction in her chest that made it hard to breathe. She intuitively felt that the shortness of breath was connected to the womb, and she said that she wanted to return to the womb in this life to find out the source of the problem.

I was terrified. The sensations of the womb are subtle, and it was still hard for me to accept that they are, in fact, real memories. I masked my intimidation and calmly said, "Okay, I'll take you back to the womb in this life, but let's first go back to an earlier life so as to have a context for the birth." She agreed, yet it was evident to me that she had little interest in the past life itself.

We began with an early childhood memory. The subject saw

herself with her mother, feeling sad and vulnerable. I asked her to go forward in time to find a happy memory with her mother, but she was unable to do so. Because I had no experience as a therapist, it struck me as odd that some subjects could not recollect happy childhood memories with a parent, although I had learned during the week that this was unfortunately the case for some people. I asked the subject to walk across the bridge and into a previous life.

She said that she was a thirteen-year-old Chinese girl walking home across some hills. She was afraid to go home because her father was abusive. She entered the lovely home and was relieved not to see her father. She found her mother in the back doing some laundry. Soon her father returned and she was filled with panic. I asked her to go back in time and to see the source of her anxiety.

She spoke of being only a few years old when her father beat her and locked her in a dark closet. I then modeled an instruction of Brian's to avoid pain. I asked her to rise above the scene and thereby not to feel endangered. As she did so her heavy, anxious breathing slowed down. She said that her father had physically and sexually abused her. I asked her to go forward in time to the last day of her life. She did so and described herself as in her seventies and very yellow. My wife, a physician, later said that it sounded like hepatitis with jaundice, which at that time was a common cause of death in China.

I asked the woman under hypnosis to allow her soul to leave her body. She did so and described a great sense of relief. I asked her to review her life and what she had accomplished. She said that although she had no children in that life she became a teacher and had nurtured many children. I asked her if her father reminded her of anyone in this life, and she said, "Yes, my current father." Brian Weiss had said that in his work he has found that people often reunite with people they had known in a previous life. I had repeatedly seen Brian Weiss link lifetimes to find recurring patterns and to foster insight for change. I then asked the woman to go forward in time to her mother's womb in this lifetime.

"I feel very anxious, as if there is so little room I can hardly breathe. It is dark and I am afraid of my future father," she said. She then spoke of how her current father had abused her physically, although not sexually, and how her mother had not protected her.

"Know that the womb is a lot like that dark closet," I responded. "But in this life you will have more choices than in the past. Although you were abused in the previous life, you will still be able to live a life of care for others. In this life, too, you will be able to nurture and give love regardless of your father's mistreatment. Don't be afraid. Allow yourself to relax and to breathe comfortably."

She then relaxed a bit and agreed to be born. It was a good thing. What if she hadn't? I led her through contractions, the birth canal, and into this life. Upon her birth I welcomed her into the world and reemphasized: "You need not fear. You can choose how to live this life. You can overcome any abuse in childhood—just as the Chinese woman did—and like her you can and will live a life of giving to others and love." I then brought her back to the present moment of sitting in the auditorium. When she opened her eyes she reached toward me and just held me. Tears streamed down her cheeks. "Elie," she said. "Thank you. I can breathe easily now." Our session had taken more than an hour.

My successful experience as a "therapist" only made me appreciate Weiss's skill more and trust that his tool of past-life regression could have a positive impact on people's lives. Throughout the week Weiss had gently and adeptly led a variety of people to uncover their past-life traumas. Past-life memory revealed a source of unhealthy barriers in some current relationships. He had shared that past-life regression was particularly helpful in resolving some phobias and anxiety disorders. A person's fear of water, for instance, might be a product of drowning in a previous life rather than trauma in this life. From what I saw, I was convinced that by extending the therapeutic quest for early trauma into previous lives there was the potential to expand and deepen the possibilities of therapeutic healing.

Among my goals in the retreat was to get a better sense of Brian Weiss in order to determine his credibility. During the week I watched him in action as therapist and teacher, and I had a short breakfast conversation with him. On the last evening of the five-day workshop, my wife and I joined Brian, his wife, Carole, and a psychiatrist in the workshop for dinner. I was impressed with their down-to-earth honesty, ease, and humor and their total lack of self-aggrandizement.

As we discussed how Brian and Carole had come to their work, I enjoyed their sense of discovery, which impressed me as sincere. By the time we parted I was convinced that the stories Brian Weiss tells in his books are honest portrayals of his remarkable experience. By virtue of engaging in past-life regression with hundreds of patients, Brian Weiss has much data to share and a solid faith in survival of the soul and reincarnation.

When Linda and I returned to California we interviewed our nine-year-old son, Joey, who had previously told us of seeing himself as different people in his dreams. We had never asked him much about these images, but now we were intrigued. He mentioned that in one life he was a high-ranking Crusader and that he was short, round chested, and had a red beard. In another life, he said, he lived in France. "What was your name?" we asked. "LeFleur," he replied. As far as Linda and I knew, Joey had no exposure to this name, which Linda recalled from her regression. Brian Weiss had shared that in his experience with past-life regression, current family members had often been present as family or close friends before, as if people traveled in clusters. We were left marveling over Linda and Joey's independent accounts of a past life as "LeFleur."

What Is Gained from Past-Life Regression?

In the aftermath of the retreat with Brian Weiss, I concluded that past-life regression with a fine therapist is a valuable tool for healing. It is still a relatively new technique, and the data is still coming in. Brian Weiss and other therapists I met at the Omega retreat have done much of the groundbreaking work and speak with confidence of their positive results. There is particular success in alleviating unresolved phobias and anxiety. These maladjustments, they say, are often linked to a violent death in the past. When these traumas are exposed under hypnosis, the event can be drained of its emotional control.

Skeptics may say that the improvement is simply a product of a therapist's attention, a kind of placebo effect. But therapeutic results are so closely linked to specific, related memories that it appears that more is at play than simply a therapist's attention. The release from anxiety in a regression is similar to the healing mechanism employed in classic therapy in which a person gains an emotional catharsis through an open and honest examination of a past trauma. Both allow a person to integrate the past in a healthful way.

In a past-life regression we may also link people in our current life with people of the past. We apparently travel from lifetime to lifetime with a related group of people. Previous behavior may offer insight into current tensions and dysfunctional patterns of relationship. Love in the past may also explain passions in this life.

Brian Weiss describes in *Only Love is Real*[1] how two of his patients shared vivid accounts of the same obscure moment 2,000 years earlier told from two different perspectives. He was tempted, he writes, to introduce them to each other, but professional confidentiality prevented him. He arranged for them to be in his waiting room at the same time, but nothing came of it. Soon after they met on their own at an airport, which led to a kind of reunification. They were powerfully attracted to each other and wed. If past-life memories exist, then there are in fact three key components of our makeup: genetics, environment, and past lives. Consequently, experiences in past lives could explain a person's innate talents, fears, and habits.

In my experience, much of the material generated in past-life regression is not true past-life memory, yet it remains potentially helpful. Under hypnosis a person is both highly suggestible and remarkably creative. When a hypnotist says, "You will now remember a past life," the subject wishes to "succeed" by pleasing the hypnotist. This need to comply is often unconscious. The imagination is remarkably capable of fashioning a good story based on bits of historical data acquired through the years.

In reference to my own past-life regression in which I saw myself as a Native American warrior, I remain skeptical that it really described me in the past. Afterwards, it felt too predictable. The hypnotist had asked me who were my heroes and I said Geronimo. It seemed like a natural flow to then see myself when regressed as a Native American. My skepticism further increased when I directed a past-life regression of a rabbinic colleague.

When I had my colleague visualize a previous life, he saw himself as a cowboy on horseback in the 1800s, surrounded by a group of other men on horseback. He then flipped into an even more vivid, earlier image.

He again saw himself on horseback, this time as a young warrior prince riding along with other men. In the next scene, a monk came out to greet him. He had arrived at a monastery in hopes of visiting with an aging monk, whom he identified as particularly wise. Moving forward in time, he saw himself in battle, feeling calm despite the clamor of swords and shouts. In the final scene—the last day of his life—he noted that he was old with long hair and a beautiful, radiant face, revealing a life well lived. He was surrounded by other men and felt respected and cared for. He had achieved a high level of wisdom, he said, but of a more worldly kind than that of the isolated monk whom he had so admired.

My friend, who did not know of my own regression as a horseback-riding, Native American warrior, said upon emerging from hypnosis that the images were vivid but also felt like the common boy-on-horse daydreams of youth. His image impressed me as a description of his striving and his core—a competent man, simultaneously dedicated to the pursuit of wisdom and courageously "fighting" to make a difference in the world. I said to him sincerely, "Just as the warrior prince lived a long life of success and gained great knowledge, know that it is also your potential."

Likewise, my Native American felt like the best parts of me: an intense inner strength; the capacity to fight with courage and coolness; identification with the shaman; and the ability to receive love. Knowing that this is how I perceive myself is very important. It gives me strength and courage. I believe that these insights are more than wishful thinking. Awareness of our core through an image draws us toward materializing that image in our lives.

In a related vein, three of the people I have regressed were women who were childless and beyond their childbearing years. In each case, among other "lives" they remembered a past in which they were fulfilled despite the absence of children of their own. Building on the legacy of those lives, they were able to affirm that despite their disappointment in not having children in this life, they could choose, as in the previous lives, to live full and rewarding lives. Such an insight feels primal and personal because it is generated from within, and it can free a person to live this life with more acceptance and joy.

The material that surfaces in past-life regression needs processing with a skilled guide. Whether fantasy, foundational insight, or past-life memory, the material may describe and influence our self-identity. In dealing with such material there is a need for interpretation, with the potential pitfalls of both over-interpretation and under-interpretation. Hence, two strong cautions: be aware that the images may not be actual past lives, and understand that there is a need to integrate the images with a skilled practitioner.

One additional warning emerges from a friend who told me of

a former girlfriend who in a past-life regression saw her current husband as her husband in the thirteenth century. In that previous life he beat her severely. She felt deep anger with her current husband for what he had done to her in the past. You can imagine his predicament in responding to her accusation. Their marriage ended in divorce, which may not have been caused by the past-life regression, but it surely did not help.

As a rabbi I tend not to use the skills I learned at the retreat with Brian Weiss. Past-life regression is a therapeutic tool that requires expertise in therapy and time for an ongoing therapeutic relationship, two requirements that I lack. When people share their problems with me as their rabbi, and when their need is for ongoing therapy, I refer them to a therapist. Sometimes, I am left wondering if the source of their problem is a past life.

For most people, I think of past lives as a kind of background music; it sets a mood that we are usually unaware of consciously. In some cases, however, the past life may create such a discordant sound track, due to abuse or a violent death in a previous life, that people are unable to act thoughtfully and are awash in anxiety. Past-life therapy may help uncover a past trauma and thereby lower the jarring, distracting sound and perhaps even eliminate it.

What we may experience with a therapist under hypnosis ranges from fantasy to core insight to actual past-life memory. Later I will describe why I believe that some past-life memories are historically real. Such a faith corresponds with reincarnation, the idea that the soul may return to a new body. Reincarnation is a belief held among large numbers of diverse peoples in our world, with seemingly little contact, if any, with each other. Those who espouse this view include Eskimos in northern Canada, villagers of the Ganges Valley in India, tribal hunters in Central Australia, and a large minority of the inhabitants of Brazil.[2] Remarkably, not as well known is that Judaism, too, traditionally affirmed reincarnation. My curiosity led me to delve deeper into

Jewish texts, which both provided support for my faith in reincarnation and challenged me to reconcile the detailed differences between perspectives.

∽

9

Reincarnation: Judaism's Views

Rabbi Lawrence Kushner of Sudbury, Massachusetts, has told me that he is often asked at public lectures if he believes in past lives. He replies, "I'm just puzzled that of all the thousands and thousands of people who have claimed to have been reincarnated, not one has ever told anybody where he hid the money."[1] His comment raises the important questions of *what proof* and *how much* should convince us? I appreciate his skepticism. It is at first impression a wild idea to think that we, or anyone else, were literally here before. I have grown to believe in reincarnation, despite incomplete proof, because of overlapping experiences, through my extensive reading, and from my developing awareness that it is a central doctrine in the Jewish mystical tradition.

Jewish mysticism holds that through the process of physical reembodiment, the soul can mend the wrongdoings of previous lives and attain further wholeness. *Sefer HaBahir*, the first kabbalistic work to gain wide circulation,[2] took reincarnation for granted. This late twelfth-century work of unknown authorship mentions reincarnation in several places without any apology or defense, suggesting that the concept was widely accepted. Biblical texts were offered in *Sefer HaBahir* as affirming reincarnation, such as from Ecclesiastes (1:4): "One generation passes away and another comes." This line was interpreted to mean that the generation that passes away also returns.[3] For the author of *Sefer HaBahir*, reincarnation helped explain why children are born crippled or blind.[4]

Nahmanides, who was influenced by *Sefer HaBahir,* believed reincarnation was the underlying principle behind the biblical commandment of levirate marriage *(yibum),* which declared that the brother of a childless widow needed to procreate with her. Nahmanides wrote that the act of the surviving brother replaced the deceased husband so that the deceased would reincarnate in the soul of the offspring. In his commentary to Job, Nahmanides understood Elihu's explanation of why the righteous suffer as being based on the claim that the suffering is punishment for the deeds in a previous life.[5] Although affirming his belief in reincarnation, Nahmanides referred to this matter in elusive terms and called it a *sod* ("secret"), evidencing the controversy between rationalists and mystics of thirteenth-century Spain concerning reincarnation.

In contrast, the *Zohar* speaks unabashedly of reincarnation[6] and offers a number of biblical examples. The following quote from the *Zohar* demonstrates the directness of the approach:

> Truly, all souls must undergo transmigration; but men do not perceive the ways of the Holy One, how the revolving scale is set up and men are judged every day at all times, and how they are brought up before the Tribunal, both before they enter into this world and after they leave it. They perceive not the many transmigrations and the many mysterious works which the Holy One accomplishes with many naked souls, and how many naked spirits roam about, in the other world without being able to enter within the veil of the King's Palace.[7]

Due to the widespread acceptance of the *Zohar* as sacred text, the concept of reincarnation, most often referred to in Hebrew as *gilgulei neshamot* (or *gilgul*),[8] became prevalent in mystical writing and began to appear in philosophic writings, too.

Reincarnation, despite the *Zohar*'s point of view, remained controversial in Judaism. On the one hand, reincarnation gained widespread acceptance, most notably in the Hasidic movement, which dominated significant portions of Eastern Europe by the end of the nineteenth century. On the other hand, reincarnation is not mentioned directly in Hebrew scripture or the Talmud. Nor is there clear documentation for the existence of the concept during the Second Temple Period (around 515 B.C.E. to 70 C.E.). Among the medieval Jewish philosophers, who were Aristotelian in their approach, reincarnation was rejected.[9] Saadiah Gaon, in the tenth century, referred to it as "madness and confusion."[10] Public debates took place on this topic in the fifteenth century, and for hundreds of years thereafter books were written both in support[11] and in opposition.[12] The reincarnation debate is ongoing and demonstrates that Judaism is not monolithic.

Even among mystics who shared a faith in reincarnation, there was widespread disagreement as to the particulars. The earlier, influential compositions like *Sefer HaBahir* and the *Zohar* only refer to reincarnation into human form. From the early fourteenth century onward, some mystics espoused transmigration into animals, plants, and even rocks[13] as a form of spiritual punishment.[14] There was also debate as to the reasons for transmigration of souls. Although the early mystics identified *gilgul* as punishment for sexual offenses, it was later characterized as a process of divine compassion enabling any soul to engage in purification or repair.

Kabbalists (practitioners of Jewish mysticism) also differed as to the number of possible incarnations. *Sefer HaBahir* states that transmigrations may continue for a thousand generations. Many of the Spanish kabbalists held that the soul transmigrates only three times after entering the original body, based on the verse from the Book of Job (33:29): "Behold, God does all these things, twice, three times, with a man."[15] In addition the *Zohar* describes *ibburim*, temporary muselike impregnations of soul who assist a living person. It offers a variety of biblical examples, such as the following: Samuel, the prophet and designator of kings, was supported by the souls of Moses and Aaron; Pinchas was aided by the *ibbur* of Nadav and Avihu when in his zeal he slew Zimri and Kosbi (Numbers 25: 6–8); and Judah was present in Boaz when he fathered Obed (Ruth 4:17).[16]

Rabbi Isaac Luria (Egypt-Safad, 1534–1572) further elaborated on resurrection as a necessary process of repair of the soul. Moreover, Luria taught that human reincarnation was an essential vehicle for repair of the entire cosmos, including God. In Luria's detailed description there are different facets of soul, each with its own specific incarnations; these were discussed in chapter 3. His influence was so great that Gershom Scholem, the great researcher of Jewish mysticism, wrote: "The Lurianic kabbalah was the last religious movement in Judaism, the influence of which became preponderant among all sections of the Jewish people and in every country of the Diaspora, without exception."[17] Due to the cosmic sweep of Luria's mystical system and his enormous influence, a separate and more detailed analysis follows that entails learning Luria's vocabulary.

What Is Luria's Cosmic Conception of Reincarnation?

Isaac Luria made an enormous impact on the study and practice of Jewish mysticism in a very short time. Born in Jerusalem in 1534, he moved as a child with his mother to her family's house in Cairo in the aftermath of his father's death.[18] He returned to Israel in 1569 and made his home in Safad, which at the time was home to some of the most influential mystics and legal scholars in all of Jewish history. Although Luria was only thirty-five years old, he quickly established himself as a charismatic teacher. Important scholars and practitioners of mysticism were drawn to him by virtue of his great learning in both Jewish law and traditional mystical texts, particularly the thirteenth-century *Zohar*. He guided disciples in praying with directed meditative intentions and presented in his oral teaching a profound elaboration of classical mystical ideas. His followers said that he possessed *ruach hakodesh,* the spirit of the Divine, which enabled him to see the past clairvoyantly, including their previous incarnations.

We know of Luria's ideas primarily from his students' books. Luria's own writings included three key works: a commentary on a short but important section of the *Zohar*;[19] a variety of liturgical poems; and a guide to penitence rituals and mystical meditations. His most prolific disciple was Chaim Vital (1542–1620), who studied with Luria for less than two years. Luria died during an epidemic only a few years after his arrival in Safad at the age of thirty-eight. In their short time together, Vital absorbed enough from Luria's teaching that he was able to dedicate the rest of his life to setting down his master's views, producing volumes of remarkable ideas.[20]

Luria held that a person has a foundational soul composed of a package of soul sparks. These soul sparks originated with Adam and are passed from generation to generation. Our goal in this life, Luria taught, is to purify and elevate our soul sparks in order to heal a fallen Adam, which will thereby enable cosmic, messianic harmony. To appreciate the significance that Luria placed on the role of reincarnation in the universe, it is important to grasp his description of the world's beginning, presented as a four-act drama directed by God:

Act 1: *Ein Sof* (infinity): God, who is infinite, filled all.

Act 2: *Tzimtzum* (contraction): God withdrew inwardly to create a sphere of emptiness into which God could craft creation. God fashioned vessels in the void into which God emanated a divine ray of light.[21]

Act 3: *Shevirat HaKelim* (the shattering of the vessels): The divine light was too powerful and the vessels exploded, a product of God's plan. Holy sparks flew in all directions and were dispersed among the broken shards. Luria's description of time and space beginning with an explosion parallels the contemporary "big bang" theory of creation.[22]

Act 4: *Tikkun* (repair): God reconstituted enough of the broken shards to enable people to help God continue the repair. Human beings would be given the capacity, free will, and duty to help gather the holy sparks. Such extraction of sparks from the shards would be achieved by the doing of God's decrees *(mitzvot)* with proper intention *(kavannah).*[23]

In Luria's worldview, God placed the first human, *Adam HaRishon,* in the Garden of Eden to repair the shattered vessels and to regather the sparks. This first human existed on a high spiritual plane. *Adam HaRishon* violated God's command by eating from the forbidden fruit and therefore fell several spiritual levels. At this point, soul sparks from Adam's body fell into lower spiritual realms, and some of the sparks were displaced more deeply into Adam's body. All future generations of people would begin life with soul sparks that originated with *Adam HaRishon.*

By virtue of Adam's fall, even the purest souls receive an admixture of evil. Luria claimed 613 bodily locations (including eyes, hands, feet, sinews, and the inner organs) of Adam's body that were the source of soul sparks.[24] These 613 locations corresponded to the 613 *mitzvot* (divine commands) of the Torah, the tools for repairing the world. For each person, the original location of the soul sparks now contained in his or her body determines that person's disposition and level of enlightenment.

For Luria, each incarnation presents an opportunity to purify soul sparks and to elevate them to the higher spiritual realm of *Adam HaRishon* before the fall. *Mitzvot* performed with the proper intention not only perfect our own soul sparks but have the potential to liberate sparks that are still caught among the shards of the divinely created vessels. The reconstituting of *Adam HaRishon*'s full spiritual body represents a return to Eden, which will be manifest as messianic harmony.

At first reading, Luria's description of soul sparks raised many questions for me. How does a soul spark translate into an actual life with a memory and personality? How does a soul spark impact on who I am? At the same time, what I found compelling in Luria's description was that the individual's work to improve his or her own soul work is linked to all the souls of creation. The elevation of each spirit furthers God's cosmic plan. Moreover, we repair our souls in this world by the combination of deeds and properly directed mindsets of focus on God and God's attributes, in Hebrew called *kavannot*. To better understand Luria's scheme, some additional vocabulary and a closer look at the makeup of soul are needed.

The nature of our soul sparks is a product of two sources: (1) their original location on *Adam HaRishon*'s body, and (2) how far up the ladder of purification they have been elevated through previous incarnations. There are five levels of soul, or five rungs of purification of the soul. These levels in ascending order are *nefesh, ruach, neshamah, chayah,* and *yechidah* (see chapter 3, "What Is Soul?"). The two highest levels are so closely identified with God that they are universal in character and are not subject to reincarnation. Elevating our sparks through the lower three levels is our life work, and our status in the process reflects different degrees of spiritual maturity.[25]

Recall that *nefesh* is the physical level of being. This animal dimension of self is shaped by physical deeds. *Ruach* is the personal self, which contains the energy that animates us and is identified with our emotional life. *Neshamah* is the transpersonal self that is shaped by our capacity of thought and enables us to reach beyond ourselves in uniquely human ways.[26] Beyond the influence of the soul sparks, a person has a primal capacity of consciousness and freedom of will that enable the process of soul repair.

Luria said that in any one lifetime our soul sparks are only purified to move up one of the rungs on the purification ladder. The performance of *yechudim,* the skilled use of specifically designed

mystical meditations designed to accompany prayer or the performance of *mitzvot,* provides an exception to the rule of one-rung-
in-a-lifetime soul growth. Each rung is also three-dimensional,
hologramlike, containing the three aspects of the soul: physical,
emotional, and intellectual.[27] Consider, for instance, that when a
person is involved in a physical act, emotions and mind might also
be employed. Each dimension of soul may therefore have a role in
a single act.

Reincarnation offers two opportunities for soul repair. First,
reincarnation enables a soul spark that has completed its work on
one rung to begin its purification on the next level. Second, reincarnation provides an additional chance to repair a mistake that
prevented the soul spark from moving upward in a previous incarnation. Luria said that a soul spark had only three lifetimes in
which to rise up each soul rung.[28] Repair of soul sparks is only
achieved by the current deeds of the living.

Luria offers a path other than reincarnation for a soul to return
to the human plane. A soul from a previous life may return as a
temporary visiting soul, in Hebrew an *ibbur.*[29] An *ibbur* will
choose to inhabit a person whose foundational sparks are derived
from the same body part of *Adam HaRishon* as his or her own.
The visiting soul may gain the merit of a specific *mitzvah* performed by the host body that is needed to complete the *ibbur's*
soul. When the mission is completed, the visiting soul returns to
his or her source in the spirit realm.[30]

The visiting soul of a *tzaddik* (a spiritually complete person)
is a second type of *ibbur* identified by Luria. The *tzaddik* is self-
less and can return a thousand times. This is comparable to the
Mahayana Buddhist concept of a *bodhisattva.* The *bodhisattva* is
an enlightened being who is exempt from the laws of reincarnation and returns to the world to commiserate with others and to
help them.[31] A *tzaddik-ibbur* provides muselike inspiration, aiding the host to elevate his or her soul, which facilitates the return
of holy sparks to the body of *Adam HaRishon.*

There is a cosmic and earthly gain in the *tzaddik*'s work of enabling the elevation of soul sparks. The more an individual perfects his or her soul sparks, the greater the capacity to effect a more integrated relationship between the individual and God and to enable a fuller integration between God and the world. When souls evolve up the spiritual ladder there is an enhanced capacity to forge connections with related soul sparks, including those of higher souls, which derive from the same body part of origin in *Adam HaRishon*. There is a correspondingly increased harmony in the manifest world when elevated sparks reunite into *Adam HaRishon*'s etheric body.

Luria's soul system is complex in theory and has a technical dimension. The following analogy to a modified ham radio offers contemporary images to convey the basics of Luria's system. Foundational soul sparks, which spring from Adam, are like transistors. *Ibburim,* the visiting souls, are special broadcasts to transistors (a kind of directed software), which enable transistor repair and improvement. The airwaves are filled with previous thoughts that a ham radio may access when its frequencies are properly aligned, which in human terms provide the capacity of clairvoyance.

The goal of the short-wave operator[32] is to receive an increasing array of sounds across a broader range of frequencies. Simultaneously, the short-wave operator broadcasts harmonious music (achieved through the performance of *mitzvot*) utilizing an appropriate radio frequency band (attuned by the proper energy of mind intention, or *kavannah*). Such a broadcast simultaneously hones the transistors and puts positive sound out into the world.

Even when a transistor is in need of repair or further refinement, it can still send out sound. All received and broadcast sound is fundamentally composed of waves emerging from the Source of sound. The ultimate goal is for all the ham operators to have finely tuned ham transistors (purified soul sparks) that are used to collectively broadcast the Oneness of all sound, thereby making the Source of sound fully manifest in the world.[33]

Beyond a systemic theory, Luria referred in concrete ways to the process of reincarnation in the lives of people around him. Chaim Vital, Luria's student, recorded in his diary that Luria described the following three *ibburim* (visiting souls) at different stages of Vital's life: at age thirteen, the *nefesh* of a great student of Rabbi Yohanan ben Zakkai visited Vital's soul;[34] at twenty he hosted the *ibbur* of an outstanding student of Rabbi Akiva;[35] at twenty-nine the soul of Rabbi Akiva himself hovered over him.[36] The timing of the first *ibbur*'s visit to Vital at age thirteen is Jewishly significant because thirteen represents the age of male adulthood. Only with adulthood is a person bound by the *mitzvot,* which empowers the use of the *mitzvot* as tools of soul repair.

Luria also described for his disciple Vital the soul sparks that comprised Vital's reincarnated foundational soul. Luria told Vital that his soul was a cluster of four primary sparks: the incarnation of a young man who died at the age of fourteen; a rich and generous man; a great rabbinic teacher;[37] and a newly redeemed spark.[38] These first three incarnations correspond to the three dimensions of a soul rung—the physical (the young man); the emotional (generous man); and the intellectual (the teacher).[39] Luria went on to tell Vital that in this lifetime he was still trying to perfect the soul sparks on the *nefesh* level, the lowest rung, which caused an apparent blow to Vital's spiritual self esteem.[40] Luria encouraged Vital to make progress through the study of the *Zohar* and through the use of *yechudim,* specific mindsets of intention often generated by prescribed repetition of verses or parts of God's sacred name that accompany the doing of *mitzvot.* Such religious discipline, Luria promised, would allow him to move steadily up the soul ladder in his lifetime.

What I gained from Luria's model is a multidimensional understanding of the soul. Growth of the soul, he taught, requires addressing the physical, emotional, and intellectual dimensions as the foundation of the spiritual. Each level is interdependent and all are nestled together. Perfection is achieved when all the rungs are purified. An engaged, directed imagination, fostered by *yechudim,* is necessary for wielding the *mitzvot* as the tools of soul repair. Luria's model emphasizes that the work we do in this lifetime prepares us for the next one and that our place in this lifetime may have been achieved by overcoming errors in a previous life.

Luria used the concept of soul repair to explain the meaning of a tragic incident. A bridal couple recited the blessing over their food, swallowed their first bites, and choked to death. The devastated parents came to Luria for understanding and comfort. He explained that the bridal couple had almost completed their life tasks in the previous incarnation, but fell short by virtue of never having eaten with the correct divinely focused concentration. When they recited the blessing at the wedding meal, they ate the first bite in the manner necessary for the purification of their souls. It was the work of divine mercy to take them from this life before they spoiled the gains of all their previous lives. [41]

In this story Luria suggested that the man and woman who had found each other were each in need of the same necessary life task. In other cases, he explicitly stated that souls in this life had known each other in a previous incarnation. For instance, Luria said that Moses Cordovero and Elijah de Vidas, two leading Safad mystics of his day, each had a soul spark from Eliezer, servant of Abraham, which explained their great friendship.

Souls divide themselves into families, Luria emphasized, as if people travel across time in groups,[42] which Brian Weiss has also found to be the case.[43] At the same time, within a family unit soul sparks generally came from different body parts of *Adam HaRishon,* enabling complementary personal and spiritual qualities.[44] Two or more people could also simultaneously possess soul sparks that emerged from the same previous incarnation.

When Luria described the previous lives of his followers he

consistently described them as incarnations of male Jews. He claimed that his own soul originated with Moses and had also existed in the body of Simeon bar Yohai, who traditionally was identified as the author of the *Zohar.* This incarnation, Luria explained, was a voluntary return to help others, an act of a *tzaddik* (righteous one).

In Luria's teaching, souls tend to reincarnate in the same gender, although he noted exceptions, like the two famous ancestors of King David. Tamar (daughter-in-law of Judah and later the mother of Judah's child), according to Luria, had the soul of a man, which later passed into Ruth. In order for Ruth (the Moabite who converted to the Israelite faith) to conceive, God imparted to her sparks from another female soul because a woman with a male soul was usually infertile. This seeming division between male and female sparks is jarring to the modern sensibility.

It is also hard for me to relate to Luria's description of temporary human incarnations into animals[45] or rocks as a form of punishment, a view also expressed in diverse world cultures that accept reincarnation, such as Hinduism and Buddhism. Many of the Safad kabbalists held that a person was unaware of his or her previous incarnations except when revealed by a *tzaddik,* like Luria. However, when a person was incarnated into a lower form, the soul became aware of its history and the purpose of its punishment. Moses Galante, one of Luria's students, told a story that expresses Luria's acceptance of the concept of incarnation into nonhumans as a form of punishment.

> Once Luria and Galante were traveling to the grave of the talmudic sage, Judah ben Ilai. As they approached their destination they noticed a crow on an olive tree crowing incessantly. Luria looked up at the bird and said:
>
> "Were you acquainted with Shabbethai the tax farmer of Safad?"
>
> "I knew him," Galante answered. "He was a bad man in

that he displayed great cruelty to the poor when they were unable to pay their taxes."

"This crow," Luria said, "contains Shabbethai's soul."[46]

Luria was a master of the mystical tradition that dates to as early as the rabbis of the first century and found more explicit written expression beginning in the thirteenth century C.E. Although Luria largely reworked preexisting ideas, he also introduced such innovations as the concept of a package of soul sparks and the dramatic new image of "big bang creation," which requires a human role in cosmic repair. Following Luria's teachings, each Jew could view a simple ritual deed or an act of kindness as a contribution to the regathering of divine sparks, a profound cosmic act.

Although Luria's description of the makeup of the soul is ostensibly complex, it can be simplified as a straightforward chain of souls engaged in an ongoing project of repair. Despite the existence of manifold soul sparks and soul visitors, Luria also taught that in practice, an individual normally works on only one level of soul in any one lifetime. The following are two examples, authored by those influenced by Luria, describing the chain of reincarnation of biblical and talmudic figures:

- Jacob sinned by wrongfully humbling himself upon his return to Canaan when he bowed to the ground before his brother Esau (Genesis 33:3). Mordechai repaired Jacob's soul by refusing to bow before Haman, even at the risk of endangering his life (Esther 3:2).[47]

- The good part of Cain's soul incarnated into Aaron, Moses' brother and the first high priest, who had sinned by cooperating with the crafting of the Golden Calf (Exodus 32:1-6). Aaron's soul incarnated into Eli the high priest, who died by breaking his neck from falling off a chair (1 Samuel 4:18), thereby atoning for Aaron's sin. This soul was finally purified when incarnated into Ezra, the prophet who was instrumental in the return to Jerusalem from Babylonian exile.[48]

Due to Luria's influence, the belief that one's life was linked to previous incarnations grew more mainstream in the Jewish community. Reincarnation, for instance, found its way into the *siddur* in the *Shema* prayer recited at bedtime. Sleep in the Jewish tradition offers a taste of death, a product of the letting go of ordinary consciousness and control. The version of the *Shema* prayer recited at bedtime includes an introduction not found elsewhere in the prayer book, which reads:

> Master of the Universe, I hereby forgive anyone who angered or antagonized me . . . whether in this transmigration *(gilgul)* or another transmigration.[49]

This paragraph, derived from kabbalistic ritual, is first found in a *siddur* from the mid-seventeenth century[50] and is still used in contemporary, traditional prayer books, including the popular *Art Scroll Siddur*.[51]

The Ba'al Shem Tov (literally, the master of the Good Name, Israel ben Eliezer, Podolia, 1698–1760), born a little over a century after Luria, and the Hasidic masters who followed built on the Lurianic system. They concretized his ideas by giving them a more psychological emphasis.[52] Knowledge of "past lives" offered insight into needed repairs from previous incarnations and the purpose of this life. After Luria, especially in the Hasidic movement, it became an identified goal of "*rebbe*-craft" (the art of spiritual mastery) for the rabbi-sage to see previous lives by looking at a person and provide information to effectuate *tikkun,* necessary repair of the soul.

༶

10

Tales of Reincarnation:
The Role of the *Rebbe*

Brian Weiss tells how he was once consulted regarding a study by the New York University physics department on the energy emitted by Tai Chi masters and Eastern healers. One of the participants flown in from China asked if Brian Weiss would regress him. Weiss agreed, and the man, while under hypnosis, recounted several past lives. At the end of the session the man asked Weiss, "Could you see the faces of the people I described?" "No," Weiss replied. The participant then said, "Well, my master identified the same past lives I experienced under hypnosis today and my master said he could look at me and see those previous people."[1] Weiss told the story in a tone of amusement, recognizing the limitations of his own skills.

The ability of a master to look at people and see their past lives is also part of the Hasidic tradition. A *rebbe* (the title given by *Hasidim* to their master), many followers said, could look at a person and flip back through earlier lives as if viewing cards in a deck until reaching the universal first card. From the vantage point of *Adam HaRishon,* the first human, the *rebbe* could ascertain the initial vision God had of that soul and thereby know how to direct the soul to meet its potential in the current lifetime.[2] The *rebbe* had to integrate insight into past lives and necessary repairs with an awareness of who the person was in the present, which was gleaned through observation, interviews, intuition, and others' input.

The ability to see a person's past lives was previously attributed to masters of Jewish mysticism. Isaac the Blind (thirteenth century), the most influential mystic of the French Provencal kabbalists,[3] "could tell by a person's face [as if reading an aura][4] whether he was from the new or the old [souls],"[5] relating to the number of previous incarnations. Isaac Luria (sixteenth century) had the ability, according to his students, to perceive all of a person's previous incarnations, as well as *ibburim,* visiting souls. The founders of the Hasidic community were considered by some of their disciples to have this same capacity.

On this topic we have a letter from the Ba'al Shem Tov,[6] the founder of Hasidism, to Rabbi Yitzhaq of Drohobitch. Although scholars today repudiate the historical authenticity of the letter, which was discovered close to 150 years after the Ba'al Shem Tov lived, it is widely accepted within the Hasidic community as accurate and is relevant for understanding communal beliefs:

> Know that for each soul one is to mend and raise to its root, one has to know all that has happened to it—all the incarnations from the time of the Genesis on—and then one can mend it. But, if one does not know enough, then one cannot bring about any good effects, but heaven forbid [one brings about the contrary]. Thus did I receive [the teaching] from my master. But if you are aware of this, I empower you, and you will succeed; for I trust the great justice of your heart, that you will listen and you will hear for what [purpose] the words [are intended]. It is not enough to pay attention to the soul telling of her incarnations, for my master taught me that the soul only tells of her last incarnation. I leave it to you to elaborate. If you are the master of souls, you will understand it all in its fullness. And the Holy One, Blessed be He, will gather our dispersed so that all the

souls will complete their body [the body of Adam], and then the complete redemption will come soon. Amen.[7]

The art of being a Hasidic rabbi was passed from master to disciple. The story is told of how the Seer of Lublin,[8] who lived in Poland at the start of the nineteenth century, gave his shirt to his student the Yehudi[9] so that he could read the incarnations of the souls of the *Hasidim*. The Yehudi was asked to perform the duties of a *rebbe* during his master's absence. The Yehudi then entered a room filled with *Hasidim*, many of whom were unknown to him. He surveyed the gathering to see if there was an aspirant after the *rebbe*'s leadership. The story continues:

And now something came to pass that frightened him as nothing had done during all his life. He looked at one of those who had entered, a very ordinary person, and looked involuntarily upon the man's forehead. In the next instant it seemed to him as though a curtain were drawn apart. He stood at the brink of a sea whose dark waves assaulted the very heavens. And now they too were split asunder as the curtain had been and thus gave space for a figure, totally unlike the visitor, but with the same seal upon its forehead that was seen upon his. But already that figure was devoured by the waves; behind it stood another, different again but with that same seal. It too vanished and farther and farther the depths revealed figures after figures. The Yehudi closed his eyes. When he opened them again, nothing was to be seen but the ordinary man and the people about him and the room with its ordinary furnishings.

For a long time he did not dare to look at the next visitor. So as soon as he did so the same thing took place. Again a curtain was torn asunder and again waves rolled in the abyss and again vision succeeded vision. At this point the Yehudi mastered the disturbance of his mind and decided to obey the plain and open bidding that had been given him. He observed and sought to grasp every figure. He let it sink into the depth of his memory. He forced his eyes to remain open as long as possible. And suddenly when it came to the fourth and fifth visitor he noticed that a change had been accomplished within him. His vision penetrated the depths independently; with inhuman swiftness it pierced those realms; it reached to the background of that row of figures and came upon the very being of the primordial.[10]

The *rebbe*'s goal in seeing past lives was to determine the necessary *tikkun* or repair of the soul needed in this lifetime. In addition to viewing the past, the *rebbe*, it was held, could commune with spirits in the present, like a medium. The *rebbe* might even commune with spirits in anticipation of reincarnation, as illustrated in the following Hasidic tale:

> On a certain Rosh Hashanah evening, the Maggid of Zlotchov[11] saw a man who had been a [Torah] reader in his city and who had died a short time ago. "What are you doing here?" he asked. "The rabbi knows," said the dead man, "that in this night, souls are incarnated anew. I am such a soul." "And why were you sent out again?" asked the Maggid. "I led an impeccable life here on earth," the dead man told him. "And yet you are forced to live once more?" the Maggid went on to ask. "Before my death," said the man, "I thought over everything I had done and found that I had always acted in just the right way. Because of this my heart swelled with satisfaction and in the midst of this feeling I died. So now they have sent me back into the world to atone for my pride."
>
> At that time a son was born to the Maggid. His name was Reb Wolf of Zbarazh. He was very humble.[12]

Stories proliferated among *Hasidim* on how we often travel in clusters of souls until we get it right. The following is such a tale:[13]

> A rich man once came to make the acquaintance of the Ba'al Shem Tov (also known by the acronym "the Besht"). He explained to the Master that he had no particular problem that required the *rebbe*'s blessing, but that, having heard many great and wonderful stories concerning the deeds of the Besht, he

had decided he must meet this man. In reply, the Besht asked the man if he would mind hearing another story. The man was eager to listen and so the Besht began:

There were once two men who had grown up together as friends. However, when they reached manhood, they found themselves in very different circumstances. One was a wealthy man, and the other very poor. The poor man, in order to save his life, asked help of his rich friend. The wealthy man did not hesitate, but offered his friend half his fortune. Now, with time, the situations of the men reversed, and the one who had before been wealthy was now very poor, while his friend, to whom he had given half his fortune, had become a very wealthy man. Sure that he could receive help from his now wealthy friend, the poor man sought him out and explained to him his difficulty. But instead of helping him, the wealthy man ran away in order to avoid having to part with any of his fortune. However, time once again reversed their situations so that the poor man became rich and the rich man became poor, and they were once more returned to their original situations. Now, the friend who had before refused to part with his fortune began to feel the distress of his own situation, and went to his friend begging forgiveness. The man who was now wealthy readily forgave his friend and offered to help him out of his difficulties, but this time he insisted that the friend give him a note, as insurance that if he was later in need his friend would share. Needless to say, as time passed, the two men again suffered a reversal of fortunes, but true to form the man who had written the note refused to honor it and his friend remained penniless.

The two men died. When they came before the heavenly tribunal, the full sinfulness of the one friend's life weighed against him and he was sentenced to Hell, while his friend was to go to Heaven. However, the one who was to go to Heaven would not accept the plight of his friend, and he explained to the Heavenly court that, in spite of the manner in which his friend had treated him, he still loved him and did not wish to see him condemned to Hell. The decision of the tribunal was that the only way to avoid this was to return both men to earth, so that the sinful man might have an opportunity to atone for his actions. And so the sinful man was returned to earth and established himself as a rich man, while the other was but a beggar.

When the beggar knocked on the door of the rich man, begging for sustenance, he was pushed rudely away and refused any aid. And so the beggar died.

At this point in the story the rich man . . . jumped up, an amazed look on his face. "Yesterday," he said, "I turned away a beggar. Was he the beggar of your story and am I that rich man?"

No answer was necessary, but the Besht nodded. The man was overcome with repentance, and was anxious to know how he could make amends for his sin. The Besht explained to him that his friend, the beggar, had a widow, and that he was to go and give three-quarters of his fortune to that widow in order to atone for his sin.

In sum, the Jewish sages went beyond the theory of reincarnation to become practitioners of repair of the soul through past-life counseling. The soul was understood as reincarnating with both the need to atone for past wrongs and to elevate itself through living piously and lovingly. Among the *rebbes,* many were held to have the capacity both to perceive past lives and to commune with the dead.

My goal in studying material on spiritual masters who perceived past lives was to explore Jewish beliefs and to assess the reality of reincarnation. As a rabbi, I don't anticipate acquiring the capacities that *Hasidim* attribute to their *rebbes.* I do believe that my own faith in reincarnation could serve as a source of comfort and insight to the community. That developing faith rests on both reading and firsthand experiences.

My willingness to accept survival of the soul was enhanced by my participation in Brian Weiss's workshop. I was struck at the workshop by both the accounts of past lives and by subjects' descriptions of passing "between lives," during which spirits addressed them. Later I observed "mediums" that seemingly engaged at will with the spirit world. The capacity to communicate with the dead is already described in the Bible and is present in a diverse range of rabbinic texts. What made watching the mediums so intriguing was that I could compare their "communications" with facts known to me, facts that the mediums would not otherwise have known.

ᔐ

11

Mediums: Judaism's Position

Several members of my community who lost children provided my first exposure to the work of mediums. In one striking case, the child had died suddenly at the age of seven from an asthma attack. The parents, pillars of my community, were devastated. When I learned that the father had appeared on national television to describe the ability of medium George Anderson to conjure up his son, I was shocked and even a bit embarrassed. I knew that the father had been suffering, and I treated his act as a response to his grief. When I talked with the father he shared that all the couples in his grief support group had used a medium to access their deceased children. Even more remarkable was that his Orthodox rabbi had given him permission to do so, based on, he said, guidance from the head of a national Orthodox court.

Perplexed, I asked a leading professor of Talmud in the Conservative movement if Jews are permitted to consult with mediums. Without pausing he replied, "Of course not. The Torah prohibition is clear." I double-checked the Torah's command, which seemed pretty straightforward: "There shall not be found among you . . . a consulter with familiar spirits . . . or a necromancer" (Deuteronomy 18:10–11).[1] The next day the professor called and said, "I was wrong. Jewish law does permit calling on the dead in certain cases. You can go to a medium that is simply telling you what he or she is hearing. But," he added, "Who would want to?" He left me with the relevant legal citations.

Before looking up the citations in the Talmud (a foundational rabbinic source encompassing rabbinic discussions from the second to sixth centuries), I read with renewed relish and curiosity a familiar biblical account of the use of a medium (1 Samuel 28:7–25). The story from the Book of Samuel concerns King Saul, who was terrified by the advancing Philistine armies. In the past he had turned to the prophet Samuel for guidance, but the prophet was now dead. King Saul dressed up in disguise and came to a woman known as "the Witch of En-Dor," for it was said that she could commune with the dead. The king's use of a medium was all the more remarkable in that he had previously outlawed this activity (1 Samuel 28:3). Although in disguise, at the start of his meeting Saul promised to protect the Witch of En-Dor from the law.

The dialogue then continues (1 Samuel 11–15):

> And the woman says: "Whom shall I bring up for you?"
>
> He [Saul] says: "Samuel, bring [him] up for me."
>
> And when the woman saw Samuel, she cried out loudly and said to Saul: "Why did you deceive me, you are Saul!"
>
> And the king said to her: "Don't be afraid on account of what you saw."
>
> The woman said to Saul: "I saw a godlike man going up from the earth."
>
> "What did he look like?" he said to her.
>
> And she said: "He came up looking like an old man wrapped in a mantle."
>
> And Saul knew that it was Samuel, and he bowed his head toward the ground and prostrated himself. And Samuel said to Saul: "Why did you disturb me by bringing me up?"

A conversation between King Saul and Samuel ensues in which Saul explains his great fear of the Philistines. The prophet replies that God is removed from Saul because of his mistaken pity on the Amalekites, which defied God's command. Consequently, the prophet says, the Philistines will defeat Saul and he and his sons will die the next day in battle. Samuel's prophecies come true. The text does not condemn Saul for having consulted a medium and suggests that the Witch of En-Dor had indeed made contact with the other world.

When the rabbis of the Talmud examined the Bible's prohibition against "necromancy," the act of calling on the dead, they read the prohibition quite narrowly. The biblical command is linked to idolatry, with a detailed description of the bones, incense, and the knocking of arms that were used as tools to accompany incantations in consulting the dead. The text (Sanhedrin 65b) explains:

> "Or that consults with the dead" means one who starves himself and spends the night in a cemetery, so that an "unclean spirit" may rest upon him.
>
> And when Rabbi Akiva reached this verse, he wept: "If one who starves himself that an unclean spirit may rest upon him has his wish granted, he who fasts that the pure spirit [the divine presence] may rest upon him—how much more should his desire be fulfilled."

The Talmud's discussion of the biblical prohibition of calling on the dead assumes that such communication is possible, which is reinforced by the following story about two of the leading rabbis of fourth-century Babylonia:

> Raba, seated before Rav Nahman, saw him sinking into slumber [death]. Said [Rav Nahman] to Raba: "Tell him [the angel of death], Master, not to make it painful for me."
>
> He [Raba] replied, "Master, are you not an important man?"
>
> Said [Rav Nahman] to him: "Who is important, well-regarded, or distinguished [before the Angel of Death]?"

> Said [Raba] to him: "Show yourself to me [after your death],
> Master."
> He did show himself. [Raba] asked him, "Did you suffer
> pain, Master?"
> He [Rav Nahman] replied: "No more than removing a hair
> from milk. But if the Holy One, blessed be He, were to say to
> me, 'Go back to the world as you were,' I would decline, for the
> dread [of death] is anguishing."[2]

This story shaped the sages' understanding of the prohibition
of mediums. Necromancy could not be such a clear-cut prohibition if among Israel's greatest teachers there was both a request
for a friend to appear "from the other side" and the sage complied.

In the initial legal writings following the Talmud (dating from
the seventh through twelfth centuries), the rabbis were quite
guarded against necromancy.[3] They held that Raba did not violate
the prohibition because he extracted the promise while Rav Nahman was still alive. A shift in attitude occurred in the thirteenth
century when many of the leading rabbis along the Rhine River, referred to as *Hasdei Ashkenaz,* gave permission to consult the
dead. Their rationale was that the prohibition was only against
consulting with the body of the dead, while calling on the spirit
was permitted because the spirit was not "dead."[4] There were contemporaries who disagreed and asserted that the body and spirit
were inseparable.[5]

As Jewish mysticism grew in importance, so did the view of
Hasdei Ashkenaz, because in mysticism the soul was regarded as
an entity existing separate from the body. Even opponents of *Hasdei Ashkenaz* grew to accept necromancy, asserting that the Torah
forbade only the use of idolatrous-like rituals, marked by the use of
special outfits and incense for conjuring up the dead.[6] If the practitioner conjured up the dead through the use of holy names, as
provided by Jewish mystical texts,[7] then it was permitted.

A leniency in speaking with the dead was codified in the sixteenth century in the *Shulkhan Arukh,* which remains until this

day the authoritative guide to Jewish practice. Joseph Karo (Israel, 1488-1575 and a contemporary of Isaac Luria in Safad), the codifier of Sephardic law (directed to Spanish, Mediterranean Jews), wrote: "To cause a sick person to swear that he will return after his death to tell him [his living friend] what he will ask him is permitted." And the codifier of Ashkenazic law (directed to Central and Eastern European Jews), Moses Isserles (Poland, d.1572), added as a gloss to Karo's statement: "And there are those who even permit [asking a question of the dead] after his death, if he doesn't address the body of the dead, but only his spirit."[8]

There are many examples of Jewish sages in Jewish literature using mediums or having the power to engage spirits in conversation. Chaim Vital (1542-1620), the key disciple of Isaac Luria, used several female mediums to maintain contact with Luria, which he wrote about in his diary.[9] Joseph Karo, Vital's and Isaac Luria's Safad contemporary, also kept a diary in which he recorded that for most of his adult years he was visited by a *maggid,* a spiritual being, who helped guide him in many aspects of life, including the composition of his Jewish law code, the *Shulkhan Arukh.*[10]

Contact with spirits was also accepted among opponents of Hasidism, for whom such contact was accepted practice. A disciple of the Vilna Gaon (Elijah ben Solomon Zalman, 1720-1797), said that his teacher, too, claimed contact with the realm of spirits.[11] The Vilna Gaon was a prodigy who dedicated his whole life to study. He was unquestionably the talmudic master of his day and also expert in the *Zohar,* universally considered a sacred text by his time. He was a sober rationalist. He severely criticized the *Hasidim* for their emphasis on prayer over study, their reliance on folk mysticism, and their insistence that God's sparks were found in everything in creation, even a pile of manure. Yet, in the words of a disciple of the Vilna Gaon in an account published in 1820:

> I heard from his holy mouth that many times *maggidim* from Heaven appeared to him, requesting to deliver to him the mysteries of Torah without any effort, but he would not listen to

them. . . . When one of the *maggidim* insisted persistently . . .
he answered, 'I do not want my understanding of the Torah to
be mediated [by others].[12]

I am amused by the Vilna Gaon's alleged rejection of the guidance of the spirit realm. It sounds like he rejected a gift in order to
retain rational control. At the same time, I admire his insistence
that he could gain the same insights by virtue of his intellectual
talents and concentrated study.

Engagement with the spirit realm became a widely expected
dimension of the *rebbe*'s work in the Hasidic community. It is said
that the Ba'al Shem Tov once tested Rabbi Gershon Kittover to see
if he could help him in his work with deceased souls.[13] After the
Ba'al Shem Tov showed Rabbi Gershon what *kavannah* (method
of meditative intention) to use, Rabbi Gershon followed his instructions and, suddenly faced with the uprush of countless souls,
fainted.[14] In more recent times, when Rabbi Shneur Zalman of
Lyady (1745–1813) was imprisoned, he stated that his ability to in-
voke the presence of exalted souls helped greatly to sustain him in
his suffering.[15] A later Lubavitcher *rebbe*, Rabbi Joseph Isaac
Schneerson, reported beholding similar visions during his imprisonment in Moscow.[16]

The ability to call on the deceased was not limited to rabbis.
Jews from every walk of life would visit the graves of loved ones
and venerable rabbis, asking them to intervene in healing, assist
with prayers, or solve problems. Rabbinic authorities justified such
practices. Today it is common practice, for example, for followers
of the recently deceased Lubavitcher *rebbe,* Menachem Mendel
Schneerson, to visit his grave in New York and to seek his guidance or intervention. In Israel today there are one-day bus tours to
the "holy graves of the rabbis," which are very popular with members of the religious community. I even know a couple that chose
to spend their honeymoon on such a trip, anticipating that it
would bring them good fortune.

In sum, several major streams of Judaism permit calling on the spirit of the departed and the use of mediums. The biblical prohibition against necromancy is limited to calling on the dead as an idolatrous religious act, evidenced by rituals such as special incantations, clothing, or incense. Conjuring up of the dead through the use of Jewishly acceptable mystical techniques, such as recombinations of the letters of God's name, is seen as a sacred act. Jewish tradition also discourages the use of mediums to foretell the future, for to do so contradicts the basic Jewish tenets of free will and individual responsibility for the future.

My reading of the Bible, kabbalistic and legal writings, and Hasidic stories reinforces for me that in the Jewish tradition there is widespread belief in the ability to commune with the dead. At the same time there is a "Ripley's Believe It or Not" quality to the accounts. Prior to my own firsthand encounters with mysteries at graveside and past-life regression, I related to the stories of survival of the soul as quaint folk literature. Another type of firsthand experience would reinforce that some people might really be able to talk with the dead. My exposure to the work of a leading medium would come on the heels of the Omega retreat and leave me amazed and more respectful of the stories I had read.

〜

12

Psychic Gifts of a Medium: James Van Praagh

James Van Praagh has become quite famous in recent years due to three best-selling books about his work as a medium.[1] I saw him before the publication of his first book. I learned of Van Praagh's psychic gifts from Brian and Carole Weiss during our evening out in July 1997. Brian Weiss mentioned that he had appeared on a TV talk show with Van Praagh, who had amazed the studio audience with specific information about deceased loved ones. It seemed he could reach into the spiritual space that Catherine, Weiss's patient, had accessed under hypnosis and converse with the souls of the departed. Upon returning to Southern California from the Omega retreat, my wife and I learned of an evening workshop offered by Van Praagh entitled "Developing Your Psychic Gifts."

My experience with mediums was quite limited. Although I had read about such phenomena, I had only seen a medium in action on television. A couple in my congregation, Pearl and her husband, Zane, had shared with me a videotape of their encounter with one of America's best-known mediums, George Anderson of Long Island, New York. He was the same medium that I had observed my other friend (who had lost his seven-year-old son) affirm on national television.

Pearl and Zane mourned their twenty-five-year-old daughter, Ellen, who had died six months earlier when the car in which she was a passenger crashed into a palm tree. Ellen's parents remained

unsure of the full cause of the accident and felt the natural guilt
that accompanies loved ones when a life is struck down prematurely. These congregants gained access to George Anderson by
agreeing to have their session with him filmed for a news program
on a Los Angeles television station, which resulted in the videotape they shared with me.

I knew this middle-aged couple to be conventional and trustworthy. They told me that they had never met George Anderson
before the taping. Pearl said that she had told her husband on the
drive to the studio, "I'll believe that the medium is for real if he
mentions my mother's name." Her mother, Anna, had died when
Pearl was three years old and, she said, none of her friends in California would have known her name.

I watched the video with Linda, my wife and a skeptic by medical training and disposition, in our living room one night and
grew more riveted as the encounter unfolded. The medium remained awake throughout the session. There were no incantations, no magic. The medium engaged in a kind of automatic
writing throughout the session and remained very attentive to the
couple. When he spoke he did so as if their daughter were con-
versing with him.

Anderson told the couple their daughter's name and nickname
and said that she had died as a passenger in a car accident. On
Ellen's behalf he asked that they not feel guilty, for they had been
fine parents. She also said, he reported, that they should not be
angry with the driver, who had also died and was sorry to have
caused the accident. George Anderson described her humor and
personality. At a certain point the medium said, "Your mother,
Anna, is here, too." I smiled as I observed Pearl's sideway glance at
Zane. The medium also said Esther, the family member for whom
Ellen was named, was alongside Ellen. He also named and described Zane's parents.

Pearl and Zane later told me that they had become believers in
Anderson's ability to communicate with their daughter. They found

her words to be a great source of comfort and healing. I took seriously what I had seen because I knew that Pearl and Zane were stable and credible. The medium's specificity of information was remarkable. The video softened my wariness of the ability of some "to talk with the dead." Yet, watching on television was not the same as being part of the experience. It was not my story being revealed, which allowed me to remain somewhat emotionally detached. Although the videotape impressed me, I remained unsure as to whether the experience was reproducible for others, which would have demonstrated that the communication was real.

My wife and I drove the hour to Los Angeles to see Van Praagh with playful anticipation. We arrived a few minutes after he began his session. The hotel conference room was packed with close to 250 participants. Van Praagh emphasized that the purpose of the workshop was for us to discover our psychic gifts. To observe him conduct readings we would need to return on another date, which was not an option for Linda and me due to an upcoming trip. Van Praagh appeared to be in his early forties and was dressed as if he were going bowling.

The first part of the three-hour evening was a slide show lecture on the *chakras,* an Indian-Sanskrit term for the seven energy centers that relate to our grounding and psychic ability. He led the group in a variety of exercises, including a guided imagery of our own *chakras* and a hand scan of our neighbor in the group, which produced a heat or tingling in my palms upon placement near different points of the body. Two hours into the evening he asked one person to give an object—a ring, watch, or necklace— to a neighbor whom he or she was meeting for the first time. He led us in a guided, mental imagery asking that we fasten a cable to the lowest part of our spine, our lowest *chakra,* and attach the other end of the cable to the earth. We were told that in this energy-drawing meditative state we were to hold an object from our neighbor in our palm and observe whatever came to mind, as if watching a movie screen.

When my wife finished holding the ring of her neighbor, she reported to the other participant on what she had seen. The following is her description.

> I held the ring. First I saw a purple and lavender object that appeared to be some hard material like glass. It had upturned, almost outstretched, handlike parts. If it was a vase it was unclear to me how any flowers could fit in. As a sculpture it was somehow incomplete. Perhaps it was a part of something.
>
> Then I saw a woman's bare feet in wedge-type sandals from the 1950s. There was a stripe of a color and gold. The woman's feet were her mother's. Then I saw her mother in a "housedress" in the background down a hall-like room. It was kind of dark. In the foreground was the woman (Bess) as a little girl. She didn't look the same, but I knew it was her. She was with her sister and a dog. The dog was like a collie, but so little. At the time, I didn't know there was such a type of dog.
>
> Next I saw a photo, an old photo of her and her family waving from a car on vacation in Florida. (She is still a girl there.) I drew this later in my notebook. The photo is sunny and faded. In the foreground is a huge parking lot. There are a few trees and if I thought about it I would be tempted to say it was in California. I knew I shouldn't think but rather go with my feeling sense of the picture. Otherwise the pictures wouldn't come. So I felt it was Florida. In the back on the left was an apartment or hotel building. Next to it was a car with the vacationing, happy family waving. There were a few palm trees up there, too.
>
> The next scene started with a feeling. Her mother is dead. I see green, lush grass well cared for on a low rolling hill and a white-domed mausoleum. I guess her mom is there.

When the woman heard Linda's description of the dog, she exclaimed, "That's Princess, the dog I had as a child!"

In reference to the purple object, the woman said, "Linda, the purple object you described is a vase that sits on my mantel, along with the photo you just mentioned. I was showing these objects to my niece just this afternoon."

"Last," Linda said, "I saw a white round building, which I sense was your mother's cemetery, but it wasn't exactly a grave."

"That's right, my mother died and is in a mausoleum."

The woman was staggered by the specificity of the material that Linda had shared, and Linda was even more amazed. She had never before participated in such an exercise and did not know that she had "psychic" power.

With about a half hour left in the workshop, Van Praagh said, "Okay, I'll now demonstrate what I do in my work as a medium. First, I want you to imagine your favorite cartoon character pictured on this wall. Then while holding the picture in mind simultaneously recite the ABC's and count from 100 backwards. Now, that is the kind of concentration I need to interpret signs and to sort out the comments made to me from the other side. There are many spirits who wish to convey messages, and I am aided by two spirits who serve as ushers choosing who can get through.

"Once I begin I want you to only give 'yes' or 'no' answers. At the outset the spirit will give identifying information to make it clear that the spirit is speaking to a particular person. It is very important that you acknowledge the spirit, or the spirit will go away. I will be like a telephone between you. At the same time what I'm shown or what I hear is sometimes only a symbol and often requires me to interpret, so your 'yes' or 'no' responses help me know if I'm on track." With closed eyes he offered a nondenominational prayer, asking God to be a protecting presence for him, and then he began. I continue by shifting to my wife Linda's description (referred to as LS) as related after the session in writing for me.

Van Praagh (VP) said to close our eyes and get comfortable. It had been very exciting to be so right about the ring stuff. Now I knew I'd get a chance to just relax. All those people with their sad stories of prematurely departed relatives. Such raw pain. Now we would see them with their intense hopes imagining contact with their relatives.

I closed my eyes. It had been bright and I could see a little reddish color as I felt the tops of my lids. In a microsecond I scanned my four grandparents with regret that I didn't know my paternal grandparents better.

"You can open your eyes." So I did. There was a lot of excitement in the room and a little humor. "I see a man. Someone's father. Sam. Samuel. I see a J."

We had been instructed to say very little when answering Van Praagh's questions. Just affirm or not—just 'yes' or 'no' answers. I took the word "father" literally. Though my father's father had been known as Sam, it was too exciting and too weird to think that now Van Praagh was "doing *Zayde*" [Yiddish for "grandfather"]. The J sort of threw me, I mean my grandfather's real name was Joshua and Van Praagh kept squinting and saying "it's Sam, but I see a J." There was no way I was going to believe this so I kept my mouth shut.

First of all I could not believe anyone could just call up dead people as if on an invisible cordless phone. Second, my father's parents had died thirty-four years earlier and I had been a little girl. They hadn't spoken much English and I regret to say I hadn't been that close to them. A medium talking to *my* dead grandparents—no way. Too weird. Also, VP had said the most he'd ever been able to go back was about forty years. I didn't think that he, the Sam he was speaking to, had been my relative. Plus, technically speaking, my dad's name is not Sam.

There was almost a palpable buzz in the room. First, it was exciting. Second, it seemed that VP was having a hard time distinguishing the name, and third, no one was identifying the person.

Before I continue with VP, let me share a relevant aside. The day prior to going to VP something unusual happened that I hadn't mentioned to anyone. Joey, our eldest son, scraped his leg. He wanted a Band-Aid. I knew we had lots of them around the house, but somehow I couldn't find one and I just talked Joey out of it.

Van Praagh looks in our direction. "Anyone with a father named Samuel?" He says he senses it's in our part of the room.

I'm feeling uneasy but in no way convinced. Fortunately the woman one seat up and to my right blurts out, "It could be my father-in-law, but he died before we were married." That cut the tension in the room.

VP said, "I see glasses. Did he wear glasses?"

Lady: "I don't know if he wore glasses. It could be. I never met him."

VP asked a few other questions like, "Did he have a cane?" and the lady answered them the same—"I don't really know. I didn't know him."

VP: "J, Joseph, Jon, Justin, Joe."

I feel a little queasy. In that short list of names are the names of our sons.

VP: "And yesterday you were looking for a Band-Aid for your son Joe, but you couldn't find one."

My stomach gave me a squeeze as I raised my shaky hand. I could hear my voice quiver as I said, "I had a grandfather named Sam and yesterday I couldn't find my son Joey a Band-Aid. It could be me." There was an audible sigh in the room.

So specific. I was totally focused on VP. How could he do this? But I would only answer 'yes' or 'no' as he instructed. How accurate could he be? What was the trick? I never would believe this if it were anyone but me. Anyone else, I would have been sure it was a shill.

VP: "I see a cane."

LS: "Nope, no cane." My grandfather did not walk with a cane.

VP: "He keeps saying, 'The cane, the cane.'"

LS: "No. I don't remember any cane." This went on for several rounds until we almost sounded like a comedy team. "Cane?" "No cane." "Cane?" "No cane." I wasn't going to give an inch.

VP was hearing the word cane *and looked impa-
tient. "He keeps saying, 'The cane,* the cane.'"

When I was a little girl, my very serious grandfather who spoke
little English used to entertain me with a trick. He would balance a cane on the very tip of his thumb. He was truly amazing
in his ability to balance it. It was something that he would do to
make me laugh. I had nearly forgotten.

LS: "Oh, the cane!"
    VP nodded. "He says you have his picture."

Now I have lots of old photos, but there is one picture I have
that is very different from the others. When my grandfather
came to this country he was in his early twenties. He worked
hard and had a special portrait done. It was a convex photo
about two feet long, touched with watercolor and placed in a
gold oval frame. I loved it because the *Zayde* I had known was
an old man with wispy white hair. In this portrait he was young,
vibrant, with dark brown hair and he looked so much like my
dad. This was the photo VP was describing. In all the family
only I have such a picture.
    VP went on to ask about a number of things. Each time, un-
less I could identify it exactly, I denied it. He asked about a
ring. "Nope."

VP: "Ask about it when you're home."
    He asked about a locket. "Nope."
    VP: "When you're home, ask ..."
    *VP: "You have a child you almost lost. A girl. There
was a time you were worried. . . ." "Yes," my husband
and I nodded. Our daughter had been in the Children's
Hospital intensive care unit for four days the year before for a serious illness resulting from an accident.*
    *VP: "This man seems larger than he is. He is short, but
very effective. Good at business."*
    VP: "He is dressed in a suit and looks very dapper. He

has a ring and cuff links." (This I don't remember. My Zayde was a modest elderly man when I knew him. He did wear suits, but I couldn't remember any jewelry. I think there were cuff links in the painted photo. Perhaps he had given them away or when my grandparent's estate was broken up one of the children inherited it.

VP:"He says he had lived in an eastern city. Someone in the family, a girl, is now going to live in that city. He says to stay in touch with her." (In fact, his eldest great-granddaughter, who is named for him, was going off to Boston for her freshman year that week. He had lived just outside Boston when he first came to the U.S. He died more than a decade before she was born.)

VP:"I see his wife. There's something funny about her head."

LS:"Well she had a stroke when she was old."

VP: "No, it was something about the shape of her head." (I couldn't answer this one and for several minutes VP and I argued about this.) "Ask about this at home ..."

"She says the man on your right is your husband and she wants to wave and say 'hi' to you, too. She says you are going on a big trip." (We were leaving for a sabbatical in Israel in just a few weeks.) It's well deserved and it will be very good. She says you are concerned about money. I see you with papers around you in a circle going over finances. She says everything will be fine." (In fact, the day before we had been refinancing a mortgage for our home. At the last minute I needed some records I hadn't anticipated and ended up sitting on the floor with piles of papers arranged on the floor around me in a circle. On the way to the VP talk Elie and I discussed financing our year abroad.)

VP:"I see scissors. Usually that means someone was a tailor. Were they tailors?"

LS: "No." (My other grandparents were tailors, but I could only answer "yes" or "no" and so I couldn't tell him.)

VP:"They weren't tailors? I see a Ruth or a Rose." (I had to deny this, sadly. When I asked my mother later if she knew a Rose she said, "Sure, My mother Anna Rose . . ." who was a tailor. I was applying the strict "Yes" and "No" rule to names as well.) Apparently when you don't acknowledge someone they cannot "come in." I'm sorry; I would have loved to hear from my other grandmother, too.

I was shocked at his accuracy. No one could have known all those details about us. Especially now that we were packing and I had no time to talk with anyone. Some of the things he knew I had mentioned to no one; they had been just unspoken thoughts. I was totally overcome with emotion. Literally spooked. Despite the scientific skepticism there is no doubt I had heard from my grandparents. On the long ride home I kept wondering (with a smile) if my grandparents were joyriding on the front hood of the car. Weird. Too weird. But accurate.

The next day I phoned my parents. "Dad, I saw this psychic and he said there was something funny about Baubie's head. Do you remember anything funny about her head?"

"Sure. When I was a baby, a car hit her. She was hospitalized a long time and needed some kind of surgery on her head. I am told she had a shaven head with stitches that my older brothers and Aunt Rose remember. It was a scary time for the family." I had never known about it. I asked my dad why he had never mentioned it. He really had been too young to remember it firsthand, just an infant when it occurred.

In retrospect there was sort of a flattening about Baubie's forehead. "Dad," I asked, "Do you know anything about a locket or a ring?" "No," he said. I then called his older sister, my Aunt Rose, and asked about Baubie's head.

"Oh my, yes. You didn't know about my mother's accident?

I was playing and while she was crossing the street bringing lunch to *Zayde* she was hit by a car. A lady came up to the house to tell me my mother was hit by a car and was dead. Baubie's head looked pretty bad for a long time, her hair didn't grow back for a while, and you could see those stitches."

So how had VP gotten wind of this when even I didn't know?

I asked her about a locket. There was a very long pause. Finally my aunt said, "Yes, I have Baubie's locket." I felt as if I had discovered a secret. It clearly was not something she wanted to talk about. She also has grandchildren. Perhaps she thought I was going to ask for it. I love my aunt, and I didn't want her to think I was looking for something.

"What locket?" I asked.

"When my parents got engaged, my father gave my mother a gold locket with her initials, E.I., engraved on it." Not only had I not known this, neither had my dad.

When Van Praagh finished channeling my wife's family members, he moved on to channel for others in the room. "Now, Maria is coming through," Van Praagh said. To the man who identified himself as her son, Van Praagh described how she had died. He said on behalf of the deceased, "I have been coming through to your friend Joanne in dreams, which she has told you, but you did not believe her." The man nodded agreement, weeping, with an older man's arm around his shoulder. "I see you are ready to buy a house. Know that it will go well for you," Van Praagh concluded.

There were several more departed "souls" whom Van Praagh presented. In each case he spoke with great specificity about their hobbies or work. He described the cause and process of their deaths. He reassured loved ones that the spirits were doing well. He mentioned specific events in the lives of their loved ones. In each case the people who were addressed responded emotionally and appeared comforted.

My wife was spinning from her encounter with her grandparents. She was surprised that, with all the people in the room, it was her grandfather, who died thirty-four years earlier, who had gotten to be "first in line." When the workshop ended she asked Van Praagh if he remembered anything else that was said or that happened with Samuel or his wife. He said that he didn't; that once he was done, the encounter was a bit of a blur. I saw how deeply Linda felt loved by the awareness that her grandparents had apparently wanted to communicate with her. We were both left excited and a bit overwhelmed by this new experience.

Van Praagh's presentation was comparable to the session with George Anderson that I had observed a year earlier. Following this live demonstration I read Anderson's *We Don't Die,*[2] which details many examples of his power to serve as a bridge to the other side. I began to respect the ability of mediums to offer comfort in the face of loss. Mediums and those with telepathic gifts may know uncanny bits of information that fill in gaps in our knowledge and help alleviate guilt. Yet, mediums are limited, too, both in terms of the knowledge they possess and the healing they can effect.

When a medium gathers information, based on what I have read and seen, it is as if he or she is looking at a scene through a slit in a fence. The medium doesn't see the full picture and what he or she sees (or hears) usually includes an element of extrapolation. Regrettably, some mediums may use their limited knowledge for personal gain and may suggest that they know more than they do. Some are outright charlatans who prey on people in pain and offer vague messages and spiritual pronouncements.

Conversation with a deceased loved one presents several risks. The contact can become an obsession and an obstacle to letting go, which is a necessary step in the integration of loss. There is a temptation to use a medium to foretell the future, which puts great power in the medium's hands due to the natural phenomenon of self-fulfilling prophecy. When we expect something to happen we influence that outcome. Finally, Jewish folk wisdom maintains that many spirits on the other side do not wish to be disturbed, as with the prophet Samuel, who chastised Saul in the encounter with the Witch of En-Dor.

Yet despite all these cautions, a medium that is genuinely gifted, sincere, and sensitive can assist in healing. Offering a form of communication with "the other side" can facilitate the completion of unfinished business between the living and the deceased, which may provide closure and alleviate guilt. A medium may provide comfort by simply affirming that death is not the final end.

Watching Van Praagh up close revealing information about a loved one was a turning point for me in verifying survival of the soul. This last experience fit neatly with many of my other encounters over the previous two years, including graveside mysteries and past life regressions. It was time for me to review what I had observed firsthand and assimilated through reading and to come to some conclusions.

꧂

13

Weighing the Evidence

As I reviewed the evidence for survival of the soul I could certainly imagine more foolproof evidence than what had been made available to me. In law we speak of "the smoking gun," the case where witnesses have actually observed the defendant emerge from the victim's room carrying a weapon, later correlated with the murder. Yet, even such powerful circumstantial evidence is not foolproof. All I could do was survey my encounters, conversations, and readings to determine which of the possible interpretations of the data appeared most compelling. Through that process, I grew to believe that another realm does exist, to which our souls pass upon death and from which they may return into a new physical life.

Van Praagh's accuracy of detail astounded Linda and me. His knowledge of particulars could not be explained away as information shared in advance of the session or provided by subjects planted in the audience. Linda and I had only decided at the last minute to attend the session and would not have been considered "VIPs" worthy of special attention from among the audience of hundreds. In addition, Linda was unaware of some of the information shared, verifying it only after the evening was over. Linda's ignorance of specifics cited by Van Praagh made me rule out the possibility that he gleaned certain information telepathically from Linda. We were left with Van Praagh's explanation as the most plausible. Somehow he was able to gain information from the spirits of the deceased.

The ability of mediums to communicate with the dead supported Weiss's assertion that he had regressed Catherine to a state "between lives" in which she was able to tell him the causes of his son's death and his father's Yiddish name. Catherine under hypnosis said that "masters" in the realm beyond were the source of her knowledge. Mediums can apparently reach into that realm from a wakeful state. The evidence of mediums apparently conferring with spirits reinforces my faith in survival of the soul, but still leaves open a key question: Do memories of past lives really exist? We need to make two determinations to assess whether the memories are actually based on a past life: the credibility of the subjects and historical verification.

My initial exposure to Telushkin's tape in the spring of 1997 had impressed me greatly. The woman he regressed provided a detailed account of her experience on the Oregon Trail. As I mentioned earlier, Telushkin verified the names she provided of the wagon train organizer and the head of her wagon train. He identified a nineteenth century pamphlet that contained the text she had quoted. He even found a diary entry made by a woman with the name the subject had said was hers under hypnosis. In a wakeful state, the woman said she knew almost nothing about the Oregon Trail. I tended to trust Telushkin's assertion of her trustworthiness, but I sought more data. She might have had some earlier exposure to these facts that remained tucked away in the recesses of her mind.

Since viewing Telushkin's tape I had witnessed scores of regressions, mostly over the course of the week at Omega. The overall intensity of the accounts and the ways that they differed from dream material persuaded me to remain open-minded. In the past-life regressions I observed, the vivid "memories" were logical, formed a consistent description of a set historical period, and included vivid sensory and emotional detail. The lives remembered were consistently ordinary. None of the subjects remembered being a monarch or a famous person from the past, as I had heard scoffers of past-life memory assert. Rather, the subjects described themselves as butlers, homesteaders, wives whose husbands abused them, wives whose husbands struggled but loved them. For instance, a Jewish woman, Orthodox from birth, whom I hypnotized after Omega, had no explanation as to why she saw herself as a poor boy in the South in the early twentieth century, or, in another regression, as a wealthy matron in England. Yet the imagination is powerful. I sought more data in further reading.[1]

There is an extensive literature of past-life memory accounts. Yonassan Gershom has interviewed many non-Jews in North America who report memories of the Holocaust from a previous life. To provide one example from among many, Gershom tells of a non-Jewish goat farmer in Nova Scotia who saw himself in a series of vivid dreams as a Dutch Jew during the Holocaust hiding with a family heirloom clock. In one dream the farmer saw the name of an antique store called "the Tyme" where the clock was to be found. Sure enough, there was a new antique store not far from his home in Nova Scotia named "the Tyme." He went with a friend and looked around but only saw furniture. Just as he was getting ready to leave, feeling disappointed by his lack of success, the antique dealer came out from the back room. When the dealer closed the door, the farmer saw the exact clock that he had seen in his dream, which had been hidden from view.[2]

The most experienced researcher in past-life memory that I know of is Ian Stevenson, a psychiatrist who has spent most of his career as a faculty member at the University of Virginia. Over nearly forty years he documented more than 2,600 cases of such memories, of which sixty-five detailed reports have been published. Stevenson's methodology includes on-site detailed interviews with the subject of the reports, to whom he may administer psychological tests and polygraphs. He speaks with family and neighbors to ascertain alternative sources of the subject's information, tries to verify historical data, and even seeks out "past-life families" of the subject.

Much of Stevenson's work is with children whose memories of past lives were spontaneously generated. He feels that their accounts of a previous life are more reliable than those provided by subjects under hypnosis because they are not influenced by either confounding factors of hypnotic suggestion or accumulated learning. He has interviewed children all over the world whose memories of a past life, although vivid in youngsters, tended to fade as the children approached puberty.

The following are two brief sketches of spontaneous memories of children culled from Stevenson's voluminous reporting that demonstrate the corroboration of past-life memories with verifiable facts. I apologize up front for the amount of detail that I provide, but credibility hinges on the specifics. I would be less impressed by these stories had I not personally observed so many past-life regressions and experienced my own potential past-life memories. These experiences offered me context for and openness to the reality of reincarnation.

> Gopal Gupta, born in Delhi, India, in 1956, refused at the age of two and a half to remove a glass of water for a guest, saying, "I won't pick it up. I am a Sharma." His parents were lower middle-class people with little education. The boy, who had just learned to speak, explained that he was a Brahmin, one of the highest castes, for whom such service was unacceptable. He then had a temper tantrum, breaking a number of glasses. Gopal's father asked him to explain his rude behavior.
>
> Gopal responded with many details about a previous life that he claimed he had lived as Shakipal Sharma in a city called Mathura, located about 100 miles south of Delhi. Gopal's parents had no connection with this town. Gopal said he had owned a medicine company, had a wife and two brothers, and that one of his brothers had shot and killed him.

When Gopal was close to eight, his father went to Mathura for a religious festival. While there he investigated and verified all his son's descriptions, including the murder in 1948 of Shaktipal Sharma by his brother. Later, when Gopal met with members of the Sharma family, he recognized them and spoke in even greater detail about traumas in his life, including his wife's refusal to lend him money to give to his brother, a withholding that probably only the family knew about and that led to the fatal quarrel.[3]

Suleyman Andary was born in 1954 to a Druze [an Islamic tribal group that numbers about one million people in the Middle East] family in Falougha, Lebanon. As a young child he shared that through dreams he remembered that he was from Gharife, a town about twenty miles away and in a separate region. He said that he owned an oil press, had children, and gave some of their names. Suleyman's family, with the exception of an uncle, had no contact with this difficult-to-reach village. When he was eleven, an age when most such children have forgotten details of past-life memories, he began to remember more. He said that his name was Abdallah Abu Hamdan and that he was the *mukhtar* (headman) of his town. Later Suleyman's family learned that there was an Abdallah Abu Hamdan who had died in 1942. Abdallah's family later confirmed additional specifics of Suleyman's account, including the names of most of Abdallah's children.[4]

My description of these accounts is far sketchier than Stevenson's reports. Their believability rests on (1) the credibility of the people with the memories, (2) the accuracy of the people recording the recollections, and (3) the details and verification of the accounts. To form a firmer position on survival of the soul requires reading Stevenson's more detailed profiles and studying beyond his work. Nonetheless, these sketches are a taste of Stevenson's work on the spontaneous memories of children, which is complemented by his documentation of xenoglossy.

Xenoglossy is the ability to speak a foreign language that the

speaker cannot account for. Brian Weiss relates such a remarkable occurrence.[5] A Chinese surgeon came to him for a past-life
regression along with a translator because she spoke no English.
In the course of regression she related a lifetime in San Francisco
at the turn of the century. Suddenly she began to speak in English, and the translator without pausing switched into Chinese.
The translator, when asked to pause by Brian Weiss, expressed
her astonishment.[6]

Ian Stevenson has a highly documented case—more than sixty
pages of description—of a woman under hypnosis who spoke in a
language that she had ostensibly never learned as well. A
Methodist minister in Mt. Orab, Ohio, engaged in hypnosis as a
hobby, including past-life regressions with his wife, Dolores. In one
session, while he was trying to alleviate his wife's back pain, she
answered *"nein"* to one of his questions. He was surprised because
as far as he knew, she didn't speak German. A few days later he regressed her again and she identified herself as another personality
by saying, *"Ich bin Gretchen"* ("I am Gretchen"). Over the next
few months in hypnosis sessions Gretchen spoke in German,
which left the minister (with dictionary in hand) uncertain as to
what she was saying.

The minister contacted Stevenson, who speaks German. Stevenson interviewed Gretchen over nineteen sessions, resulting in close
to 350 pages of transcript. Gretchen said she was from Eberswalde,
Germany, and lived in a stone house on Birkenstrasse. She identified
her family members by name and described her appearance. In conversation she mentioned Pope Leo several times and repeatedly
spoke of religious tensions. Stevenson was unable to find records of
the people she mentioned, but the historical assertions were verified. Based on these historical details, it appeared from Stevenson's
research that she lived until at least 1878.

In their interviews Gretchen demonstrated a German vocabulary of more than 237 words. She spoke with good pronunciation
and, when writing sentences, used correct German spelling rather

than spelling words according to their sound in English. Dolores could not explain her facility for the language. She had grown up in Clarksburg, West Virginia, where there were few German speakers, and she maintained that she had not known any German speakers growing up, nor had she studied the language in school. In reference to "genetic memory," the possibility that some memories are DNA-bound, Gretchen had died, Dolores said, unmarried and with no children. Dolores's own German ancestors had immigrated to America before 1847.[7]

Stevenson's premise is that the ability to speak a foreign language cannot be acquired without study and practice. Dolores did not ostensibly learn German in this life. Some qualities of her conversation, such as repetition of ideas with great emotion (perseveration) and a focus on trauma, were matched by another one of Stevenson's subjects, Jensen. Under hypnosis Jensen spoke, based on all linguistic and historical detail evidence, as a seventeenth-century Swedish peasant living in a colony of old Sweden that thrived only during the seventeenth century.[8]

These accounts impressed me greatly. Stevenson's investigation documents that more than a creative, self-generated story is involved. His subjects provide specific information to which they lacked access in this lifetime. His follow-up, which includes finding obscure historical records, corroborates the specific names, past jobs, and causes of death that the subjects spontaneously reported as small children. His work affirms that a phenomenon exists that cannot be accounted for as simply a good guess or coincidence. Stevenson's case studies of xenoglossy powerfully reinforce the notion of reincarnation.

People who debate the source of past-life memories offer a variety of opinions. Some say that the memory is drawn from the collective unconscious or a general sphere of collective thought, as if picking up designated radio waves.[9] My objection to this explanation for past-life memories is that the subject's recollections appear to be deeply rooted in the specifics of the person who

lived the experiences being recalled, which is why its telling provides a profound therapeutic effect. Others say past-life memories
are genetically based, as if rooted in a person's DNA itself. There are
many problems with this suggestion. One is that the memories span
cultures that there is no reason to believe are part of the subject's
heritage and hence genetic past. Some say the memories are simply
material gathered in this life unconsciously, but the amount and
specificity of the information (as in the example of two-year-old
Gopal Gupta), like the ability to speak a foreign language (as in the
experience of Gretchen), make this suggestion unconvincing.[10]

The stories I have shared are dramatic, well researched, and
only a sampling from a large collection. Nonetheless, without the
context of having witnessed firsthand past-life regression and
mediums, I would probably push these stories aside as too weird.
There are endless questions that may be asked of each account
that render their significance uncertain. But in the words of the
philosopher Immanuel Kant in regard to psychic phenomena,
"The same ignorance makes me unwilling to deny utterly the
truth in diverse ghost stories, because I have the curious reserva-
tion that, although I doubt each one taken by itself, when they are
considered as a group I have some belief in them."[11]
Likewise, some accounts of past lives delivered under hypnosis appear to be true. Reincarnation most persuasively explains
the phenomena of children who spontaneously remember verifiable accounts of having lived somewhere else and people speaking foreign languages to which they were not exposed in this life.
Yet as soon as I acknowledged that I could accept reincarnation as
real, a host of questions emerged, including:

- How could I reconcile the remarkable differences between
  accounts of reincarnation? As an example, while Weiss's subjects consistently described having lived in a diversity of cultures, traditional Jewish accounts of past lives are usually of
  other Jews.

- Why is it that such stories are exceedingly rare in those cultures that do not believe in reincarnation?

- If past-life memory accounts, as well as near-death experiences, are profoundly shaped by culture, then how can I know that the stories correlate with anything other than the creativity of the mind?

These questions warranted careful consideration before I could take a firm stand on the nature of the soul's journey.

෴

14

Discrepancies in Afterlife and Reincarnation Accounts

The cultural perspectives on survival of the soul with which I am most familiar are those of traditional Judaism and contemporary Western society. Examining collections of accounts from each uncovers both similarities and differences. What lessons are derived from the similarities, and how can I reconcile the differences?

Near-death experience accounts of recent decades present several shared images: life review, telepathic knowledge, out-of-body experience, being drawn into the light, being greeted by loved ones, and life review. These phenomena are likewise presented in traditional Jewish literature, as demonstrated in talmudic and *Zohar* quotes presented earlier (see chapter 5). An examination of life review is a good starting point for comparison of the traditional Jewish and modern Western systems.

Jewish sources speak of a life review that occurs upon death. A selection from the Talmud (written between 200–500 C.E.) states, "When a person departs to the eternal home all his [or her] deeds are enumerated and he [or she] is told: 'Such and such a thing have you done, in such and such a place on that day.'" Admitting to the rightness of the assessment the person replies, "Rightly have you judged me."[1] The review process, according to rabbinical sources, may be unpleasant. In the words of an early Palestinian *midrash* (written during the first several centuries of the Common Era):

> When a righteous person arrives at the end of his days, his recording angels precede him into heaven singing his praises. . . . But when a wicked person dies, one who did not bring himself to turn in repentance to God, the Holy Blessed One says: "Let your soul be blasted in despair! How many times did I call upon you to repent and you did not?"[2]

Similarly, the relatively recent Hasidic rabbi, Yitzhak Meir of Ger (d. 1866), asked:

> Why is a person afraid of dying? For does he not then go to his Father! What a person fears is the moment he will survey from the other world everything he has experienced on this earth. In the World to Come a person obtains a clear retrospect of all his deeds on the earth.[3]

Another source, the diary of a nineteenth-century Turkish rabbi who engaged in exorcisms, describes souls from the other world as in terrible anguish due to errors, including ritual lapses, committed while alive.[4]

The Jewish tradition, therefore, described a complex picture of life review encompassing the potential of spiritual embrace, as well as the possibility of terror.

Dr. Raymond Moody, the first author to generate widespread recognition for near-death experience, recorded in his ground-breaking book, *Life After Life* (1975), an account of the following life review:

> When the light appeared, the first thing he said to me was, "What do you have to show me that you've done with your life?" or something to this effect. And that's when these flash-backs started. I thought, "Gee, what is going on?" because all of

a sudden, I was back in my childhood. And from then on, it was like I was walking from the time of my very early life, right up to the present.

It was really strange where it started, too, when I was a little girl, playing down by the creek in our neighborhood, and there were other scenes from about that time—experiences I had had with my sister, and things about neighborhood people, and actual places I had been. And then I was in kindergarten, and I remembered the time when I had this one toy I really liked, and I broke it and cried for a long time. . . . I remembered when I was in Girl Scouts and went camping, and remembered many things about all the years of grammar school. . . .

The things that flashed back came in the order of my life, and they were so vivid. The scenes were just like if you walked outside and saw them, completely three-dimensional, and in color. And they moved. For instance, when I saw myself breaking the toy, I could see all the movements. It wasn't like I was watching it all from my perspective at the time. It was like the little girl was somebody else, in a movie. . . .

Now, I didn't actually see the light as I was going through the flashbacks. He disappeared as soon as he asked me what I had done, and the flashbacks started, and yet I knew that he was there with me the whole time, that he carried me back through the flashbacks, because I felt his presence, and because he made comments here and there. He was trying to show me something in each of these flashbacks. . . .

All through this, he kept stressing the importance of love. The places where he showed it best involved my sister; I have always been close to her. He showed me some instances where I had been selfish to my sister. . . .

He seemed very interested in things concerning knowledge, too. He kept pointing out things that had to do with learning, and he did say that I was going to continue learning.[5]

Harold Bloom, a prominent Yale literature professor, addresses the issue of near-death experience in his book, *Omens of the Millennia.* In his review of the contemporary literature, he points out that the afterlife, including the life-review phase, is consistently presented as a loving and pleasant experience. He notes that the afterlife literature of past centuries was more varied and colorful, often filled with infernolike descriptions. He attributes the difference to a lack of imagination in our own time, suggesting, while not stating, that the accounts are colored primarily by cultural projection.

Bloom's analysis, however, fails to consider the negative accounts of the life-review process. In 1943 George Ritchie, who was among the first to introduce Raymond Moody to encounters with near-death experience, described regions in the afterworld that were hellish in nature.[6] In the 1990s a literature concerning distressing near-death experiences emerged.[7] Maurice Rawlings, a cardiologist, describes attending a patient as he was fading in and out of consciousness screaming, "I am in hell!" The patient later described near-death phenomena, but without recalling the hellish aspect of his experience. Both doctor and patient were transformed by the experience, each becoming religious. Rawlings's subsequent research indicated that frightening experiences were more likely to be forgotten than pleasant ones.[8] In addition, patients are naturally more reluctant to share with researchers negative self-images and memories than positive ones.

Most contemporary near-death experiencers recount that in the life-review phase they, and not a "Figure of Light," perform the judgment. The "Figure of Light" serves to provide a standard of judgment. The recurring theme that emerges from accounts of those who have had such experiences is that each person is responsible for every thought, word, and deed of his or her life and that all are judged lovingly.[9]

The joy and pain of life review recounted in near-death experience is paralleled by descriptions of the calm and anguish of afterlife in Jewish sources. The *Zohar* (thirteenth century) describes *Gehenna,* a phase of purification of the emotional dimension of personality soon after death. In this phase a person's past wrongs—both ritual and ethical—are brought into sharp relief. It is understandable how a person from a culture that emphasizes the need to fulfill ritual obligation could remain psychologically tormented by a yearning to return to earthly existence for spiritual repair. In that light, it is understandable how people who were deeply religious and expected God to judge them for their ritual failures would feel anguish in the world to come.

Mediums such as Van Praagh also report that in the other world all is not peaceful. Before he begins a session, Van Praagh engages in a short, generic prayer to protect himself from harm. He says that angry and hurtful people exist on the other side, too, as well as spiritual masters. He says that his contacts as a medium are limited to forty years from the time of a person's death, and during that time personalities largely remain intact. He affirms that a person's station and role in the next world may vary and are based on his or her spiritual evolution in this world.

In sum, there are remarkable core similarities between Jewish discussions and the experience of contemporaries in regard to life review and the afterlife. The power of culture to shape these descriptions must be accounted for as well. When we turn to past-life memories and reincarnation, we are even more profoundly aware of the extent to which culture serves as a filter for recounting experiences. For starters, among the faithful of Catholicism and mainstream Islam, which reject reincarnation, there are hardly any accounts of past-life memories. This absence of such experience may well be due to selective memory. After all, in these cultures such memories would not be elicited and, if presented, would be discounted as fantasy.

Traditional cultures, such as Judaism, also present a different pattern of reincarnation than the reports widely witnessed in contemporary past-life regressions. In contemporary reports, people commonly describe having lived in a multiplicity of cultures and as each gender. In contrast, most Jewish accounts, whether reported by the early mystics or among *Hasidim,* consistently specify that in earlier lives the person lived as a Jew, usually of the same sex. There are accounts of Jews having been non-Jews in the past and of the opposite gender, but these are exceptions to the rule.[10]

At first impression these differences so neatly fit their respective cultures that it is natural to attribute the memories to cultural projection. In our contemporary Western culture people are drawn to diversity and by and large accept the equality of the sexes. The emphasis is on autonomy and acceptance of people's behavior as long as it is not hurtful. Traditional cultures, like Judaism, were more closed. Men and women were separated by discrete roles and rarely mixed in public. For centuries Jews lived as a closed, persecuted community that looked outward at other communities with distrust and even disdain. It is understandable that for most of Jewish history, Jews could have hardly imagined living as non-Jews.[11]

The idea that the souls of people choose to return to their same culture and as the same gender[12] is actually quite common among peoples who believe in reincarnation. In fact, in the case of the Burmese, the Igbo of Nigeria, and the Eskimo tribes of the northwestern United States, spirits almost always reincarnate in the same family.[13] Among the Druze, people tell of returning always as a Druze and doing so soon after their death.[14] A return to the same culture is also a tenet of the Tibetan Buddhists, who hold that the same soul has served as the Dalai Lama, the leader of Tibetan Buddhism, for fourteen incarnations. According to Tibetan belief, a cluster of other souls who serve him as Tibetan monks accompanies the enlightened soul.[15] The idea that a person has to have experienced many cultures to develop a soul is largely a contemporary bias. Religious Jews and Buddhists might argue the opposite: Mastery of a religious tradition and enlightenment are aided by having been steeped in that tradition over centuries!

One explanation for the differences between traditional

cultures and contemporary accounts may be selective memory—remembering only that which matches an existing cultural norm. Another explanation is that there exist two general categories of soul: those who prefer to remain in their own culture and those who are more universal in orientation. This possibility rests on the assumption that souls have input in choosing their future body and culture, which both Weiss and Stevenson say is consistent with many of the accounts they have gathered and is also a common belief in Buddhism.[16] Some souls might prefer to continue to evolve in the setting that is most familiar and where there is the most work to do. The idea that Jewish souls are drawn to remain as Jews is reinforced by the Jewish mystical image that the souls of at least 600,000 Jews stood at Mount Sinai when God addressed the Israelites. The soul sparks of those witnesses continue to reincarnate as Jews to testify to God's revelation and to undergo purification.[17]

There is also a gap between the multifaceted Jewish description of the soul's reincarnation and some contemporary accounts. Jewish mysticism, particularly the Lurianic system, speaks of soul sparks, which means that more than one person may share a previous life at the same time and a spark may enter a person after birth. In contrast, most contemporary past-life regression accounts present a seemingly clear-cut chain of personalities imbedded before birth. Upon further examination, Judaism is not unique in this regard, and the differences from current accounts are more often a matter of language and metaphor than one of fundamentally different understandings.

Many cultures beyond Judaism provide sparklike images of soul, including Eskimos, Tibetans, and the Igbo of Nigeria. These diverse peoples believe that a human mind can effectively split or duplicate so that one personality can reincarnate into two or more bodies.[18] At the same time, in the traditional Jewish literature there is also a consistent description of a chain of discrete incarnations. In the theoretically elaborate Lurianic system of reincarnation, we normally work on only one level of our soul in any one lifetime, which simplifies the analysis and provides a more straightforward chain of incarnations in practice.

Finally, there are some contemporary accounts in which incarnations enter a person after birth. Stevenson writes of at least ten documented cases in which the subject was born before the person whose life he or she remembered died.[19] There is also much literary precedent for the "muse" or spirit guide who visits, influences a person, and departs. This idea is comparable to the kabbalistic concept of *ibbur*, the visiting soul. James Van Praagh, in his book *Talking to Heaven*, describes different kinds of spiritual guides:

> The first group of guides is personal guides. These are persons we have known in previous incarnations or in between lifetimes with whom we share an affinity. . . . Personal guides may make vigorous attempts to guide us through our daily lives and impress us with the best way to remedy certain situations . . . mastery or specialized helpers . . . are spirits who are drawn to us based on certain activities or work in which we are engaged. . . . For instance, if you decide to write a mystery story, your thoughts will draw to you an author who has worked or has specialized in that type of writing. . . . [Last] our spirit or master teachers . . . [are] individuals [who] may be quite spiritually evolved, or may never have lived in the physical world, or may have been involved in some aspect of spiritual work during many lifetimes upon this earth. Like our other guides, they, too, gravitate to us based upon our level of spiritual evolution and understanding. . . . Most of us will have one or two of the same master teachers throughout our soul's evolution lifetime after lifetime.[20]

This description of spirit guides aids us to see that although the vocabulary may differ, both Judaism and a contemporary medium each present a similar claim: A spirit, whether called "guide" or "*ibbur*," may serve as a source of wisdom.

In sum, there is a strong cultural overlay to near-death

experience accounts and to past-life memories. At first impression, the influence of culture is strong enough to prompt me to discount all "twilight zone" accounts as simply coincidence and the unconscious desire to find meaning in the random. Likewise, all the stories of conversation with the "other side" can be viewed as simply wishful thinking or the working out of guilt. But I stop short of taking the position of the debunker, although there is a strong cultural filter in making meaning of paranormal experience.

The fact that the mind shapes our experience does not mean that there is no reality beyond the cultural filter. We may learn the possibility of authentic phenomena beyond the mind from the medical use of placebos, dummy pills (often made from starch or sugar) that are prescribed to patients in studies for comparison to actual medication. Placebos may have a profound effect on relieving symptoms such as headaches, arthritis, or ulcers, and they can include similar side effects as real medicines. The "placebo effect" evidences the healing power of the mind. Yet, the fact that a starch pill has a medical impact does not mean that medicines don't actually work. Indeed, the ultimate test of a new medicine is precisely its greater effectiveness over the placebo. Likewise, the fact that people's imaginations come into play in describing their near-death experiences or encounters with spirits does not mean that their experiences were only in their minds.

Despite differences in the accounts, I am persuaded of the reality of soul survival by the compelling similarities in descriptions of the afterlife in Jewish mystical texts, texts of ancient cultures such as Tibetan Buddhism, and contemporary findings. These divergent systems of wisdom affirm the survival of the soul and describe stages following death that include being drawn into the light, life review, purification, levels of soul achievement, and reincarnation. Some of the differences in the description are a product of vocabulary and not a denial of the category.

What I gain from the study of Jewish sources on survival of
the soul is an affirmation of my growing faith in another realm of
reality. In the study of Jewish text, I join a centuries-old conversation on the meaning of life and learn that, among the most sensitive and mystically oriented of my ancestors, many saw this world
as only a passageway to another world. Reincarnation in the Jewish mystical literature was consistently viewed as real and as another opportunity to develop our souls. The Jewish tradition
affirms that we have spirit guides, or visiting souls, that come to
aid us on our spiritual path.

Judaism teaches that our inner life is composed of different dimensions, and on the highest level our souls are an extension of
the Divine. The purpose of our striving in this world is, paradoxically, to rise after death to a level where we are no longer conscious of personality but enveloped by the One. There are also
areas in the Jewish conversation that leave me perplexed. I am
aware that my forebears viewed the non-Jewish world distrust-
fully, which limited their ability either to imagine that souls flow
freely through reincarnation among cultures or to accept the ability of souls to choose beforehand to return as anything other than
a Jew.

I remain humbled to know that survival of the soul and reincarnation are largely a matter of mystery. I cannot always clearly
discern where cultural influence ends and actual experience begins. Nor can I fathom the actual workings of reincarnation in all
its subtleties. On the practical level, for instance, I was recently
asked: "What if a person is reincarnated and then his or her loved
one dies? Will the reincarnated person not be there to greet the
deceased in the world to come?" I could only reply, "I don't know."
Experiences in the realm of spirit have a quality of being beyond
time. Consequently, in that transcendent level we cannot speak of
past, present, and future or of a linearity of reincarnations.[21]

In sum, my personal experiences and reading have led me to
believe in the reality of soul, its survival, and reincarnation. My

faith is reinforced by traditional Jewish and contemporary accounts. My evolving belief in survival of the soul has changed my
perspective on life and transformed my approach to illness and
death of friends and family.

ᔕ

15

The Impact of Affirming
the Soul's Survival

In the aftermath of my affirmation of survival of the soul, my ability to console the ill was severely tested. A forty-five-year-old congregant, a good friend and mother of two children, developed a mysterious form of brain cancer. Months of oncological and neurological diagnostic tests at the University of California Irvine Medical Center, the Mayo Clinic, and Johns Hopkins, including two brain biopsies, proved inconclusive. After the family's hopes of improvement had given way to resignation, Barbara underwent a relatively routine minor surgery and became comatose.

During eight months of silence she physically wasted away— her wrists and ankles grew stiffly arched, her muscles grew thinner, and her mouth was often open. It was painful to see such a witty, kind, and creative person physically disintegrate. Devoted friends came to visit, but it became harder and harder for them and for the children to see her in this condition. Although she was always in a moderate-to-severe comatose state, there were times when she reacted to stimuli with changes in respiration or emotion, sometimes manifest as dramatic changes in body temperature and heart rate, flushing and sweating, and clenching. Her vigilant husband, Ed, correctly surmised, "She's on a train with a one-way track; she's the one who has left, and I'm the one at the station."

As her condition grew worse I met with her children, ages nine and twelve, and had them draw spontaneous pictures to elicit their emotions, offering a springboard to conversation. During our discussions, I told them that their mother would most likely die soon, saying, "Your mother is in a cocoon and will emerge as a butterfly," an image I borrowed from Kübler-Ross, the famous author of *On Death and Dying* (1969). I not only said it; I believed it. I shared with Ed and the children why I had grown to believe that when our body ceases to function, a part of us—our soul—endures. My faith in survival of the soul comforted Ed and his children, despite the unanswerable question of why this was happening to Barbara.

As Barbara's physical condition grew more grotesque I remained calm in her presence. When I visited her I would speak to her, either out loud or within myself, and I believed that she was aware of my presence as people maintain awareness while in an out-of-body state. I encouraged Barbara to let go, to fly more freely. When she died after eight months in a coma, there was a little smile on her face. The family experienced both relief that their ordeal of watching and waiting was over and a serene sense that Barbara had moved on to a higher realm. My faith in survival of the soul helped me remain consistently present and purposeful and helped the family accept their tragic loss.

During that same year (1997), I had to cope, along with my siblings, with my own mother's diminishing health. In the previous year my family and I had visited my mother in Phoenix a few days after she returned from a long trip to Israel. As we stood in a hallway talking, she began to lose her balance and we placed a chair beneath her. My wife, the neurologist, told us that our mother was in the midst of a stroke.

We called the paramedics, who quickly arrived and took my

mother to the same hospital where she had given birth to her four children. The first day in the hospital my mother, who knew seven languages, did not speak. She remained almost motionless. When she began to speak she spoke in a mix of Hungarian and Yiddish, her first languages. Her recovery of speech and the ability to walk was slow, frustrating, and painful.

My mother had been a successful, independent business-woman her entire adult life. She was a folk celebrity around Phoenix due to her late-night television ads for her wig stores and the wigs she supplied to the local cartoon show personalities, who reciprocated by performing skits about her from time to time. She was a devoted mother who had a strong relationship with her children. I could hardly imagine life without her. Her stroke meant that we, her children, were for the first time responsible for our mother's care.

We arranged for twenty-four-hour coverage so that she could maintain her dignity while recuperating at home. Due to her limited mobility she rarely left the house. Despite the traumas of her young adulthood, including the Nazis taking her and her family from their home, the horror of imprisonment at Auschwitz, and the murder of family, throughout her life my mother actively affirmed life and God. Now, however, there were more evident flashes of resentment and anger. When her last wig store was closed, she mourned.

In the course of two years of poor health she prepared two medical directives requesting that no extraordinary efforts be used to revive or sustain her, including the use of a respirator. During this time she continued to suffer small strokes and heart problems, which slowly ratcheted down the quality of her life. She knew I was going to Israel for a year in the fall with my family, and she encouraged me to plan the trip.

Her major goal was to attend the bar mitzvah of her eldest grandchild, which was scheduled for the end of the summer of 1997. She flew to the event in Denver with her caregiver but was so overcome by the altitude and a weak heart that she was hardly able to get out of the hotel bed for lack of breath. Her eleven grandchildren came to visit her in the hotel room and sang for her, as did her brother and her nieces and nephews. She managed to make it in her wheelchair to the synagogue for an hour to see her grandson chant from the Torah.

When she returned to her home in Phoenix she said to me over the phone, "I've done what I wanted to do and I'm done." The next time we spoke she asked, "When is your departure date to Israel?" I told her it was a month away. She again encouraged me to go. Two weeks later she was admitted to the intensive care unit. I received the call at six o'clock on a Shabbat morning. My sister told me that my mother was on a ventilator and her condition was not good. I decided to wait until the evening to travel to Phoenix because there was little I could do and my mother would not have wanted me to travel during the Sabbath, which would have been a violation of Jewish law unless it was to save a life.

When I arrived that evening at the hospital my mother was conscious, but she could only respond in subtle ways, such as squeezing my hand. She was on a ventilator and did not speak. My sister told me that when the paramedics reached her house they were unaware of her medical directive, and they did all they could to ease her difficulty in breathing. Soon after I arrived, my siblings and I met with her treating physician. He told us that he wanted to keep her on the ventilator because she might get stronger. We were ambivalent: We knew how much she had suffered, she had said that she was "done," and she had prepared not one but two explicit medical directives.

The first day I sat at my mother's side and expressed my love for her both out loud and silently within myself. Frankly, I was glad that she had initially been put on the ventilator because it allowed me the time to fly to Phoenix to be with her. The next day the treating physician asked for permission to feed her intravenously. We deferred to the doctor, but with even greater mixed emotions.

When the two nurses arrived to put in the tube, they asked me to return an hour later.

When I came back I saw that my mother's respirator was turned up and she had no feeding tube. They said that she had fought them for the entire hour and would not let them put the tube in. My siblings and I were persuaded that my mother had made a conscious statement, both in writing and now affirmed in deed. We decided to remove her from the ventilator the next day.

The following morning my brother brought his two children —her oldest grandchildren—and my sister brought her daughter who lived in Phoenix and was closest to her. My children, who were still quite young, had remained in California with my wife. My nieces and nephew were at first uneasy at the sight of their grandmother covered in tubes and staring straight ahead unresponsively. I told them that their grandmother could hear their thoughts and that they should tell her of their love, which they did. After the grandchildren left, the doctors turned the respirator off. My brother, a neurology professor, sat and watched the monitors, and I commenced my daily, routine morning prayers.

While praying I had the odd sensation of being held as if I were a baby in my mother's arms and gently being swayed. Afterwards I sat down, closed my eyes, and meditated on my breath. About fifteen minutes later, with my eyes still closed, I noticed light around my mother's silhouetted head. At that same moment my brother said, "She's gone." I opened my eyes and the EKG was flat. I experienced an initial spasm of emotion that welled from deep within, a profound wailing of loss and of love for my mother. Shortly after, I felt a sense of peace rooted in my faith that she was being drawn into light and that my father and other loved ones were greeting her.

We held only one night of the *shiva minyan* (the traditional nights of prayer following a death) because Jewish law prescribes that a Jewish holiday cuts short the usual seven days of mourning. I went directly from my mother's house of mourning to the airport and from there to the *bimah,* the platform from which I would lead Rosh Hashanah services. My congregants offered me much strength and comfort.

Despite knowing that there was no replacing my mother, I felt at peace. I knew that she had lived a good life as a source of love for her husband and children and as a model of compassion in the larger community. My mother had taught us, "We are only here for a visit." In the past I had smiled at her faith as simply the folk expression of her Hasidic youth or a way of putting off her doctors. As a result of my growing affirmation of the survival of the soul, her words rang true and eased my sense of loss.

There is no replacing the hug or the familiar touch of the hand or voice of a loved one. But letting go is easier when one believes that death is not final. In the words of my mother, "I'm not afraid. I know that my loved ones await me on the other side." Although I used to think my mother's words were a *bubbe meisa,* Yiddish for a "grandmother's tales," I have learned to take her folk wisdom more seriously. I am comforted to know that my mother's soul, her essence, endures.

My mother's life and death prompted me to affirm the value of a Jewish life, a life that embraces Jewish ritual, values, and thought. The soul can't be seen, but it is not an abstraction. How we live determines the impact we make on loved ones and the elevation of our own soul. The quality of how we live is a product in part of whether we see ourselves, as my mother did, as passing visitors in this world.

In the last several years I have visited many congregants in the hospital in life-threatening situations and on their deathbeds. My faith in survival of the soul has provided me with a greater calm and a context within which to offer the traditional Jewish perspective on death as a door to another realm of life. In recent months, I joined a family from my congregation at the bedside of their dying mother and grandmother. My faith in an afterlife enhanced my ability to facilitate closure of her life and to ease the elderly woman toward death.

During that afternoon, Jackie called me and said that her mother's condition had deteriorated. I had known Gertie for several years, including visits with her two and a half years before, when she had suffered a severe heart attack. She never regained her strength, which had continued to decline upon her husband's passing a year before.

Jackie tells me on the phone, "My mom stopped eating almost two weeks ago. When she refused to eat her favorite foods, ice cream and chopped herring, I knew she was really ill. As of yesterday, the doctors are speaking of impending renal failure. Hospice nurses are caring for her at the Board and Care Home, where she has lived for the past year. Would you come to see my mom before she dies?"

I leave an evening meeting early and arrive at the Board and Care Home at nine o'clock. As I enter the dimly lit room, I am surprised by how many people are gathered there. In front of me is Gertie, the eighty-seven-year-old matriarch of her family. She is propped up slightly with pillows in her bed, her hazel eyes wide open, her jaw clenched. Seated around her, lining the walls of the room in chairs, are nine family members, including Jackie, Ian (Gertie's son), and several grandchildren.

There is an uneasy silence in the room, conveying uncertainty and sadness. I sit along the left side of Gertie's bed. My goal is to provide comfort, which requires first gauging the situation and Gertie's needs. Jackie begins to quietly fill me in on her mother's condition.

"My mom has been quite agitated today. Just before you got here the nurse gave her some morphine, which has settled her down. The nurses are uncertain how much time Mom has left. They say it could be days, even a couple of weeks, or just moments away."

I reach over and put my hand on Gertie's arm, letting her know that I care and that I am present.

"Gertie," I say. "You know me. I am Rabbi Spitz. I have come to see you and your family. How are you?"

Gertie continues to stare forward and makes no response. From previous encounters with Gertie I know that she is a fighter for her life. I also sense that she is afraid to let go of this life, a fear both of the unknown and of leaving her family. I therefore address that fear.

"I see that you are frail and weak. Know that in our tradition when the body ceases to function life does not cease. There is a part of us, the soul, that is contained within the vessel of the body. Consider your body to be like a cocoon. When you die your soul will emerge like a butterfly rising upward toward a great light. At death our souls return to God, their source." As I speak I am focused on Gertie but aware that my words are for her family, too, offering a context for their mother's death.

"In our tradition," I continue, "a person who is in the phase of moving toward death is called a *goses,* and it is customary for the *goses* to recite a confessional prayer, called the *viddui.* With your permission, I would like to say the *viddui* for you." She does not respond verbally, or look at me.

I gently take Gertie's hand and recite the traditional paragraph in Hebrew. I then say in English a prayer inspired by the *viddui* (the traditional confessional prayer recited before death): "*Rebbono shel HaOlam,* Master of the Universe, May You do Your will with Gertie. If it be Your will to take her, do so gently and with a loving embrace. May she feel whole in her leaving this world, forgiven for all her shortcomings. May she know of Your abiding love and care for her family. Amen."

I conclude with the last line of the traditional *viddui:* "*Shema Yisrael Adonai Eloheinu, Adonai Echad.* Hear O Israel, the Lord our God the Lord is One." These words are the touchstone of Jewish faith, a line that Gertie knows well. The *Shema* affirms her identity and prompts an association with death because this line is among the last words that our tradition directs us to say before dying.

"Gertie," I say. "Are there any closing words that you would like to say to your family?"

She remains silent.

I look to her family. "This is your opportunity to speak to your mother and grandmother and to say good-bye."

Jackie breaks the extended silence, gets up from her chair, and leans close to her mother. With tears streaming down her face, she speaks gently of her love.

After Jackie sits down, her brother Ian rises. He is a tall man, well over six feet. He sits on his mother's bed, leans over, and whispers privately in her ear for several minutes.

In turn everyone in the room approaches Gertie and speaks— some in stage whispers for all to hear, expressing both their love of their Granny and asking for pardon for unfulfilled expectations. Although Gertie does not answer, she takes her grandchildren by the hand and even pulls them closer to her. Gertie remains wide-eyed and attentive.

When everyone finishes addressing Gertie, I say to her, "Know, Gertie, that you need not fear death. You will leave your body gently, surrounded by God's caring light. With your permission, let me lead you in a guided imagery that will ease your way." My intent is to relax her, ease her pain, and aid her in letting go of this life.

With my eyes closed, sitting upright with my feet flat on the floor in a meditative posture, I speak in a calm voice. "Gertie, see yourself walking on a path. Alongside the path is a river with fresh flowing water, water that comes down from a tall waterfall. At a certain point some of the water of the stream gathers to form a pool, a kind of *mikvah*." I anticipate that Gertie knows the word *mikvah*, Yiddish and Hebrew for a pool of water used for ritual purification.

"Take off your clothes and enter the pool of water. The water temperature is just right. Feel the water all around you. The water soothes your muscles and relaxes you. Drink some of the water. As it moves down your throat, you feel refreshed. There is a basket next to you in the pool. Take all your pain and place it in the basket. Send the basket down the stream away from you. Now, relax. Take a moment to just feel safe and comfortable.

"Come out of the water. There is a towel there and some soft clothes. Dry yourself off and put on the clothes. You are in a lovely meadow. Before you is the setting sun. Walk forward toward the sun. Know that as it goes down, you will be fine. You will never be in darkness. You will be surrounded by God's light. Just keep walking forward, feeling calm and safe. See yourself surrounded by a gentle light, a divine light."[1]

I open my eyes. Gertie is breathing quite shallowly, and her eyes have begun to close. There is a peaceful feeling in the room, as if everyone is in a calm, meditative space. I say to her family, "Now is your time to send your mother and grandmother your love. See yourself sending light toward Gertie, as if surrounding her with the light of your love."

Gertie's breathing continues to slow. Her face looks peaceful; her jaw is no longer clenched. We all sit calmly. There are moments where Gertie's breath is imperceptible, and then a clear breath. After four or five minutes Gertie's breathing stops. "Is she dead?" they ask of me. Frankly, I have not been with many people at the moment of their death and I am a little uneasy about checking. I admit, "I am not sure."

Ian gets up and feels for the beat of the carotid artery. He puts his ear to her chest. "I think she has stopped breathing." He gently closes her eyelids.

Someone goes out to get the attendant, who returns with a stethoscope. He listens to her chest and says, "She is gone."

We are all amazed. Gertie has passed gently and calmly, surrounded by the family that was the center of her life. Family members quietly embrace. I hug the family and excuse myself, telling them that I will see them tomorrow.

As I drive home, I am grateful to God for the tools that have allowed me to help Gertie and her family. I am also amused by and self-conscious of my shamanlike image for the family. When I get home, I tell my wife what happened. I'm glad that my son, who often depends on my guided imagery to fall asleep, is already sleeping. I have no desire to use my guided imagery with him tonight. My wife teases that when I lead imagery in synagogue the next time, word will be out to keep your eyes open.

The next day I join Jackie and her family at her home. They are in good spirits, evidencing acceptance and even relief in their loved one's death. I am in my rabbinic mode, a touch paternal. "Do you have any questions?" I ask. Adrian, Gertie's grandson, speaks. "Rabbi, about what happened last night, have you ever done that before?"

I smile, saying, "Frankly, I was amazed myself. I have led this imagery before, and it has offered calm and a greater ease in letting go of this life. The last time I used it was with a man dying from cancer. He was able to say loving good-byes to his family. After the *viddui* and the same imagery he stopped speaking and died the next day. But the elegant timing of your grandmother's death was new for me."

The family begins to speak all at once. "Rabbi," Ian says. "I have never seen anything like that scene last night. Even the lighting was just right, and the events were perfectly paced."

Beyond the awe of their mother and grandmother's timing, there was a genuine sense among the family members that the previous evening had allowed them closure and that Gertie had died peacefully, embraced by her tradition and her family's love. There was also a newfound respect, articulated by the grandchildren, for the possibility of survival of the soul.

I have learned in my work that dying is similar to falling asleep. We may fight sleep even when tired, and we fall asleep when we let go. Similarly, we have significant control in choosing the timing of our death. Faith in another realm beyond this bodily life and closure with family enables a person to let go, easing gently into death.

I could comfort the family and lead the imagery with Gertie because I have much experience with meditation and guided imagery. But my ability to aid Gertie was largely a product of my sincerity. I genuinely believed everything I told her. I do believe in survival of the soul and that we pass from this earthly realm into light. I believe that Rabbi Yaakov was right when he said that this world is but a passageway for the soul to a higher plane of existence, and, I would add, to yet a return to the earth in a new incarnation. The key question that remains is how do we live our lives now so as to cultivate our souls before our departure from this realm?

16

Cultivating the Soul

The story is told of a tourist who traveled from America to Eastern Europe to visit the renowned scholar and *tzaddik* the Hafetz Hayyim (Israel Meir Kagen, Lithuania, 1838-1933). He came in and saw a bed, a chair, a table, a cupboard, a closet, and a bookcase. The tourist was shocked and asked the sage:

"Where are your possessions?"

"Where are yours?" the Hafetz Hayyim replied.

"What kind of question is that?" the tourist said. "I'm a visitor here."

"I am too," the sage replied.[1]

The Hafetz Hayyim's sparse living situation is admittedly an extreme. Judaism does not require asceticism. Indeed, one of the questions the Jerusalem Talmud (edited in Palestine by the fifth century) says God will ask a person as he or she reaches the next world is, "Why did you not enjoy all that was permitted to you?"[2] This world is a gift to be enjoyed, but the Hafetz Hayyim and the tradition emphasize that material possessions are only an aid to comfort and not the goal of life.

As physical creatures in a competitive world, it is easy for acquisition to dominate our lives. We naturally seek safety, good food, comfortable homes, and the immediate gratification offered by television, stereos, and computers. Most people say they believe in God and engage in regular prayer, but the inner life is marginalized. Our energy is primarily placed on externals. We live more responsibly and compassionately in the here and now when we believe in an accounting at the end of our days. We are taught that each day is precious and our calling is to use our days purposefully, the same lesson that was conveyed by the children who had survived death that Dr. Melvin Morse studied (see chapter 2).

There are many images used to convey the nature of the soul, which resides within us and endures. Images are important in that they offer a concrete form for what is otherwise invisible. An image allows us to better grasp the contours of process, even as we also acknowledge that all analogies are incomplete descriptions. In that light, the kabbalah used the image of fire to convey that all aspects of our life—the physical, emotional, intellectual, and intuitive—are united in soul just as the colored bands are united in the flame. Our task is to nurture that flame so that it burns brighter, enabling a greater unity within us, which in turn instills a feeling of being more fully alive and prompts service on behalf of the source of life.

The major religions and insights of contemporaries offer guidance on care of the soul. The description that follows is culled from my own reading and life experience and has an admittedly Jewish slant because it is the religious system that I know best. To begin, let me share an image that I have developed to help me conceptualize how to better nurture my soul.[3] This description of soul work is modest in intent, serving only to point to possible pathways of action.

> Imagine soul as a hollow, glasslike bead, composed of light, at the center of our being. The bead has three colored bands nestled one on top of the other, kind of like the concentric circles of color on a Jawbreaker candy. Spirit flows through the center

of the bead. It is a warm, sweet light that passes through the bead in all directions. This spirit emerges from the Divine.

The three bands of the bead, from the outer to the inner, represent the physical, emotional, and intellectual dimensions of our life. The degree of transparency of these bands is ever-changing, reflecting in auralike ways our accumulated experiences. We are born with this hollow three-banded, vessel-like bead, in which are imbedded the memories of previous lives. When we die, this glasslike bead, composed of light, rises into an ethereal realm, in most cases destined to return into a new body. The divine spirit, which flows through the bead, remains unchanged, always flowing. The divine light flows to all parts of our person, emerging through the bead, as if through a prism.

Our goal is to purify the three bands of color. The more transparent the glass, the greater is the flow of light from the center. Lines of discoloration or foggy patches form in varying degrees corresponding to the severity of injury that has occurred, whether by harm that has befallen us or harm we have caused to others. Scars are manifest as dark lines through which light can barely pass. When light from the spirit passes through the bead, it may resolve discolorations on the bands. Simultaneously, our deeds impact on the color and transparency, too. Acts of mindfulness and compassion can dissolve some of the discoloration. True healing is a joint product of our own efforts (will) and the light from within (grace).

The center of the bead is often clogged as if by sediment that builds from anxiety, selfishness, anger, fear, violence, and apathy. To cleanse the obscuring buildup requires an awareness of our past injuries and our current dysfunctional reflexes. There is a part of us (somehow removed from the elements of the bead) that allows us to examine the bead.

Soul repair work begins with our willingness to look at ourselves honestly and to change if needed. A therapist, who with skilled listening metaphorically holds up a mirror for us to see our true selves, often aids this process. A form of therapy that is particularly insight provoking is "wakeful dreaming," in which a

skilled guide provides dreamlike settings, which allow unconscious material to easily and clearly rise to the surface, offering
revelations of our inner lives.[4]

Prayer is also a window into our center. In personal prayer we
express ourselves honestly and openly. Since God already knows
us, there is no reason to avoid the truth. God's judgment of us
won't change, and God will maintain our confidences. By sitting
down and writing God a letter we may experience this kind of
personal prayer. Theology, the examination of the nature of God,
emerges from acts of relationship and can therefore wait. In writing the letter we write as if God is a caring, knowing presence.
Such letters usually end with words of gratitude because we imagine God as the source of our entire life, and after expressing our
needs we naturally acknowledge what we have. The letter, therefore, also offers perspective.

Seeing life in all its parts as a gift from God can dramatically
shape our outlook. When we see good fortune or success as a gift,
there is surprise and gratitude. When events go poorly, there is the
possibility of acceptance if there is a faith in a guiding, purposeful
presence. In contrast, when we see our achievements as the products of only our own efforts, we run the risk of arrogance in response to success and we may then turn cynical and blame others
when we confront hardship. The attitude of gratitude allows us to
experience life as constantly fresh, awe inspiring, and as an unfolding gift. Gratitude enables us to open up the soul bead's center
more widely by cleaning out the harmful buildup of cynicism
through the dual currents of delight and acceptance.

Blessings—statements of gratitude to God in response to an
event before us—also serve to elevate our consciousness and link
the facets of the bead. Traditional Jewish blessings include thanks
for waking in the morning, eating a piece of bread, and viewing a
rainbow. Indeed, the Talmud records that we are to recite 100 blessings a day.[5] In making gratitude a consistent response to God, we
are conditioned to express thanks to the many people who make

our lives richer. In slowing down to recite a blessing we may consider the web of partnership that goes into producing most of the objects in our lives, to use our senses more fully and to experience awe. In performing such religious acts, the directed imagination guards against even blessings becoming a series of dull, rote reflexes.

Soul work is also achieved by directing our attention to the inside of the bead, which offers a taste of the sweetness of spirit and an increased access to spirit's flow. We draw from the center of our being through a variety of meditative techniques, which are shared by all traditional religions. Meditation, which includes certain forms of prayer, keeps our minds narrowly focused (often through a repeated phrase combined with the steady rhythm of breathing) while we passively observe the flow of thoughts that dart through our minds. There are varying degrees of inner quiet achieved through meditation. The deeper the stillness, the greater the access to intuitive insight and the feeling of "oneness." All meditation techniques are honed by a constancy of disciplined practice.

One way to get a taste of the spirit at the center of the bead is through "cosmic empathy." After writing a letter to God, answer your letter as if God is responding. We who are fashioned in "the image of God" have the capacity to empathize and to see ourselves from a larger point of view, which paradoxically seems to emerge from our very core. In leading this exercise with groups over many years, I have found that the reply is consistently that of a loving, wise parent. The replies do not provide yes-or-no answers, but are process oriented and call on our best values and deepest insights. Such experiences reflect the prophet Elijah's description of the Divine in "the still, small voice" (1 Kings 19:12), to which we become attuned in quietude.

Encounters with spirit lead to service. In holy moments we are filled with love and the desire to give. All of the major religions demonstrate the commitment to compassion on behalf of the needy by providing shelters, staffing soup kitchens, and visiting the ill. This desire to affirm and assist others also includes an enthusiasm for celebrating life-cycle events with friends and family and marking communal anniversaries of key historical events. When engaged in acts of compassion and joy we become a vessel, unified and illuminated by the light of spirit.

Soul work is our life's homework assignment. There are no shortcuts, only the opportunity to live with increasing awareness and generosity. Every act is potentially "soulful" when we bring our entire person to the act. Sex, for instance, may just be a physical release. But when we bring emotional commitment and spirit to the act it may be an expression of love, an intertwining of lives, and a touch of "oneness." The more consistently we utilize our imagination to access all dimensions of our being, the more our lives are lived fully and all facets of soul are simultaneously engaged. When we live with our attention focused on the present moment, whether performing a deed or simply being, we are less self-involved and drawn closer to God, the source of spirit. The religious quest is to transform more and more of life into divine encounters.

No religion has a monopoly on soul work. Indeed, as a Jew I have found wisdom outside my faith that I then seek to integrate into spiritual practice. At the same time, as a religious Jew I appreciate that Judaism provides a toolbox to nurture the soul. Among its tools is the *siddur* (the traditional prayer book), which is a distilled collection of "letters to God." Communal prayer cultivates gratitude and connection and serves to prompt personal prayer.

A key Jewish tool is the Sabbath, "a palace in time"[6] in which we have the space to appreciate family and creation and to link ourselves to community and God. Dietary laws serve as tools that foster the discipline of placing limits on appetites and forge identity. Sacred texts inculcate values that help prioritize how we spend our hours. Among the key lessons of the Jewish tradition is that each person is given life for a purpose, which it is our task to discover. Although that purpose may emerge from unfinished business in a previous life, it is in this life that we have choice and the ability to elevate our soul.

Living now with purpose is the key to cultivating soul. Past-life memory does not solve our problem of how to live. Just as classic therapy looks to uncover traumas early in our lives in order to diffuse them of their psychic toxins, so past-life work extends the range of possible memory. The traumas of the past may shape patterns of behavior that warrant examination and healing.

A belief in reincarnation influences our moral sensibilities. Due to reincarnation of souls, the stranger may have been our brother or sister in a past life. If we were the opposite gender in a previous life from what we are now, we are more empathic with the other gender and more outraged by discrimination. Because in past lives we may have lived in other cultures, we are more motivated to respect "foreign" cultures.

On a theological plane, because all people possess a divine spark, we are called to see a divine connection with every other person and to perceive the oneness of humanity. In Lurianic terms, we are to see our inner sparks as linked to the sparks of every other person, and we are charged with elevating our sparks to enable the healing of *Adam HaRishon,* the source of all soul sparks. Our life deeds not only shape our own lives but also serve to heal creation and even God.

It is our challenge to understand the uniqueness of our own souls and the particular purpose for which we were placed on this earth. In that light, there is the following Hasidic story:

> Before his death, Rabbi Zusya said, "In the coming world, they will not ask me: 'Why were you not Moses?' They will ask me: 'Why were you not Zusya?'"[7]

The deeds that define our lives may be quite simple, but they define us when they are done with an open heart and a sense that they emerge from our core.

Soul work is done on earth because in this realm we have

choices and relationships that allow us to succeed or fail, grow or deteriorate. The choices we make, the priorities we assert, and the love we share shape our spiritual lives. Just as we need a body as a vessel for the soul, so we need the structures of community, symbols, and a system of discipline to ground our consciousness.

For many, an awareness of soul leads to living without an attachment to any one particular religious tradition. The reasoning is that if the "light" is universal and each person is created in the image of God, then it is limiting and even elitist to pick any one religious tradition. But in daily life there are advantages to commitment. Consider the analogy of a person who does not want to live in any one place and spends his or her life in hotels. Although a house limits our mobility, it also provides a constancy of space that allows us to assert our identity more fully and invest more deeply in friendships and community. While we remain committed to a primary tradition, we can still reach out to other faiths and worldviews and integrate their learning into our own lives.

Cynthia Ozick, a great contemporary Jewish writer, says that the symbol of Judaism is the shofar, the ram's horn blown on the High Holy Days. The air for the blast, a symbol of soul, emerges from the Divine. There is a need to channel the air through a small hole, symbolic of a distinct people and tradition. The sound that emerges through the large hole, which symbolizes the world, is a universal call to return in faithfulness to the source of life and in partnership to heal the world. Our ability to make an impact in the world is enhanced by our belonging to a religious community, which provides an entire system of religious living. Judaism, in this case, offers the wisdom of the survival of the soul and tools with which to cultivate the soul in this life.

Although Judaism is a rich soil in which to grow the soul, this terrain remains untilled by most today. Judaism teaches that there is a larger organizing presence in the cosmos who calls on us to see our lives as purposeful. We are taught that we have the capacity to repair past lives and even the cosmos. Although there is a future world and a divine, caring presence, it is how we live now that matters. This last point was illustrated in the following parable by a current Hasidic rabbi, Levi Isaac Horowitz, also known as the Bostoner *rebbe*:

> Once upon a time there was a king who wanted to give a treat to the workers in his diamond mine. He told them that for three hours only they could keep for themselves all the diamonds they could pluck from the ground. Some got so excited that, as soon as they found a stone, they would polish it and fantasize what they would do with it once the three hours were over. Others just tried to collect as many diamonds as possible, leaving the polishing and the fantasizing to later. Needless to say, these collected much more than the others. "Why?" asks the *rebbe,* and answers: "Because they used the time for what was meant to be."[8]

Our challenge is to use the time we have now to live gratefully and responsibly, knowing that how we choose to live shapes our soul. Each of us has a unique inner potential that we are to discover and to share with others. The ability to accept death as part of life provides comfort and the awareness that each day is precious. Our challenge is to make the best of every day in this life.

∽

Conclusion: Live Now Gratefully and Responsibly

My faith in the survival of the soul emerged in stages through first-hand experience and reading. These experiences had a dreamlike quality: elusive, in need of interpretation, and, unless noted quickly, vanishing. Yet my experiences at graveside, my personal paranormal awareness of the death of loved ones, my exposure to past-life regression, and my observation of expert mediums produced a clear pattern. That pattern revealed realms of knowledge that transcended the five senses and pointed to the survival of the soul and its return.

There is no proof for the survival of the soul, only evidence. As in a court of law, the evidence requires analysis and largely hinges on the credibility of the witness. Our openness to the veracity of the accounts rests in significant part on our own experiences with the paranormal. Each piece of paranormal evidence can be interpreted away or minimized. It is only with the accumulation of anecdotes that we may conclude that our soul survives and returns.

Although there is a strong cultural filter at play in all of these accounts, the phenomena do not plausibly stem from wishful thinking or coincidence alone. An examination of the near-death experiences of children with culturally diverse childhoods reveals that there are common elements that cannot simply be products of education or acculturation. Two examples are the failure of children to see a parent greet them in the light unless the parent was already dead (even if the parent had died only seconds prior to the vision) and the ability of patients in near-death experiences to recount events in vivid detail despite having been medically unconscious.

There are transsensory methods of communicating and gathering information. My wife's ability to hold an object and describe to a stranger her childhood dog or the items on her mantel is more than coincidence. James Van Praagh's ability to give my wife details about her grandfather was more than a good guess or our willingness to give meaning to general information. Although I have not observed a person demonstrate xenoglossy, the ability to speak in an "unlearned" language is documented extensively. The spontaneous, corroborated memories of past lives related by children from around the world add weight to the claim that under hypnosis, too, people may access actual past-life memories.

Modernity offers new tools, including hypnosis and electronic communication, that aid in accessing and gathering stories of the paranormal. The accumulating data have engaged influential writers who have begun to make an impact on our mainstream culture. The evidence of paranormal phenomena points to a soul and challenges the ingrained materialistic assumption that reality is limited to what can be tested, seen, or controlled.

Once the topic of the supernatural is opened up for discussion, it is remarkable how many people have a story to tell. For many, these stories were kept private because they were unsure how their friends and family would respond. They often feared that they would be judged as weird or gullible for holding that an encounter they had with a spirit was real. When people tell me their stories, they consistently well up with emotion and vividly remember their encounters precisely because the experience touched a primal part of their inner being. Hence, an additional reason that supernatural accounts are treated as private material is that they are experienced as profoundly personal.

Attention to soul survival is growing rapidly. It is evident in the popular culture, where in recent years such films as *What Dreams May Come* with Robin Williams, *Ghost* with Whoopi Goldberg, *Dead Again* with Kenneth Branagh and Emma Thompson, and *The Sixth Sense* with Bruce Willis were successful. The closing scene from the film *Titanic* presents the heroine dying and being greeted on the other side by people who have died before her. For many in the younger generation, survival of the soul and reincarnation are plausible.

We see the growth of interest in survival of the soul in our bookstores. James Van Praagh's *Talking to Heaven* (1997) and *Reaching to Heaven* (1999) reached the top of the New York Times best-seller list, and Brian Weiss's *Many Lives, Many Masters* (1978) is an international best-seller in more than thirty translations. The focus on the paranormal has also broken into academic circles. In a 1996 book on the influence of culture on mystical accounts, Jess Hollenback of the University of Wisconsin collected tales of mediums, telepathy, and out-of-body experiences to document an underlying core reality that transcends culture, even though it is influenced by culture.[1]

The insights of contemporary researchers parallel the accumulated wisdom of Judaism. Traditional Jewish texts offer nuances of understanding survival of the soul. To realize that new insights are really old is both to gain greater confidence in that which is "new" and to gain motivation to examine anew the guidance that Judaism offers on how to nurture the soul.

Faith in survival of the soul also evokes interest in the Divine. If the soul survives, there is a greater likelihood of an enduring, unseen dimension to reality. If we are destined to return to cultivate our soul, then our lives are purposeful, which indicates an organizing consciousness in the cosmos. Faith in the existence of God is not a product of intellectual proofs (including compelling stories of survival of the soul) but a consequence of living in relationship to God. With a faith in the Divine and in the timeless paradox of free will coexisting with destiny, we see meaning and purpose in what would otherwise be considered a "coincidence."

Faith in survival of the soul changes how we view death. Death is not an end but a door into another realm. Faith offers greater grace in dealing with friends or family who are gravely ill. We may share with those who are terminally ill that they need not be afraid and that their loved ones will greet them on the other side. Such assurance may aid them to die with greater acceptance, comfort, and dignity. Belief in survival of the soul also makes closure on this life even more important. Reconciliation with loved ones, holding hands and expressing love, saying good-byes, and feeling completion offer both an easier transition and the promise of less work to do in the next realm or upon our next return.

A faith in survival of the soul adds greater urgency to living our days meaningfully, which is aided by like-minded friends. Just as our soul needs a body as a vessel of expression, so our body and soul gain from the grounding and reinforcement of a religious community and the tools of a particular, coherent tradition. Adherence to a specific religion is not an end of the religious journey, but a home from which to interact in the larger world. We learn from the wisdom of those who have lived before us, gaining tools for deepening our gratitude to and awareness of the mystery and presence of God. As inheritors of an ancient heritage, Jews are members of an extended family in pursuit of holy living. When we live with a faith in our people's covenant with God, we gain purpose. When we respond to God's call we serve as God's partner in completing creation.

A religious perspective is a product of life experience, but autobiography is shaped as profoundly by our decisions and our goals for the future as by our past. A therapist told me that my wife would shape me in the future as much as my mother had in the past, and he was right. In addition, our aspirations both describe who we are and shape whom we will become.

In that light, I am optimistic about Judaism's future despite the persistence of ignorance and apathy because Judaism offers a richness of values, sacred texts, and tools to transform the mundane into sacred moments. As soul work gains in importance, Jews will look to find tools and community that are offered by Jewish involvement. Judaism's future depends on decisions we make now and on our aspirations.

Although Judaism affirms a world to come and even reincarnation, the emphasis is on how we cultivate our soul in this world through good deeds. In that light, the same Rabbi Yaakov who described this world as only a passageway into the next world also said: "Better is one hour of bliss in the world to come than the whole life of this world; better is one hour of repentance and good works in this world than the whole life of the world to come."[2]

Judaism affirms the lesson of the children that Dr. Melvin Morse studied, who after their near-death experiences all finished school, were drug-free, did not fear death, and said that they were brought back to this world for a purpose. The purpose of one's life may be profound in its simplicity. In the words of the Ba'al Shem Tov, "A soul may wait for a millennium to descend to earth, and then live a whole lifetime for the one moment when he will be able to do another a favor."[3]

We live this life with an opportunity to grow our soul so that we will be ready to respond when needed. We are responsible for how we behave in this world and can use our free will to shape our soul for good. Again, in the words of the Ba'al Shem Tov: "A wise man does not have to wait for his next incarnation; he can begin it [any necessary repairs] in this life.[4]

Our challenge is to live now in simplicity, with gratitude to God, and with a willingness to act generously and responsibly. In the words of Rabbi Menachem Mendel of Kotsk (1787–1859), "Take care of your own soul and of another man's body."[5] We don't live in the sixteenth century, even if we remember it, or in heaven. Our past has meaning and our future has relevance only if we live with awareness and compassion in the present moment. When we are fully focused, that moment is a sacred window through which we may catch a glimpse of our soul's source, the Divine.

〰

Appendix:
Torah and Immortality of
the Soul: A Hot Debate

What is the biblical view of the afterlife and, specifically, does the Bible acknowledge the immortality of the soul? These questions are hotly debated among contemporary scholars. A review of academic scholarship demonstrates both the elusiveness of a definitive reading of the Bible and the nature of the emergence of ideas.

I have saved this scholarly assessment for the appendix precisely because the goal of the book was to personalize my journey, including my reactions to the Jewish tradition on survival of the soul, and not get bogged down in academic debate. It is my hope that this appendix will provide a fuller foundation for some of my conclusions and enable a richer reading of Jewish text.[1]

Defining *Sheol*

Scholars do agree that Hebrew Scripture *(Tanakh)* is remarkably vague as to the nature of the afterlife. There is no straightforward description of what happens to the body or soul after death. Death is of course mentioned and a key term, *Sheol* (שְׁאֹל), is used in the *Tanakh* sixty-five times to signify the afterlife or the grave. Other terms used as synonyms for *Sheol* include *bor*[2], *shakhat*,[3] and *avedon*[4]. Analysis of these terms is especially difficult because the context is usually poetic rather than technical in nature. For each usage of the term the reader must decide whether the description is meant metaphorically or literally. The reader is also left to assess in each case whether the biblical author's imagery is a response to clinging to this life or a presentation of the awaited fate upon death.

Jacob is the first in the Torah to use the term *Sheol*. Afraid that his youngest son, Benjamin, will suffer harm if he accompanies his brothers back to Egypt, Jacob pleads, "My son must not go down with you, for his brother is dead and he alone is left. If he meets with disaster on the journey you are taking, you will send my white head down to *Sheol* in grief" (Genesis 42:38). Does Jacob use *Sheol* to designate the grave or a developed concept of a fate after death? The later uses of *Sheol* can support either position.

Sheol is used as a synonym for the grave. In the words of Isaiah, "Your magnificence has been flung down to *Sheol*, underneath a bed of maggots and over you a blanket of worms" (Isaiah 14:11). Job says, "For soon I shall lie down in the dust; when you seek me, I shall be gone" (Job 7:21). And there are images of *Sheol* as a particular place with a semblance of life. Proverbs describes, "Her house is a highway to *Sheol*, leading down to Death's inner chambers" (Proverbs 7:27). *Sheol* is described as a place with gates (Psalm 9:14), secured with bars (Job 17:16), and as a monster with gaping jaws that devours all and is never sated (Isaiah 5:14; Proverbs 27:20).

In some descriptions, death leads to an absence of consciousness. A sampling: "A dead man's sons come to honor [him] and he knows it not" (Job 14:21); "The living know that they will die, but the dead know nothing" (Ecclesiastes 9:5); "The dead cannot praise YHVH . . . [it is] a realm of silence" (Psalms 116:7 and 94:7).[5] In other citations, even in death there is activity and awareness: "The shades tremble beneath the waters and their denizens" (Job 26:5); "*Sheol* was astir to greet your coming— rousing for you the shades of all earth's chieftains, raising from their thrones all the kings of nations. All speak up and say to you, 'So you have been stricken as we were, You have become like us!'" (Isaiah 14: 9–10); and the image of the deceased Rachel, "Thus said the Lord, 'A cry is heard in Ramah—wailing, bitter weeping—Rachel weeping for her children. She refuses to be comforted'" (Jeremiah 31:15).

And there is diversity within the text over whether death is final. In the following citations death is portrayed as a one-way road: "All who go to her [death] cannot return and find again the paths of life" (Proverbs 2:19); "The dead shall not awake nor be raised out of sleep" (Job 14:12); "They are dead, they can never live. Shades, they can never rise" (Isaiah 26:14). There are also images of return from death: "I kill and make alive"

(Deuteronomy 32:39); "Take away their breath, they perish and turn again into dust; send back your breath, they are created, and you renew the face of the earth" (Psalm 104:29–30). Accounts of the revival of the dead occur with the prophet Elijah (1 Kings 17:22), with his disciple Elisha (2 Kings 4:35), and in the statement, "As soon as the [dead] man touched the bones of Elisha, he revived and stood on his feet" (2 Kings 13:21).

The disparity of perspectives on *Sheol* and death is imbedded in the very word *Sheol.*[6] The origin of the term is uncertain. It might come from the Hebrew *sho'al* (שֹׁאַל), meaning "a hollow hand," and suggesting a place of emptiness, decay, and silence. Alternatively, the same root is found in *sha'al* (שָׁאַל), meaning "to ask" and implying that in the netherworld are spirits who remain conscious and who may be called on. This second view is reflected in the case of King Saul conjuring up the deceased prophet Samuel, who retained his personality, memory, consciousness, and even prophetic ability (1 Samuel 28:5–25).

Scholars reach different conclusions as to the nature of the term *Sheol* and the reason for the many ways the term is used in Scripture. One possibility is that the concept of *Sheol* evolved in the nearly thousand years that passed between the time of the patriarch Jacob and the prophet Daniel. Among the earliest academics to assert a clear pattern of change in the use of *Sheol* was R. H. Charles. He wrote in 1899 that in the early phases of Israelite history the reward-punishment aspects of the afterlife were absent and the person after death was completely removed from God. Only later did the Israelites conceive of *Sheol* as a realm in which God had moral jurisdiction.[7] The problem with Charles's confident analysis is that it is based on the assumption that if the text fails to express a concept, then that concept did not exist in the contemporaneous society. In addition, he assumed that the chronology of the texts is determined by the complexity of ideas that they contain.

Interpreters of the text face two obstacles inherent in the biblical style. First, the text is full of holes and silences on foundational concepts and rituals. There is scant presentation of burial customs, marriage rites, divorce procedures, or the celebration of a newborn. The text assumes that the audience has a working knowledge of these key ideas and customs. Rather than describe a complete culture, the primary goal of Hebrew Scripture is to take an ongoing, organic community and shape its self-identity as a people living in relationship with God. The approach is largely emotional, anecdotal, and poetic rather than philosophic, consistent, and clear.

The second obstacle is the biblical tendency to present key concepts like *Sheol* as a collage of ideas. We are left to compare how terms are used in context, knowing that language is not static and much of the life and beliefs of the people remains out of view. The difficulty in ascertaining the biblical view of the afterlife and the "true meaning" of *Sheol* was framed by the contemporary scholar Herbert Chanan Brichto as follows:

> Scripture is a fragment, a residual deposit of a society, a culture and a history of development whose immense substance and shape are only imperceptibly suggested in the surviving writings. To change the figure, the Hebrew Bible is the visible tip of an iceberg: the mass below the surface, respecting quantity, distribution, and contours, lends itself not to precise knowledge but to informed guesses.[8]

Modern Readers

After surveying the biblical evidence on afterlife, Johannes Pederson wrote an influential assessment in 1926.[9] He maintained that the Hebrew Bible presents the individual as a vital unity of the physical and spiritual elements. *Nefesh* is used to refer to "man in the totality of his being" and is used interchangeably to refer to parts of the body.[10] As in life, so in death there is no separation of body and soul.[11] Death is simply life in its weakest state.[12]

Ephraim Urbach, an Israeli talmudic scholar, in *The Sages* (1969), concurred: "In the Bible a monistic view prevails. Man is not composed of two elements—body and soul, or flesh and spirit."[13] He examined two words in the Bible that were later used by the rabbis and mystics to signify soul. *Nefesh*, he showed from parallelisms, is used for flesh and spirit and simply signifies existence. *Ruach* in the Bible meant spirit or breath and is only a manifestation of life. "The body and *Ruach* form an indivisible entity, and it may be said that man is a psycho-physical organism."[14] Like Pederson, Urbach concluded, "even death is not the antithesis of life but its extreme enfeeblement."[15]

The noted Israeli biblical scholar Yehezkel Kaufmann offered an explanation for why the afterlife "plays no part in the religion of YHVH."[16] In paganism, he wrote in 1945, death brought the soul to the divine or demonic realm. "Entering this kingdom, the soul becomes 'divine.' When all Israelite religion placed all divinity in YHVH, the spirits of the dead ceased being 'gods.'"[17] Kaufmann concluded, "The biblical age had not yet succeeded in forming a conception of a judgment of the soul and its deliverance from death that would be vitiated by the images of an infernal god or the apotheosis [deification] of the dead."[18] Kaufmann's analysis emerged from awareness that among Israel's neighbors, including both the Babylonians and Canaanites, the deceased in their spiritual form could pose a physical threat to a god, a divine vulnerability that the Israelite religion rejected.

In a recent work, Jewish philosopher Neil Gillman surveys the evidence and continues along a similar path. "The idea that human beings will live again after death," he writes, "cannot be found in Jewish writings much before the second century B.C.E. and the idea that we possess a soul which never dies is not found until roughly a century later."[19] He offers two possible explanations for the Bible's denial of survival of the soul:

> Worship of the dead was prevalent in all the surrounding cultures and biblical religion feared any pagan contamination. . . .
>
> Another answer might lie in the biblical insistence on preserving a sharp demarcation between God and human beings: Only God is immortal, humans die. That is precisely the difference between the two. Only much later, when the community faced new religious challenges, was it possible to look at this doctrine anew and revise it.[20]

Much of Gillman's book, *The Death of Death* (1997), is an examination of the emergence of the doctrine of resurrection. Resurrection in the biblical context refers to the process by which the dead are awakened by God to a new life in their own bodies in this world. The concept of resurrection affirms monism, the unity of body and soul. Belief in resurrection offers people a national reward for good behavior. The miracle of resurrection will provide evidence that God's supreme power extends to death. Gillman begins his analysis with three late texts: Isaiah 25: 7-8,[21] Isaiah 26:18-19,[22] and Daniel 12.[23] He notes an evolution of the idea from resurrection for Israel's righteous alone (Isaiah) to resurrection for all peoples, who will then be judged (Daniel). Gillman identifies resurrection as a dramatic shift from denial of an afterlife to the wholehearted acceptance of the afterlife concept. He believes the shift resulted from the clash of contemporaneous history with traditional theology.

Two biblical sources refer to the evolving concept of resurrection. The Book of Isaiah deals with the conquest and dispersion of Judea in

586 B.C.E. , but some biblical scholars date the Isaiah passages that shed light on the concept of afterlife to the late second century B.C.E. and refer to the author of these chapters as "Isaiah Apocalypse."[24] The Babylonian conquest raised a moral dilemma: Many of the vanquished were innocent of any wrongdoing. Resurrection promised vindication of God's fairness by bringing the righteous back to life. In the Book of Daniel, the Jewish people are also faced with a time of national trauma. The text of Daniel, widely accepted as the most recent work in Hebrew Scripture, describes the persecution of the Jews by Syrian Antiochus IV (Epiphanes) in approximately 167–164 B.C.E., popularized by the Hanukkah story. Daniel could not say, as did earlier prophets, that the people's suffering was due to their straying from Torah. Antiochus persecuted the Judeans precisely for their loyalty to Torah while the ungodly among the Jews prospered because they ignored the commands of the tradition.

Gillman attributes a shift in Israelite afterlife beliefs to the national trauma of the second century B.C.E.:

> The earlier strata of biblical religion could not contemplate human immortality, probably because that would muddy the distinction between God and human beings. But, with the authors of Daniel and Isaiah Apocalypse, the need for an alternative theodicy to those proposed in the Torah and in Job, the need to reconcile God's justice with God's power, served as the existential impetus for overturning the classical biblical message. No longer does death mark the end of the individual's destiny. God's power now extends beyond the grave.[25]

Gillman notes the possibility that resurrection is a cultural borrowing from the Persians, among whom the Jews lived from the middle of the fifth century B.C.E. The Zoroastrian religion, founded by the Persian prophet Zarathustra in the sixth century B.C.E., taught both resurrection and judgment. At the same time, Gillman does not deny that the biblical concept of resurrection could just as well have evolved within the Israelite culture, although the only texts he identifies with the idea are those of Isaiah Apocalypse and Daniel. The Jewish view could have emerged internally from the belief in God, "the ultimate force Whose power extends over all of nature and history . . . then why cannot God raise human beings from the grave?"[26] However, Gillman is certain that the concept of immortality of the soul, which is distinct from the concept of resurrection, is strictly a later idea borrowed from the Greeks.[27]

Post-Modern Readers

Leonard Greenspoon, in an article published in 1981, also examines the biblical concept of resurrection, finding textual references throughout Hebrew Scripture.[28] He writes, "It emerges that Dan. 12:2, which is in general the starting point for any discussion of the Biblical concept of resurrection, is the end product of countless generations of speculation concerning man's place in the afterlife."[29] He locates the underpinning of resurrection in the core Israelite belief in "God as Warrior," which affirms that God has supreme power over nature and can combat chaos and even death.[30] God as warrior is already expressed in Deuteronomy—"I deal death and give life" (32:39)—and made manifest in the reviving-the-dead stories of Elijah (1 Kings 17: 17-24) and Elisha (2 Kings 4: 34-37 and 13: 21).

When Greenspoon examines Jeremiah's words, he concludes: "We have no doubt that Jeremiah was as familiar with the full Biblical concept of resurrection as the later author of the Isaiah Apocalypse."[31] He points as an example to Jeremiah's condemnation of Israel's enemies: "[they shall] sleep a perpetual sleep and not wake,' says the Lord" (51:39).[32] In addition, he reads Ezekiel's image of God reviving the dry bones of Israel (Ezekiel 37) as a motif already familiar to the people. "Ezekiel," he writes, "was working with a concept of resurrection of the dead well enough known to his audience to allow for the simultaneous application of this belief to "literal" resurrection and national restoration."[33]

Greenspoon proposes a model for the evolution of Israelite thought on the topic of resurrection. On the one hand, he acknowledges that the concept of resurrection evolved within Scripture, reaching its most developed phase in Daniel's description of the awakening and judgment of both good and evil people. On the other hand, for Greenspoon, biblical ideas are "recrudescent," meaning they break out anew from older mythic motifs and language. Ideas are not borrowed from others, he writes, but drawn from a collective pool of concepts and images of the deities that were shared by the different cultures in the ancient Near East.[34] Although the Israelites came to the unique view that God was the sole creator, who was eternal and moral, the language, images, and concepts used to convey this description of the Divine were drawn from and shared with the larger culture. Moreover, "the development of the Biblical view of resurrection is not to be charted in terms of growth from simple to complex, but rather in terms of changes of emphasis in response to changing historical and theological concerns."[35]

Greenspoon examines the widely espoused claim that the Israelites borrowed the concept of resurrection from the Persians and rejects it. "Supposed linguistic parallels between texts in the two traditions," he wrote, "have not always been carefully drawn."[36] The specific images of resurrection are also different. In the Bible, God reawakens those asleep to renewed life. The Persian image is different: Among the Zoroastrians, resurrection is a reconstituting of the creature by a reunion of its several elements. Despite the distinctions, the two cultures may have influenced each other, for example, in making resurrection a more significant religious motif, but the respective cultures were not dependent on each other for the inception of the idea.[37] In Greenspoon's words: "In reality, neither the crude term 'borrowing' nor the seemingly loftier 'inner-Israelite development' can do justice to the complex, creative process we have touched on."[38]

The early rabbinic assertion that resurrection is found throughout the biblical text, Greenspoon concludes, may have more merit than academics have formerly conceded:

> At certain periods during which the Biblical text was being composed, we can detect an interest in resurrection even when it went largely or entirely unexpressed. At these periods, if not at others, writers could have given shape to interests through language and imagery that have little or nothing in common with the criteria with which we have been working. If this is the case—and we should be willing to admit the possibility—then we need to give more serious attention to the efforts of those within early post-Biblical communities who might well have retained sensitivity to the text that is frequently lacking in modern, scientific approaches. As a result, our understanding of the complex process through which the Biblical belief in resurrection will undoubtedly be enhanced.[39]

The contemporary scholar Herbert Chanan Brichto, quoted earlier, also emphasizes that modern bias may shape our biblical readings: "Our perception of the normative religion of Israel is often conditioned—if not determined—by what we think it should have been in keeping with our own notions of superstition, truth or theological validity."[40] He accuses his academic colleagues of wrongly ruling out immortality of the spirit as an ongoing biblical belief. "Why has a millennium and more of good Bible scholarship failed to discern the basic view of afterlife permeating Scripture?" He answers his question, "for the biblical evidence for immortality presents a model of afterlife which would have constituted a rebuttal of resurrection!"[41] Many scholars assumed that if the Israelites believed that body and soul were inseparable and destined for renewed life on the earthly plane, then there was no place for an immortality of an independent spirit in the heavenly realm.

Brichto acknowledges that biblical scholars trained similarly may reach mutually exclusive conclusions because the text is written cryptically and ideas are often submerged. In contrast to many of his colleagues, he concludes:

> Biblical genius rendered the inherited model of afterlife theologically acceptable. . . . It made one's condition in the afterlife contingent not only upon his own obedience to the moral norms, but upon how well he succeeded in inculcating his children and children's children in God's moral norms.[42]

Brichto cites as evidence the verses in Isaiah that describe the shades in *Sheol* that greet newcomers (Isaiah 14:9–21). He emphasizes the story of Samuel coming back from the dead and speaking through the Witch of En-Dor. Citing Yehezkel Kaufmann, he says that the biblical prohibitions against necromancy are not founded on the belief that such activity is nonsense, but rather a presumed efficacy that tempts people to pursue their goals without reference to the norms of God.[43] He looks at the laws of levirate marriage, which required that a man reproduce with his brother's widow when the brother died without progeny. The levirate laws, the importance placed on a proper burial, and the expression of the patriarch's longing for progeny, he holds, were rooted in the belief that the status of the deceased in *Sheol* was tied to the ongoing loyalty of his offspring to God in this world.

Both Brichto and Greenspoon work backwards. Each brings a developed religious concept with which he is able to read elusive statements more clearly. The lens through which Greenspoon reads the text is the description of resurrection presented in both Daniel and rabbinic writings, dating from the first century B.C.E. to the fifth century C.E. Reading with the assumption in place that resurrection is a Jewish idea, he identifies early biblical allusions to the concept that may not be readily discernible without this operational premise. Likewise, Brichto brings a key idea that he uses to read the collage of scriptural verses in a fresh way.

Brichto's point of view is defined by the presumption that the Israelites had and were exposed to ideas about an afterlife. Belief in the afterlife, he states, is a given in the ancient world. The idea emerges from the human awareness that flesh decays and "that the recently alive or long-dead appear in dreams."[44] He quotes Fustel de Cuolanges:"The most ancient generations, long before there were philosophers, believed in a second existence after the present. They looked upon death not as a dissolution of our being, but simply as a change of life."[45] Brichto says that the reason the Bible does not explicitly present immortality as a central idea is that it was "*de rigueur* in ancient Israel" and the Bible is more concerned with practice than with creed.[46] At the same time, immortality met the important need of reward and punishment. The prophet Daniel, Brichto writes, implicitly displaced the *Sheol* model with the concept of resurrection to eternal life. "Afterlife gave way to resurrection, and tacit assumption to explicit prescription."[47]

On the topic of whether the Bible describes an enduring soul, Brichto avoids a definitive answer, whereas both Greenspan and Gillman respond with a firm no. Before we turn again to the issue, it is useful to follow the tangent to the study of Jewish mysticism. Two key issues faced in analyzing Scripture on the topic of the afterlife—the validity of working backwards with a point of view already in place and the assertion that a culture may learn directly from internal experience—also apply to the study of Jewish mysticism.

Jewish mysticism is largely an academic discipline of the twentieth century. Much of the groundbreaking work was accomplished by Gershom Scholem (Germany-Israel, 1897–1982), the first to hold a professorship in Jewish mysticism.[48] Among Scholem's important works was *Major Trends in Jewish Mysticism* (1941), in which he surveyed Jewish mystical tendencies from the *Merkavah* mystics (already mentioned in early rabbinic writings) to the latest manifestations in Hasidism. Scholem largely used a historical model. His implicit assumption was that a given cultural and religious phenomenon is closely intertwined with or dependent upon its historical predecessors and outside influences. For instance, he attributed many of the ideas in *Sefer HaBahir* (Provence, twelfth century), the oldest of the Jewish mystical texts, to the infiltration of non-Jewish Gnostic writings and Neoplatonism.[49] Gnosticism was the outlook of closed circles of mystics, dating from the first and second century of the Roman world, who saw the world as ruled by two opposing powers.[50]

Moshe Idel, currently a professor at Hebrew University in Jerusalem, challenges Scholem's assumptions.[51] Idel views Jewish mysticism as primarily an internal development. Although Jewish mystics were influenced by the cultures and ideas of the communities to which Jews were exposed, the wellspring of ideas dates to the earliest layers of Judaism. The body of mystical ideas was largely conveyed as an oral tradition. Idel rebuts Scholem's claim that foreign Gnostic ideas shaped early kabbalah on several counts:

1. It is inaccurate historically. Contemporary scholars of Gnosticism refer to the Jewish influence on the emerging Gnostic literature, rather than the "Gnostification of Jewish mysticism."[52]

2. Scholem's view fails to take into account how the "foreign ideas" came to be accepted by Jews without significant opposition during the first hundred years of their appearance in the late twelfth and thirteenth centuries and with only limited and ineffective protest after the late fifteenth century. By contrast and at about the same time, Maimonides (Spain-Egypt, 1135–1204), who was widely acknowledged as a halakhic authority, stirred a bitter debate over his philosophic writings.[53]

3. Believers who embraced *Sefer HaBahir* asserted that the mystical concepts were an ongoing part of Judaism's esoteric tradition. Many of them were masters of a critical reading of the sacred text, who identified with the conservative rabbinic mindset that distrusted new ideas.[54]

"Far from being a total innovation," Idel concludes, "historical kabbalah represented an ongoing effort to systematize existing elements of Jewish theurgy, myth, mysticism into a full-fledged response to the rationalistic challenge."[55] The failure of most university scholars to affirm the mystical elements in early Jewish texts is due to academic bias. The mystical elements "were neglected by scholarly analyses that commonly preferred a nonmythical reconstruction consonant with the theological inclinations prevalent in the rationalistic approaches to Judaism of the *Wissenschaft des Judentums*" (scientific study of Judaism).[56]

Idel teaches two more points that are relevant for our continued discussion. You may read back, chronologically speaking, and find fragments of the same concept in earlier strata of the tradition. As an example, explicit images in kabbalah of anthropomorphic perceptions of the angelic realm illuminate earlier *midrashim* and talmudic and Gnostic texts.[57] Second, ideas often emerge internally rather than being borrowed, because experiences generate ideas. Consequently, there are common elements in mysticism across cultures because people encounter similar mystical phenomena. In sum, Idel's work represents a new phase in the study of Jewish mystical texts: a phase that acknowledges that much of the mystical content of the Jewish tradition was preserved as oral tradition and was only hinted at in earlier Jewish writings. This post-modern phase honors the influence of history and culture on the shaping of ideas but also says that profound ideas may arise spontaneously across cultures due to the inherent similarities of human experiences.

My Reading of the Bible on Immortality of the Soul

As I approach Hebrew Scripture to determine if there is recognition of the soul, I admittedly come with a bias. I believe in survival of the soul. My observations of the telepathic knowledge of the death of loved ones and the uncanny ability of mediums to identify specific facts concerning the deceased, plus the testimonies of near-death experiences, have persuaded me that there is a part of us that survives our earthly existence. I am not surprised that contemporary anthropologists and scholars of comparative religion affirm the universality of a belief in the afterlife.[58] Regarding soul, Roger Lipsey writes in *The Encyclopedia of Religion*, "Very nearly all traditions speak of the mortal body and of an undying or potentially undying presence within it."[59] Isolated, illiterate, Stone Age Aborigines in Australia espouse it,[60] as did the Egyptians and Sumerians more than six millennia ago.[61] This primal belief in soul persists as a tenet in nearly all religions around the globe.[62] I am skeptical that the soul was unknown or rejected by the Israelites and culturally borrowed by the rabbis due to the influence of the Greeks. The following are some of the reasons that I am unconvinced:

1. The concept of soul is too common a human idea for the Israelites not to have come up with it independently.

2. The rabbis were very sensitive to the intrusion of foreign ideas into their faith and would have fought such a nonbiblical idea. In fact, there are no recorded protests in the Talmud.

3. There are fundamental differences between Plato's concept of soul, widely claimed by modern scholars as the greatest influence on the rabbis, and rabbinic beliefs. For Plato the body was a prison of the soul and for the rabbis it was the medium of development and improvement. Plato described the soul as without beginning or end, while the rabbis maintained that all

souls began at the time of the six days of creation. The soul
progressed, according to Plato, through elevated ideas. The
rabbis emphasized righteous deeds as the path to elevation.[63]

In the Talmud the rabbis held immortality as a fundamental belief.
The nature of that immortality is largely described in terms of resurrection, an eventual return to an earthly, bodily existence. But dualism, the
belief in an independent soul, is also widely present. In the Talmud, immortality of the soul and resurrection are "fused and confused."[64]

There are many statements reflecting rabbinic dualism. The following compilation represents only a sampling of these references: The soul
preexists the body (*Haggigah* 12b); While yet alive and when asleep the
soul departs and draws spiritual refreshment from on high (*Genesis Rabbah* 14:9); The soul is a guest in the body here on earth (*Leviticus Rabbah* 34:3); Upon death, the soul departs and is capable of a fully
conscious, disembodied life (*Ketubot* 77b and *Berakhot* 18b–19a).

Like Idel, we may review Jewish texts in reverse, beginning with a
fully developed idea and reading backward chronologically to identify
early examples in the development of the idea. In our case, we are able
to begin with the developed idea of immortality expressed in the Talmud, which encompassed both resurrection and dualism. Using this lens
to read the Bible, we find dualism in the text. The independence of spirit
from the body is implicit in the familiar account of creation: "The Lord
God formed Adam from the dust of the earth. He blew into his nostrils
the breath of life, and Adam became a living being" (Genesis 2:7). The
image of God's spirit resting in humans continues in Hebrew Scripture.
The book of Proverbs says, "The lifebreath of man *[nishmat adam]* is the
lamp of the Lord" (20:27). And in Ecclesiastes, "And the dust returns to
the ground as it was and the spirit *[ruach]* returns to God who be-
stowed it" (12:7).

Some modern scholars maintain that these expressions of God-
endowed spirit refer only to the capacity of animation, a kind of imper-
sonal battery charge. It reminds me of the image of the Golem, the ro-
botlike being designed by Rabbi Judah Loew ("Maharal," d.1609, Prague).
The folktale describes the Golem as having gained its energy source
from God's divine name placed in its mouth.[65] But unlike the Golem, humans are endowed with the capacity of self-reflection, creativity, and
will. These qualities are linked in the later mystical tradition with *nishmat chayim,* the [divine] soul-breath.

Some of these same scholars say that the Hebrew words for spirit are used in the Bible as synonyms for "alive" and that the same words are used for body parts and spirit. Interestingly, Ephraim Urbach makes such a case, but he only looks at the Hebrew words *nefesh* and *ruach*.[66] He ignores the important term *neshamah,* the precise term used in the animation of Adam. In contrast, the classic biblical commentator Abraham Ibn Ezra (Spain, 1089–1164) pointed out that *neshamah* is only used to describe humans,[67] suggestive of a unique dimension with which God endows humanity.

Granted that the creation story alone does not provide a clear-cut description of a consciousness that survives, can we find such an idea elsewhere in the Bible? Remarkably, there is a valuable expression on this topic that appears ten times in the Five Books of Moses but was given scant attention by those who asserted that there was only monism in the Bible. In describing six key deaths, the text states a variation of the phrase "*ve'nesaf el amav*"—"and he was gathered to his people."

Ve'nesaf el amav—*and he was gathered to his people*

Already in 1948 there was an article written in French in a scholarly German periodical that scrutinized this phrase.[68] The author, Bern Alfrink, pointed out that the idiom "*ve'nesaf el amav*" is positioned between death and burial and is separate and distinct from each of them. For instance, regarding Abraham the Torah says, "And Abraham expired and died at a ripe old age and he was gathered to his people. And Isaac and Ishmael buried him."[69] Variations of the phrase are also used to describe the deaths of Ishmael,[70] Isaac,[71] Jacob,[72] Aaron,[73] and Moses.[74] The idiom cannot refer to burial in a familial tomb because that was not the case for Moses or Aaron. Likewise, it is said of Jacob long before his body was brought from Egypt for interment in the Cave of Makhpelah. Alfrink concluded that the phrase means "reunited with one's ancestors and refers to the afterlife in *Sheol*."[75]

Ephraim Urbach only mentions the phrase in passing.[76] Neil Gillman pauses and analyzes its biblical origins. The repeated idiom, he says, simply suggests a good death:

> Instead of going down to *Sheol,* Isaac and Jacob are each portrayed as being "gathered to his kin" (Genesis 35:29 and 49:33), and David "slept with his fathers" (I King 2:10). There are no references to *Sheol* here, though presumably, that's where the "kin" and the

"fathers" are to be found. In general, then, the term *Sheol* is used to characterize a particularly tragic or premature death, one that follows a painful life or experience.[77]

Preceding this paragraph, Gillman emphasizes, "In all these cases, however, the rewards of a good life are experienced here on earth, not in some afterlife."

In contrast, I believe that "gathered to his people" signifies a duality of body and soul and suggests an afterlife. First, I am impressed with the regularity of the appearance of this idiom to describe a phase after death—ten instances in the Five Books of Moses. Second, the solemnity and importance of the phrase is conveyed by the attribution in the text of the words to God in each of the cases in Numbers and Deuteronomy.[78] My reading is that "gathered to his people" presents a reward experienced by the disembodied spirit for a life well lived. I am reassured in my judgment by the recent writings of some of America's most prominent biblical scholars in their JPS Torah commentary.[79]

Nahum Sarna, who cites Brichto, surveys the possible meanings of "gathered to his kin" in light of its imbedded contexts and concludes:

> The existence of this idiom, as of the corresponding figure "to lie down with one's fathers," testifies to a belief that, despite his mortality and perishability, man possesses an immortal element that survives the loss of life. Death is looked upon as a transition to an afterlife where one is united with one's ancestors. This interpretation contradicts the widespread, but apparently erroneous, view that such a notion is unknown in Israel until later times.[80]

Jacob Milgrom summarizes the forty-year-old article by Alfrink and adds: "This biblical idiom has its counterpart in the bordering river civilizations of Egypt ("going to one's Ka") and of Mesopotamia ("joining the ghosts of one's ancestors"), all of which is evidence for a belief in the afterlife that permeated the ancient world and for the concomitant fear that a wrathful deity might deprive man of this boon."[81] Jeffrey Tigay concurs: "This [expression] refers to the reunion of the spirit with those of one's kin in *Sheol* after death."[82]

The recognition of a spiritual afterlife is not new in the Jewish tradition. The JPS commentators reclaim a perspective that consistently appeared among the medieval biblical commentators. Some traditional interpretations said that the phrase "gathered to his people" simply suggests a "gathering to one's ancestors in peace" and takes no stand on the nature of the gathering. More commonly the phrase was understood as acknowledging the existence of an independent spirit and as the promise of a spiritual reward. Due to the importance of *ve'nesaf el amav*, I share a survey of major premodern rabbinic commentators on this biblical phrase:

- Rashi (Sholomo Yitzhaki, France, 1040–1105): The term used for the placement of *nefashot* in the place of their storage.[83]

- Ra'ava (Abraham ibn Ezra, Spain, 1089–1164): There are those who say that [this phrase] refers to *nefesh*, which is separate and distinct from the body. And when it separates from the body, the glory is gathered to his people. And there are others who deal with the phrase as gathering with one's ancestors in peace.[84]

- Radak (David Kimchi, Provence, 1160–1235): To one's family that had died, one is gathered, and this is the language of Hebrew Scripture, whether ancestors were righteous or wicked.[85]

- Ralbag (Levi ben Gershon, Provence, 1288–1344): The expression is connected with the soul, for while it is in the body it is, as it were, in isolation; when the soul leaves the body, it rejoins its Source and is gathered back to its glory.[86]

- Sforno (Ovadia ben Yaakov, Italy, 1470–1550): He was gathered into the bond of eternal life with the righteous of all generations, who are his people because they are similar to him. The plural, "his people," implies that there are many nations in the World to Come. . . . Everyone's share in the World to Come is a product of his own unique accomplishments during life. Therefore, no two portions in the Hereafter are alike.[87]

The review of the literature prepares us to squarely address the central question: Does Hebrew Scripture acknowledge a soul? My best response is *yes*. Although not conclusive, the evidence is nonetheless persuasive. The Torah's description of creation is dualistic in nature. There is a spirit endowed by God (Genesis 2:7) and a body that "is of the dust . . . and to the dust you shall return" (Genesis 3:19). The deaths of key figures in the Bible are described by the idiom, "gathered to his people." The phrase is not a synonym for death, which is expressed by two other Hebrew terms, *gevah* and *mut* (מות, גוה), which either alone or together usually precede the idiom.[88] The implication of the spirit being gathered to its people, whether family or the righteous of the world, is that the spirit remains with an identity after the death of the body.

Elements of survival of the soul in Hebrew Scripture mesh with the reality of the Israelite experience and with reading of the text. First, the Israelites lived among other peoples who held such a view. Second, human experience all over the globe has fostered a belief that there is a part of us that is touched by the Divine and survives this plane of existence. Third, an interpretation of survival of the soul makes sense when we work backwards from the rabbinic tradition. The fact that it is espoused in the Talmud without opposition and is a common understanding of classic biblical commentators puts the burden of proof on those who assert that dualism is a later foreign intrusion—a burden that I have not seen met.

It is natural to then ask: Why does the Bible not make an explicit statement regarding the afterlife and survival of the soul? First, I think that Samson Raphael Hirsch (Germany, 1808–1888) was right when he responded: The belief in immortality of the soul was so routinely accepted in ancient times that there was no need to "teach" it as dogma. It was taken quite for granted that just as the dead body returned to earth, its source, so the soul would return to the spiritual plane from which it originated.[89] Second, the Bible is implicitly responding to the death obsession around it in the pagan world. Death is played down as a religious focus. Third, the primary focus of the text is on shaping a communal covenant with God. The text strives to convince the audience that there is only one God who plays an active role in the people's lives and that living in covenant with God in their earthly existence is their major responsibility.

Reincarnation

Although I am persuaded that there are literary allusions to afterlife throughout Hebrew Scripture, I am unconvinced that the same is true for reincarnation. The idea that our soul will return into another body is a given in Jewish mysticism, beginning with *Sefer HaBahir* (Provence, twelfth century) and continuing in a more developed fashion in the *Zohar* (Spain, thirteenth century). Contemporary anthropologists document that belief in reincarnation spans the globe and history and seemingly has arisen independently in diverse societies. The belief in preexistence and reincarnation in isolated Stone Age peoples, J. Bruce Long writes in *The Encyclopedia of Religion*, indicates that "this belief arose contemporaneously with the origins of human culture, per se."[90]

Plato, too, espoused reincarnation, yet unlike dualism, reincarnation does not appear explicitly among the early rabbinic writings.

Jewish mystics identified hints of the concept of reincarnation in Hebrew Scripture. *Sefer HaBahir* (twelfth century) points as a proof-text to the line from Ecclesiastes, "One generation goes, another comes" (Ecclesiastes 12:4).[91] Ramban (Nahmanides, Spain, 1194–1270) commented on the Book of Job that the words of Elihu, Job's friend, are implicitly a statement that Job's tragic fate is a punishment for wrongs in a previous life.[92] It is possible that reincarnation was part of Jewish oral tradition from the earliest times, but I cannot identify the concept in Hebrew Scripture. There is too wide a time gap between Scripture and the *Sefer HaBahir* to convincingly work backwards and read the concept into poetic phrases. Among the biblical proof-texts for reincarnation cited by the mystics, not one makes the case clearly and there are too few to form a persuasive pattern.

Admittedly, my curiosity as to whether the concept of reincarnation can be identified in the Bible arises from the popularity of the idea in our own day. In a related way, the survey of scholarship on the topic of soul in the Bible is humbling. It demonstrates the extent to which our conclusions and methodology are influenced by the times in which we live. There are fundamentally different assumptions made by readers living in pre-modern, modern, and post-modern times.

Styles of Reading

The pre-modern period for Jews encompasses the earliest rabbinic writings from the dawn of the Common Era until emancipation in the eighteenth century. During this long stretch, Jews read Scripture as God's literal revelation. The words contained truths that transcended place or time. Readers unself-consciously and creatively found their respective understandings of Judaism and all "truth" in the text. There are still Jews today who read Scripture in this way. Indeed, the categories of pre-modern, modern, and post-modern are descriptions of the reader's assumptions rather than the chronology of when they read.

The revolution of modernity was the recognition that ideas do not exist as absolutes but are shaped by culture and history. Modernity for Jews was influenced by the eighteenth-century philosophy of enlightenment and enabled by emancipation, the cultural release from living as a closed community. Through the spectacles of modernity, the Bible was read as a human document. Scholars sought to identify the history of the text and its ideas by identifying its chronological layers.

The scholars of Judaism of the mid-nineteenth century called their enterprise *Wissenschaft des Judentums*, the "scientific study of Judaism." They believed that they could read texts objectively, the way a scientist approaches a problem. The modern enterprise of literary archaeology relied on the tools of philology (the chronological development of language), the choice of words (particularly for God's name), and the study of comparative language and religion. Scholars assumed that ideas moved in a linear fashion (from simple to complex) and that the emergence of ideas was largely the product of cultural borrowing.

Post-modern readers view the confidence of their predecessors with skepticism. The key insight of the last several decades is that the reading of any text is the product of context, both the author's and the reader's. The author was shaped by the ideas of his or her time and chose from among those ideas, whether consciously or unconsciously, to pursue an often unexpressed agenda. A text is a window into another time, but not a random window, rather a showcase.

The reader is also the product of manifold influences, including psychological disposition, a specific culture, and idiosyncratic taste. No two readers are identical and there is no uniform understanding of what is "reasonable." A sixty-year-old male reader, for instance, is usually more cautious, keenly aware of his limitations, and less physically pleasure-based than a twenty-year-old. Different cultures, as well, have different priorities and values. And last, we are individually inclined to find what we are looking for in a life situation or a text. As the folk adage goes, "Show a man how to use a hammer and he will see nails everywhere."[93]

Reading a text is, therefore, a very different exercise from performing a scientific analysis. By definition, the scientific method uses variables that are subject to measurement and control. Such measurement or control is not possible in the analysis of the inner workings of an individual or a community. A text is only a partial public display of a larger array of feelings and beliefs. More is hidden than revealed.

In a post-modern view, ideas evolve and are shaped by culture, which includes foreign influences. At the same time, ideas may originate from primal human experiences, creating a pool of shared concepts and images that come in and out of fashion. Each culture is distinctive as to which of these ideas are given prominence and how they are expressed. Ideas do not necessarily move from simple to complex, as evidenced in popular music trends such as the progression from Bach to the Backstreet Boys. It is also hard to categorize ideas as simple or complex. In the area of soul, for instance, which is more complex—Plato's dualism or Aristotle's teaching of the inseparability of body and soul? And a question evoked by former President Boris Yeltsin's recent pilgrimage to Jerusalem for Christmas services: Was communism or the return to Russian Orthodoxy more complex?

During my research, I could not help but wonder (and at times marvel) at how much the respective biblical interpretations matched the worldviews of the scholarly readers over the centuries. Most of the academics that identify with the "modern, critical" reading of Scripture were and are rationalists who view survival of the soul with skepticism, if not downright disdain, as superstition. For those who hold that the body and soul are inseparable and that when we die, we die, there is a repeated finding of strict monism in Scripture, too. For some of the Christian scholars who reach this same conclusion, there is the affirmation that a new revelation was needed to introduce the elevated concept of an enduring soul.

I identify with a post-modern approach. I acknowledge that I come to the question of soul and the Bible with a bias. I believe that in life we are intertwined, body and soul, and that with death our soul survives and rises to a higher plane retaining consciousness, identity, and memory. And I believe that, more likely than not, our souls return into a new life, bringing potential talents and inclinations and emotional scars from the past. With humility, I assume that the most profound experiences in life are filtered through an individual's way of seeing the world, a product of culture and disposition. Yet, a person can form judgments of meaning and understanding. With self-awareness, another person or text need not be a mirror for oneself.

I have one last bias to share. I believe that the Bible is unlike any other book. It is different by virtue of being read as a sacred text across the world by so many divergent cultures. Its special status is a product of powerfully organized religious movements that convinced or coerced others to follow their faith. The enduring relevance of Hebrew Scripture is also due to large gaps in the narrative and figurative language, which enable the reader to read him- or herself into the text. The large number and variety of *midrashim* (rabbinic interpretations) are due precisely to the repeated gaps in the text. But last, and most important to me, I believe that the text resonates with transcendent wisdom because it emerges from human encounters with the Divine. The revelation is not pure, but filtered through the minds of the recipients and therefore impacted by history and culture. In the words of Abraham Joshua Heschel (Poland-Germany-U.S., 1907–1972), "as a report about revelation, the Bible itself is a *midrash*."[94] Yet the biblical text remains sacred because it embodies the mystery of and response to transforming encounters with the Divine.

I am more engaged by viewing Torah as an intricate, coherent whole than by the enterprise of unraveling the Torah's individual strands. In anthropomorphic terms, at some point one stops asking how a person became the way they are and instead relates to that person directly in all of his or her complexity. Likewise, we draw out from our partner those qualities that reflect our own interests, and so it is with our reading of Scripture and rabbinic texts. There is the possibility of genuine empathy and hearing the other honestly, and in doing so, the influence goes two ways. When we listen openly to Hebrew Scripture and Judaism there is an integrity and distinct consciousness that shapes how we see the world. And like a person, the text has many layers, not just historically but internally.

Conclusion

A review of scholarly writings, both traditional and academic, provides nuanced readings of the *Tanakh*. Thoughtful scholars differ as to the ideas behind the words, a difference due in part to how they weigh the words and what they surmise is behind them. Many scholars say that the *Tanakh* precludes survival of the soul, presents the human as undivided body-soul, and changes only toward its chronological end, with the introduction of resurrection as an answer to the suffering of the righteous. Some recent scholars find clues of resurrection threaded throughout the text. Others find literary fragments that piece together a portrait of belief in an afterlife determined by the kind of lives people lived, manifested in part by the loyalty of their descendants to them and to God.

My best reading is that the biblical phrase "and he was gathered to his people" evidences faith in survival of the soul. The research of fine academics and a long line of traditional commentators support this interpretation. The ambiguity of the term *Sheol* reflects a collage of ideas as to the nature of the afterlife, influenced by the images of Israel's neighbors. Jewish expressions of soul were affected by Israel's neighbors, too,

which culturally for the rabbis meant the Greeks. Yet, the Israelite concept of soul emerged, developed internally, and persisted as a product of
a shared human awareness that we are more than our bodies and that
how we live this life shapes our fate for a realm to come.

Notes

Introduction

1. *Pirkei Avot (Ethics of the Fathers)* 4:21.
2. The rabbi who shared this story is Allen Krause of Aliso Viejo, California. I later called his wife, Sherri, to learn more about her experience in the hospital. She shared that with the aid of a psychologist friend she entered into a deep trance to cope with her horrible pain. She became aware in this relaxed state of a blue light passing from her feet and emerging from her head. She found herself feeling peaceful and became aware of a cocoonlike structure around her that served to help her breathe and to turn her. The prayers people said on her behalf formed the translucent cocoon.

   After her deep trance experience, her treating physician commented that her blood gases had moved from a dangerously low reading to normal. She remained aware of the cocoon around her and the prayers said on her behalf. One particularly difficult night she heard praying in a language she could not discern. Later she learned that a relative by marriage who is Ethiopian had stayed up that entire particular night praying for her in Amharic.

   On the fifth day in the intensive care unit she felt ready to die. She had heard doctors speaking of her low probabilities of healing, but mostly she was wracked with excruciating pain she felt she could not take anymore. Suddenly she felt herself rising out of her body. She knew she was outside because she felt no more pain. Before her she saw a series of doors, some of them opened. She understood them as places and experiences of her life. At the end of the hall she could see a bright light, unlike any light she had ever seen before. It was the brightest of the bright, but it did not hurt her eyes and it seemed to have texture, almost like the fluids of the womb. As she was moving down the hall she felt calm and eager to enter the light. Then she saw a beloved rabbi who had died of a heart condition a few years before. He was sitting on a fire hydrant, as he was often seen doing during his daily walks while alive. He held out his hand and telepathically communicated that she was not to continue toward the light and that she was to go back. Suddenly she was back in her body, once again wracked with pain, but it was a turning point in her recovery.

Once she recovered, which involved close to two weeks in the intensive care unit, she was a changed person. She had previously identified with the Jewish tradition but was an agnostic about God. After these experiences she felt convinced that there was a God and that prayer actually mattered. She said that she had lost all fear of death. She viewed these experiences as a gift and has since used her experiences to help two people overcome their fear of death, enabling them to die peacefully and with dignity.

Chapter 1: Telepathy

1. Recently, Ching-Lan described to me just how profoundly butterflies are identified with Al: "At the time of Al's death, I was not at the hospital. I had gone to Kubbi's apartment to rest. I was standing out on the balcony, and there was a pine tree within a long arm's reach. While I was standing there a beautiful monarch settled on a branch so close that I could almost reach out and touch him. He stayed on the branch for quite a long period of time and I was able to enjoy his beauty. A tremendous sense of peace came over me while watching him, and then he slowly lifted into the air, circled several times, and lifted off into the sun. It was at the same time that Al died in the hospital."

   [A couple of months after Al's death, his daughter Holly Anne got married.] "During the wedding when they were saying their vows, a beautiful monarch butterfly fluttered over Holly Anne and her husband. This was a marriage he had blessed and wanted to see very much."

2. Louis I. Newman, "The Battle," in *The Hasidic Anthology* (New York: Schocken, 1934, 1963), p. 70, citing *Esser Tzachtzochoth* by I. Berger

(Piotrkov, 1910—Hebrew), p. 89 and *Priester der Liebe* by Chaim Bloch (Vienna: 1930—German), p. 196.

3. Newman, "The Lamentation of the *Shekhina*," in *The Hasidic Anthology,* p. 71, citing *Priester der Liebe* by Chaim Bloch, p. 86.

4. There is extensive literature on telepathic communication, including accounts of such accomplished people as H. M. Stanley, the African explorer and "discoverer" of Dr. Livingstone; Lord Brougham, a notable British orator and statesman, who was Lord Chancellor in the Whig government of 1830-34; and L. I. Vasilev, who became professor of physiology in the University of Leningrad. See Ian Stevenson, *Children Who Remember Previous Lives: A Question of Reincarnation* (Charlottesville, Va.: University Press of Virginia, 1987, 1992), pp. 9-20.

5. Cited in Stevenson, *Children Who Remember Previous Lives,* pp. 13-14.

Chapter 2: Near-Death Experiences (NDEs)

1. Elisabeth Kübler-Ross, *On Death and Dying* (New York: Macmillan, 1969).

2. Elisabeth Kübler-Ross, *On Children and Death* (New York: Collier, 1983), pp. 206-211.

3. Raymond A. Moody, Jr., *Life After Life* (New York: Bantam, 1975), pp. 21-23.

4. Melvin Morse, with Paul Perry, *Closer to the Light: Learning from the Near-Death Experiences of Children* (New York: Villard Books, 1999), pp. 1-8.

5. Elisabeth Kübler-Ross, *On Life After Death* (Berkeley, Calif.: Celestial Arts, 1991).

6. Kübler-Ross, *On Life After Death,* p. 14.

7. Ibid., p. 33.

8. Sherwin Nuland, *How We Die* (New York: Vintage, 1993, 1995), pp. 137-139.

9. Carl Sagan, *Broca's Brain* (New York: Random House, 1979), pp. 301-302.

10. For a broader and more in-depth review of physiological explanations of near-death experience see Patrick Glynn, "Intimations of Immortality," in *God: The Evidence,* (Rocklin, Calif.: Forum, 1997), pp. 99-137, and Melvin L. Morse, David Venecia, and Jerrold Milstein,

"Near Death Experience: A Neurophysiologic Explanatory Model," *Journal of Near-Death Studies,* no. 1 (Fall 1989): 45–53.

11. Peter Fenwick and Elizabeth Fenwick, *The Truth in the Light* (New York: Berkeley, 1995), pp. 211–214.

12. Carl B. Becker, "Why Birth Models Cannot Explain Near-Death Phenomena," in Greyson and Flynn, *The Near-Death Experience* (Springfield, Ill.: Thomas, 1984), pp. 104–162.

13. Peter Pitzele, my friend and mentor, shared these examples of mystery with me.

Chapter 3: What Is Soul?

1. Jack Canfield and Mark Victor Hansen, *Chicken Soup for the Soul* (Deerfield Beach, Fla.: Health Communications, 1993); Thomas Moore, *Care of the Soul: A Guide for Cultivating Depth and Sacredness in Everyday Life* (New York: Harper Collins, 1992); Joan Borysenko, *Fire in the Soul: A New Psychology of Spiritual Optimism* (New York: Warner, 1993); Gary Zukav, *The Seat of the Soul* (New York: Fireside, 1989); James Hillman, *The Soul's Code: In Search of Character and Calling* (New York: Random House, 1996).

2. Moore, *Care of the Soul,* p. xviii.

3. Ibid., p. 5.

4. *Berakhot* 10a. For similar imagery see *Midrash Psalm* on 103:1; *Vayikra Rabbah* 4:8; and *Devarim Rabbah* 2:37.

5. Peter Pitzele, *Our Father's Wells* (New York: HarperSanFrancisco, 1995). The book is a collection of bibliodramas expanding on the narrative of the Genesis accounts.

6. Ibid., p. 13.

7. This line is inspired by a sentence from Thomas Moore: "Tradition teaches that soul lies midway between understanding and unconsciousness, and that its instrument is neither the mind nor the body, but imagination." In Moore, *Care of the Soul,* p. xiii.

8. "The *nefesh* is bound to the *ruach,* the *ruach* to the *neshamah,* and the *neshamah* to the Blessed Holy One." *Zohar* III, 25a (top).

9. *Nefesh* is linked to *assiyah,* the physical world of action; *ruach* is in the domain of *yetzirah,* the world of feelings, *neshamah* is in the world of *beriah,* thought; the next realm of creation is *atzilut,* divine transcendence identified with intuition and later linked by Isaac Luria with the highest levels of soul, *chayah* and *yechidah.*

10. The *Zohar* is traditionally ascribed to Shimon bar Yohai. Gershom Scholem persuasively demonstrated the authorship of Moses de Leon (Spain, d. 1305), a suggestion first made by the historian Heinrich Graetz—see "The Zohar I: The Book and Its Author," in *Major Trends in Jewish Mysticism* (New York: Schocken, 1941), pp. 156-204. Moshe Idel, the great contemporary scholar of Jewish mysticism, teaches that much of de Leon's material was part of an extensive oral tradition, rather than self-generated material, which helps explain its rapid and widespread acceptance among mystics.

11. The idea of five levels of soul emerges from rabbinic commentaries from as early as first-century Palestine. See *Bereshit Rabbah* 14:9 and *Devarim Rabbah* 2:37.

12. Analogy presented by Aryeh Kaplan in Sutton, Abraham, ed., *Inner Space: Introduction to Kabbalah, Meditation, and Prophecy* (New York: Moznaim, 1991), pp. 17-20, and in Aryeh Kaplan's *The Light Beyond: Adventures in Hasidic Thought* (New York: Moznaim, 1981), p. 110, fn. 23; also in David Zeller, audiotape *The Tree of Life* (Boulder, Colo.: Sounds True, 1996), tape 3. Based on writing of Chaim Vital's *Nefesh HaChaim* 1:14; *Etz Chayim, Shaar* 5:5, from Psalm 23:31.

13. Utilizing one of the descriptions in the *Zohar* (second section, *Parshat Mishpatim*, p. 94b).

14. Kaplan, *The Light Beyond*, pp. 110-111.

15. This formulation is inspired by an undated taped lecture of Rabbi Noah Weinberg of Aish HaTorah, Jerusalem, on "The Five Levels of Pleasure." At the same time, Rabbi Weinberg does not correlate his "levels of happiness" with soul. I have reduced his five levels to four, and I use my own language. With gratitude to Gary Winkler for sharing this tape.

16. *Mishneh Torah,* Book One: Knowledge, "Laws of Repentance," 10:6, using the translation of Isadore Twersky, *A Maimonides Reader* (New York: Behrman House, 1972), p. 84.

17. *Sanhedrin* 91a; *Vayikra Rabbah* 4:5; *Tanhumah Vayikra* 12. Among the collage of rabbinic writings there is also a *midrash* that emphasizes the separateness and greater responsibility of soul over body: "In *olam haba* the soul and body will stand in judgment. What will the Holy Blessed One do? He will overlook the body and censure the soul, and when it pleads, 'Master of the Universe! The two of us sinned alike, so why do you overlook the body and censure me?' God

answers, 'The body comes from below where people sin; but you come from above where sin is not committed. Therefore I overlook the body and censure you'" (*Vayikra Rabbah* 4:5).

18. *Midrash Tanhumah, Vayikra* 11.

19. *Ketubot* 77b; *Berakhot* 18b–19a: for Philo, the first-century B.C.E. Alexandrian philosopher influenced by Plato, there was a complete separation between body and soul.

20. During the medieval period a multiplicity of rabbinic views was expressed on the nature of the soul, influenced in part by the intellectual currents of the day, which include the following:

   • Abraham ibn Daud, like the Moslem philosopher Avicenna, espoused immortality of the individual soul.

   • Maimonides, influenced by Aristotle, saw soul as "intellect" linked to the great "Intellect" of the Divine, which on the highest level enabled merger and obliterated the individual soul's identity (*Moreh Nevukhim*).

   • Spanish neoplatonists such as Bahya and Solomon ibn Gabriol believed that although the soul was derived from the Universal Intellect, those powers were invested in an individual soul that had its own identity.

   • For Hasdai Crescas (*Or Adonai* 2:6) and Joseph Albo (*Sefer Halkkarim* 4:29), love, not intellect, is the highest good, and the soul remains immortal after separation from the body.

21. Saadiah Gaon, *The Book of Beliefs and Opinions (Emunot veDeot)*, treatise 6.

Chapter 4: Survival of the Soul: Judaism's Views

1. In addition, there is a statement in Genesis that Enoch "walked with God and he was no more, because God had taken him" (Genesis 5:24). This line comes in sharp contrast to all the surrounding genealogy in which it is said of each person that "he died." This led some Jewish writers to assert that Enoch's spirit entered paradise without physically dying. See *Targum Yerushalmi* and *Derekh Eretz Zuta* 1, end (post-talmudic tractate).

2. See Abraham, Genesis 25:8; Isaac, Genesis 35:29; Ishmael, Genesis 25:17; Jacob, Genesis 49:33; Aaron, Numbers 27:13; Moses, Numbers 20:24, 20:26, Deuteronomy 31:16, 32:50. Also King David and

Solomon's deaths are described with the words "slept with his fathers"(1 Kings 2:10; 1 Kings 11:43).

3. Commentary on Genesis 25:8.

4. Ibid.

5. See Dr. J. H. Hertz, "Israel and Egypt: The Spiritual Contrast," *The Pentateuch and Haftorahs* (London: Soncino Press, 1936, 1964), pp. 396-397); Rabbi Jack Riemer, "Do We Believe in an Afterlife?" in Riemer, ed., *Wrestling with the Angel: Jewish Insights on Death and Mourning* (New York: Schocken, 1995), pp. 309-311.

   There are other possibilities as to the Torah's reticence on the afterlife. Some say that God in addressing the Israelites avoided the afterlife because the people were then unable to absorb the idea. This is similar to Maimonides' explanation of the silence on resurrection of the dead. Just as God chose to lead the Israelites in a circuitous route to avoid the Philistines, Maimonides states that God wrote the Torah "in the language of man" and only presented what they were able to hear.

   Others say that the Israelites at this phase did not believe in the concept of survival of the soul and that it only entered Judaism much later due to foreign influences. None of these possible explanations is definitive. Regardless of the Bible's original motive for near silence on the afterlife, the rabbis' later glosses on the Torah and worldview will define Jewish faith.

6. See Leviticus 11:24-31, 11:39.

7. Throughout *Tanakh* (Hebrew Scripture) there is reference to *Sheol*, a place of ethereal, shadowy existence after this world. *Sheol* description varies in *Tanakh* and remains vague. See for example, Numbers 16:33; Psalms 6:6; Isaiah 38:1-10; Job 7:9-8, 10:20-21, 11:7-8, 14:21-22, 17:13-16; Proverbs 27:20. For a fuller discussion of the meaning of *Sheol* see appendix of this book.

8. Samuel 28:11-15.

9. *Sanhedrin* 10:1; also the preamble to *Pirkei Avot*.

10. A key example of individual reward is the story in *Hullin* 142b of a boy's fatal fall while obeying his father's request to climb a ladder and bring down nestlings from the roof, which would have complied with the two biblical mandates for which the reward is a "prolonged life" (honoring parents—Exodus 20:12; and removing baby birds from a nest only when the mother bird is away—Deuteronomy 22:7). R. Jacob ben Korshai explained the seeming contradiction of

obedience and death by interpreting "that your days be prolonged" to refer to the next world ("the world that is wholly long"). As an aside, the boy's death, according to the Talmud, led one leading rabbi, Elisha ben Abuya, to apostasy.

11. *Sanhedrin* 91b.

12. *Berakhot* 28b.

13. R. Joshua b. Hananiah, *Tosafot* 13:2; later codified by Maimonides in *Mishneh Torah*, "Pious of the nations of the world have a portion in the world to come" (*Yad, Teshuvah* 3:5).

14. Said of a Roman executioner who kindly speeds up the death of Rabbi Hanina ben Teradyon (*Avodah Zarah* 18a); also said of a Roman nobleman who saves the life of Rabban Gamaliel from death (*Ta'anit* 29a). Twenty-four examples from early rabbinic writings of a *bat kol* promising the "world to come" are provided in Arthur Marmorstein, "The Doctrine of the Resurrection of the Dead in Rabbinic Theology," in *Studies in Jewish Theology* (London: Oxford University Press, 1950), pp. 174–178.

15. *Avodah Zarah* 2a–b: The image continues with both the Romans and Persians presenting representatives who describe their military and material successes, which fail to impress God.

16. The seven laws are: forbidden acts—idolatry, blasphemy, bloodshed, sexual sins, theft, and eating a living animal—and fulfilling the duty of establishing courts. *Sanhedrin* 56–60, later codified by Maimonides in *Yad, Melakhim,* 8:10, 10:12.

17. *Pirkei Avot* 4:29.

18. *Pirkei Avot* 3:1.

Chapter 5: What Happens After I Die?

1. *Sifre Deuteronomy* 356.

2. *Berakhot* 34b.

3. *Berakhot* 17a.

4. Said by Harold Kushner in a public lecture at Temple Beth Shalom, Santa Ana, California, in 1996.

5. There is a discussion in the tenth chapter of *Sanhedrin* on the nature of the world to come. Maimonides expresses disdain for speculation on the world to come because of our own inability to grasp a disembodied state. In his words: "Just as a blind person can't grasp

color, or a deaf person the nuances of voice, or a eunuch the lust of sexuality—so those who are in a body are unable to grasp the joys of the soul. Just as fish do not know the nature of fire, because they live in its essential opposite, so from the material world are the delights of the spiritual world unknown" (Maimonides' introduction to his commentary on the tenth chapter of *Mishnah Sanhedrin*).

6. Although the first handwritten copies of the *Zohar* were produced by Moses de Leon in the thirteenth century, the first editions of the *Zohar* were published in Mantua (1558–1560) and Cremona (1559–1560).

7. For the classic description of Moses de Leon's authorship of the *Zohar,* traditionally attributed to the first-century Rabbi Shimon Bar Yohai, see Scholem, "*Zohar* I," pp. 156–204; Daniel Chanan Matt's introduction, *Zohar: The Book of Enlightenment* (New York: Paulist Press, 1983), pp. 3–10.

8. Simcha Paull Raphael, "A Contemporary Psychological Model of the Afterlife," in *Jewish Views of the Afterlife* (Northvale, N.J.: Jason Aronson, 1994), pp. 357–402.

9. *Berakhot* 22b.

10. *Moed Katan* 28b.

11. *Zohar* III, 53a.

12. *Zohar* II, 218a.

13. *Taanit* 11a.

14. *Zohar* I, 79a.

15. The Cave of Makhpelah is the burial place near Hebron of the patriarchs and the matriarchs, with the exception of Rachel. The site is also used figuratively as the ethereal passageway for souls to the Garden of Eden.

16. *Zohar* I, 127a.

17. TJ *Moed Katan* 3:5, 82b; TJ *Yevamot* 16:1, 15c.

18. *Zohar* II, 26a.

19. *Berakhot* 18b; *Shabbat* 13b.

20. Zalman Schachter-Shalomi, *Spiritual Intimacy: A Study of Counseling in Hasidism* (Northvale, N.J.: Jason Aronson, 1991), p. 42.

21. *Zohar* I, 226a.

22. Raphael, *Jewish Views of the Afterlife,* p. 390.

23. *Sifre Deuteronomy* 10:67a; *Maaseh de R. Joshua ben Levi,* cited by Raphael, p. 391.

24. *Zohar* II, 209a.

25. Raphael, p. 394, citing in fn. 71 Louis Ginzberg, ed., *Legends of the Jews,* vol. 1, trans. Henrietta Szold (Philadelphia: Jewish Publication Society, 1967-1969), pp. 57-58. Complete English text is found in Moses Gaster, ed. and trans., *The Chronicles of Jerahmeel, IX* (New York: Ktav, 1971).

26. Another monastery that has a large collection of human bones is the Capuchine Monastery in Rome. Hundreds of years ago, one of the monks had a dream in which all the bones were arranged artistically. Afterwards he took the bones, such as the bones of the spine, and arranged them to form flower patterns and other designs, which are available for public viewing.

27. "Certain things whose literal meanings are impossible such as the corporeality of God must be interpreted (allegorically). However, that which is possible remains as is." Moses Maimonides, *Treatise on Resurrection,* translated and annotated by Fred Rosner (New York: Ktav, 1982), p. 45; *Mishneh Torah, Hilkhot Yesodei Torah* 1:7. Yet, Maimonides accepted the supernatural category of miracles that he believed were woven by God into creation.

Chapter 6: Traditional Judaism on Resurrection

1. Josephus, *The Jewish War* 2:8, 14, 163; *Antiquities* 18:1, 4, 16. English translations of Josephus are, *The Jewish War* (Middlesex, England: Penguin, 1959, 1984), and *Loeb Classic Library Edition* (Cambridge, Mass.: Harvard University Press, 1978). Vol. 2-3, *The Jewish War,* vol. 4-9, *Antiquities.*

2. Discussed in *Sanhedrin* 92b, where Rabbi Judah understands Ezekiel as speaking allegorically.

3. An additional relevant citation from *Isaiah* (25:7-8a): "He [God] will destroy on this mount the shroud that is drawn over the faces of all the peoples, and the covering that is spread over the nations: He will destroy death forever."

4. *Ketubot* 11a; *Sanhedrin* 90b; TJ *Kilayim* 9:4, 32c; TJ *Ketubot* 12:3, 35b; *Ecclesiastes Rabbah* 1:4.

5. The idea of resurrection for the rabbis was clearly and literally corporeal. Into modernity this literalness has created concern over which clothes to use for burial, whether there is a complete interment of all organs, and the desire to be buried in Israel. See

"Resurrection" in *Encyclopedia Judaica* (Jerusalem: Keter, 1972), vol.14, p. 99.

6. This bone does not correspond to a bone that is visible to inspection of the spine. There are a variety of sources on the *luz: Bereshit Rabbah* 28:3; *Vayikra Rabbah* 18:1; Louis Ginzberg, *Legends of the Jews*, vol. 5, p. 363, fn. 345; Saul Lieberman's "Some Aspects of Afterlife in Early Rabbinic Literature," in *Harry Austryn Wolfson Jubilee Volume* (English Section), vol. 2 (Jerusalem: 1965), p. 502.

7. Contained in Maimonides' introduction to his Mishnah commentary to the tenth chapter of *Sanhedrin*, also called *Helek*. This list was put into poetic form, the *Yigdal*, and is contained as a popular hymn in traditional prayer books.

8. The thirteenth. For insight into the controversy after his death, see "Maimonidean Controversy" in *Encyclopedia Judaica*, vol. 11, pp. 745-754.

9. Moses Maimonides, *Treatise on Resurrection*, translated and annotated by Fred Rosner (New York: Ktav, 1982).

10. Based on *Berakhot* 17a; see Maimonides, *Treatise on Resurrection*, p. 25.

11. In the words of my Jewish philosophy professor, Rabbi Harlan Wechsler,"If God can create from nothing *(ex nihilo)*, then God can create from something."

12. Maimonides wrote that to attain love of God, a Jew needed to know math and science because love of God emerged from knowledge of God's works (see, for example, *Guide* 3:51). This emphasis on knowledge outside the realm of traditional Jewish texts was seen as particularly offensive. See "Maimonidean Controversy" in *Encyclopedia Judaica*, vol. 11, pp. 745-754.

13. "The Gate of Reward," in *Ramban (Nahmanides): Writings and Discourses,* translated and annotated by Charles B. Chavel (New York: Shilo, 1978, 1995), pp. 424-551.

14. See Hasdai Crescas's *Or Adonai* (Hebrew).

15. "*Ikkarim*" i.iv. 35-41, xxiii.

16. The Reform Movement's Pittsburgh Platform of 1885 rejected bodily resurrection and *Gehinnom* (purgatory) as "ideas not rooted in Judaism."

17. Neil Gillman, *The Death of Death: Resurrection and Immortality in Jewish Thought* (Woodstock,Vt.: Jewish Lights, 1997).

18. *Zohar, VaEra*, 28a-29b.

19. I take solace from a similar conclusion by the great contemporary thinker Rabbi Louis Jacobs: "We ought to be frank enough to admit that all the speculation regarding life here on earth after the resurrection simply does not 'ring a bell' for us whereas the more spiritual interpretation of a Maimonides does." Louis Jacobs, "The Hereafter" in *A Jewish Theology* (New York: Behrman House, 1973), pp. 318-322.

20. There still remains room to grapple with this issue. Some have resolved the seeming contradiction of the choice between resurrection and reincarnation by suggesting that both could simultaneously be true: Each of the bodies would come back with its respective soul, because the soul, like a flame, can be divided and can exist in each body with no loss.

21. Menachem Kallus, a doctoral candidate in Jewish mysticism at Hebrew University, has said in private conversation that for Isaac Luria reincarnation may have meant the reconstituting of the ethereal body of *Adam HaRishon,* a gathering of fallen sparks that will usher in the messianic era.

Chapter 7: Past-Life Regression: An Introduction

1. Brian Weiss, *Many Lives, Many Masters* (New York: Fireside, 1988).
2. Ibid., p. 54.
3. Ibid., p. 56.
4. My first meeting with Elisabeth Kübler-Ross was in November 1996. I met with her six times during the next twelve months.
5. The seminar at the end of 1996 was part of a collection of workshops co-sponsored by the Omega Institute and *New Age* magazine, and held at a hotel near Los Angeles International Airport.
6. We met in New York in the spring of 1997.

Chapter 8: Training with Dr. Brian Weiss

1. Brian Weiss, *Only Love Is Real* (New York: Time Warner, 1996).
2. Stevenson, *Children Who Remember Previous Lives,* pp. 25-27, includes a list of the following cultures that believe in reincarnation: Hindus, Buddhists, Shiite Moslems of western Asia, native tribes of Northern, Western America, Trobriand Islanders, the tribes of central

Australia, and the Ainu of northern Japan. For sources on reincarnation in a variety of religious traditions see Joseph Head and S. L. Cranston, eds., *Reincarnation: The Phoenix Fire Mystery* (New York: Julian Press, 1977).

Chapter 9: Reincarnation: Judaism's Views

1. Shared with me in a private conversation.
2. Redacted in the south of France in 1180.
3. Gershom Scholem, "*Gilgul*: The Transmigration of Souls," in *On the Mystical Shape of the Godhead* (New York: Schocken, 1991), p. 203.
4. "Why is there a righteous person who has good, and [another] righteous person who has evil?

   "This is because the [second] righteous person was wicked previously, and is now being punished.

   "Is one then punished for his childhood deeds? Did not Rabbi Simon say that in the Tribunal on high, no punishment is meted out until one is twenty years or older?

   "He said:'I am not speaking of his present lifetime. I am speaking about what he has already been previously.'" From *The Bahir*, translation and commentary by Rabbi Aryeh Kaplan (York Beach, Maine: Samuel Weiser, 1979, 1990), part 1, section 195, pp. 77–78.
5. Nahmanides commentary on Job 33:30.
6. For the main part of the *Zohar* reincarnation is a process restricted to a childless man and his wife, but a broader view of reincarnation is presented in *Saba d'Mishpatim* (*Zohar* III, 94a–114).
7. *Zohar* III, 99b.
8. *Gilgul* has the root "to roll" (from body to body). See Gershom Scholem's analysis of the origin of the term in *On the Mystical Shape of the Godhead,* pp. 197, 209, fn. 23.
9. Saadiah Gaon, *The Book of Beliefs and Opinions,* treatise 6, ch. 7; Abraham ibn Daud, *Emunah Ramah*, treatise 1, ch. 7; Joseph Albo, *Ikkarim,* treatise 4, ch. 29. Yehudah Halevi and Maimonides are silent on the topic, but Maimonides' son, Abraham, rejects it completely.
10. Saadiah Gaon, *The Book of Beliefs and Opinions,* 6:7.
11. Menasseh ben Israel's *Sefer Nishmat Hayyim* (Amsterdam, 1652); Elijah ha-Kohen ha-Itamari's *Ana Gilgul* (Smyrna, 1736); and Meir

Bikayam's *Golel Or* (Smyrna, 1736)—cited in "Gilgul," *Encyclopedia Judaica,* vol. 7, (Jerusalem: Keter, 1974), p. 573.

12. Abraham ha-Levi ibn Migash's *Sefer Kavod Elohim,* 2 (Constantime, 1585), pp. 10–14, and the writings of Leone Modena and Ben David—cited in "Gilgul," *Encyclopedia Judaica*, vol. 7, p. 573.

13. See *Sefer ha-Temunah*; *Ta'amei ha-Mitzvot* of Yosef of Hamadan (1290–1300); also see the work of mid-thirteenth-century teacher Joseph ben Shalom Ashkenazi. The doctrine of transmigration into all forms of nature as a flow up and down the ladder of creation was a rejection of Aristotle's notion of fixed forms.

14. Joseph of Hamadan said that transmigration into animals was a form of hell.

15. See, for example, *Zohar* III, 216b *(Ra'aya Mehemna)*.

16. *Zohar* II, 104a–b and III, 217a—cited in Scholem, "Gilgul," p. 222, fn 57.

17. Scholem, "Isaac Luria and His School," in *Major Trends in Jewish Mysticism,* pp. 285–286.

18. Luria, also know as *HaAri* (an acronym which means "the lion" and is derived from *Ha-elohi Rabbi Yitzhak*—"The Divine Rabbi"), was born in Jerusalem in 1534 to an Ashkenazic father and a Sephardic mother. When his father died, the young boy and his mother moved to a relative's home in Egypt. Scholars differ as to whether the relative was her great-uncle, uncle, or her brother. Luria studied traditional texts, including mysticism, with leading Egyptian rabbis of his day.

19. *Sifra di-Zeniuta*, "The Book of Concealment," composed while still in Egypt. Luria also wrote comments on the *Sabba* of the *Zohar,* which deals with reincarnation.

20. *Eitz HaChayim*. Vital began *Eitz HaChayim* shortly after his master's death and worked on it, according to some scholars, for more than twenty years. Divided into eight sections, or "gates," the work contains writings by Luria plus Vital's accounts of Luria's teachings.

21. This divine ray of light is also called *Adam Kadmon,* the primordial human, which is different than *Adam HaRishon,* the Adam of the Bible.

22. Parallels between Luria's ideas and contemporary "big bang" cosmology are developed in Richard Friedman's *The Disappearance of God* (New York: Little, Brown, 1995) and Daniel Matt's *God and the Big Bang* (Woodstock, Vt.: Jewish Lights, 1996).

23. This description of Luria's creation is a minimal outline of Chaim Vital's description of the Lurianic system. Vital's writing is exceedingly difficult to grasp in all its multifaceted layers. During my sabbatical in Jerusalem in 1997 I had the opportunity to study with Menachem Kallus, a student of the writing of Vital and a doctoral candidate at Hebrew University advised by Professor Moshe Idel. The following is a fuller description of Luria's vision of creation, which is still a simplification and yet conveys the complexity of Luria's description of creation.

   When we say "God created" we are speaking of an infinite God who emanated infinite light, referred to as *Or Ein Sof.* God wished to allow for the potential of finitude to be expressed, which returns in process to infinity. Initially in the sphere created by God's evacuation is an impression of previous infinite light and emptiness. God reenters the emptiness halfway, as if to the center. As God reenters from the top, moving inward, concentric circles of *sefirot* (divine attributes) are formed. With God's finite potential at the center, the *sefirot* also take the form of pillars, which constitute *Adam Kadmon. Adam Kadmon,* the primordial human, is the root of the vessels themselves. *Adam Kadmon* is in a realm above the highest spiritual levels of the world as we know it (*atzilut*). All on the level of divine self-creation is perfect.

   After a complex process whereby the lights return to the infinite and then return again to the finite, the lights become differentiated and vessels begin to form. Then God brings the lower levels of the lights to the upper part of *Adam Kadmon* and emanates ten vessels of light back to the lower level. Three light vessels in the highest sphere represent the levels of transcendence, will, and intelligence and contain the reemanated light. The seven lower vessels, intentionally fashioned in an unbalanced way, shatter. The lights return above, and the vessels descend to the levels that will later become the lower worlds. Then God emanates a "new face" that is balanced, and this divine emanation begins to reconstitute the fallen sparks.

   In order to re-create the divine realm of *yetzirah, Adam Kadmon* mates internally, thereby allowing for a reconstituted world (*olam hatikkun*). *Adam Kadmon* is still composed of ten *sefirot,* divine emanations, which are now organized as five faces, *partzufim,* composed of the five main *sefirot* (emanations or attributes of God): *keter*; *chokhmah* and *binah* (which face each other); and *tiferet* and *malkhut* (which below were back-to-back but are raised up by *keter* to return face-to-face). *Adam HaRishon*, the Adam of the Bible, is formed through the merger of *binah* and *tiferet* as they rise up to *keter* and *chokhmah*. *Adam HaRishon* was supposed to return *malkhut* and *tiferet* face-to-face on the lower level, so as to make an uninterrupted chain of *tikkun* from *ein sof* (the highest *sefirotic* level) to the lower levels.

After eating the forbidden fruit, *Adam HaRishon*, as the *Zohar* says, falls into the physical world (*Olam haAssiya*), a lower spiritual plane. Sparks scatter in all directions when *Adam HaRishon* falls because *Olam haAssiyah* is filled with profane shards (*kelipot*) from the breaking of the vessels. Some of the sparks are thrust deeper within *Adam HaRishon*, inner sites from which he will pass the sparks on to his descendants. Other sparks fall among the *kelipot*, a scattering that leaves *Adam HaRishon* and God, the source of the sparks, incomplete.

Each person's soul is constituted by sparks from *Adam HaRishon*, identified by their point of origin, their root in the spiritual body of Adam. Family members are rarely from the same soul root. This allows for complementary cooperation in a family because souls that are not yet rectified but come from the same root are in competition for the same scarce resources in the shattered world. This is analogous to different personality types in astrology, which complement each other by their differences and can clash when the same types are brought together. Souls of the same root, however, are able to use intentionality to rise higher and gain by combining forces. When the soul spark is purified through acts of intentionality, the spark may rise, enabling a reunification and healing of *Adam HaRishon*. Luria provided specific contemplative exercises to accompany the performance of *mitzvot* as the tools of intentionality.

24. The sparks originating from the primary 613 body locations are also called "great souls."

25. The idea that the three components of the soul transmigrate separately was first mentioned in the *Zohar* (III, 178b—*Ra'aya Mehemna*). This idea, which is not emphasized in the *Zohar*, becomes a central description of soul, as accounted in Vital's description of Luria's teaching. More original was Luria's claim that each facet of soul, or *tzelem*, was three-dimensional: the *nefesh* (the physical component) had a *nefesh* (the doing of the body), a *ruach*

(feelings concerning the body), and *neshamah* (thoughts rooted in body).

26. As used in the Bible, Ibn Ezra points out, the word *neshamah* only refers to *nishmat adam*, the soul of Adam. Commentary on *Genesis* 7:23.

27. Ken Wilber, the contemporary philosopher of science and consciousness, in *The Marriage of Sense and Soul: Integrating Science and Religion* (New York: Random House, 1998), also describes levels of inner, human life that are likewise hologramlike, composed on each level of all levels: "But in a more sophisticated integration, *each of those levels* (sensory, mental, spiritual) *is also divided according to the differentiations of modernity* (art, morals, and science). Thus—and I must put this very loosely for an introductory statement—there are the art and morals and science of the sensory realm, the art and morals and science of the mental realm, and the art and morals and science of the spiritual realm" (p. 25).

28. An exception to the three-lifetime rule may be made for a soul in the midst of a *tikkun*, a soul repair. To my knowledge, Chaim Vital does not say what happens to the soul if it fails to rise a level in the course of three lifetimes. Vital's style of writing is more stream-of-consciousness than linear, which explains such omissions.

29. According to Gershom Scholem, early kabbalists used the terms *gilgul* and *ibbur* interchangeably. Toward the end of the thirteenth century the two terms began to be used differently: *ibbur* designated a temporary soul impregnation into a living body, and *gilgul* the incarnation of a soul into an unfolding body in the womb from the moment of conception. *Dybbuk*, a term popularized in Hasidic folk tradition, is a negative *ibbur*. The term *dybbuk* appears by the seventh century, but as the concept of "wandering souls," *dybbuk* is first described by Chaim Vital. See Scholem, "Gilgul: The Transmigration of Souls," in *On the Mystical Shape of the Godhead*, pp. 222–223.

30. The repaired soul spark returns to the higher realm with a "karmic" debt paid by helping the person whose deeds were the vehicle of purification.

31. Jane I. Smith, "Afterlife," in Mircea Eliade, ed., *Encyclopedia of Religion*, vol. 1 (New York: MacMillan, 1987), p. 110.

32. There is a core consciousness and freedom of will that transcends

the soul sparks, otherwise we would not have the capacity to repair our soul sparks.

33. The analogy is my own and emerged in conversation with Menachem Kallus.

34. Rabbi Elazar ben Arakh.

35. Rabbi Elazar ben Shamu'a.

36. *Sefer HaHizyonot* (Jerusalem: Mosad HaRav Kook, 1954—Hebrew and out of print), p. 135.

37. Rabbi Vidal de Tolosha, author of *Maggid Mishnah.*

38. Contained in Vital's diary, *Sefer HaHizyonot,* p. 134.

39. An insight of Menachem Kallus.

40. Conclusion of Menachem Kallus.

41. S. Baruchovitch, *Sipurey HaAri,* p. 44.

42. The idea that souls are divided into families predates Luria, according to Scholem, who also finds it present in the writing of R. Solomon Alkabetz (ca. 1550) and Luria's teacher (and Alkabetz's brother-in-law), R. Moses Cordovero (1522-1570). See Scholem, "Gilgul . . . ," pp. 224-225.

43. In Brian Weiss's *Only Love is Real,* he tells of two clients who seemingly reunite from a previous life. The book concludes that people travel in repeated groupings across time. Likewise, in *Many Lives, Many Masters,* Weiss shares that Catherine identified people in this life with incarnations of people she had known in previous lives.

44. Harold Bloom, in *Omens of the Millennium: The Gnosis of Angel, Dream, and Resurrection* (New York: Riverhead Books, 1996), p. 213, writes: "Luria fascinatingly taught that parents and children almost never have an affinity of sparks, almost never share the same root. So much for Freudian psychology!" The claim that a family doesn't share the same root does not mean that families don't have much in common, including incarnations as a cluster in an earlier life. It may mean that there are spiritual core qualities that enable otherwise unenlightened people to live peacefully together. Those who share the same soul sparks have the potential to either be exceedingly close or clash like the same poles of a magnet.

45. The concept of nonhuman reincarnation reminds me of a story. Sam and Jake were close friends. They agreed that when the first of them died he would return and tell his buddy what life was like on the other side. When Jake died, Sam grieved greatly. One night Sam awoke upon hearing a familiar voice.

"Jake, is that you?" Sam asked hesitantly.

"Yes, Sam, it's me. I promised that I would come back and tell you about the other side."

"You're the best friend!" Sam said. "So, what's it like?"

"Well, each morning I get up and have this great breakfast of fresh lettuce and sprouts. I feel the sun and see the beauty of the flowers around me, and then I have sex until lunch. For lunch I also eat fresh vegetables, and afterwards I have sex until dinner. I watch the sunset, and the sky is bigger and more magnificent than ever."

"Wow," Sam says. "Heaven sounds wonderful."

"What Heaven?" Jake says. "I'm a rabbit in Montana!" (With gratitude to Dr. Ray Lederman for sharing this story.)

46. *Shibhei haAri*, p. 29.

47. Israel Sarug, quoted in *Sefer Gilgulei Neshamot,* 115; cited in *Perush Meir Ayin.*

48. Natan Shapiro (first half of the seventeenth century), *Machberet HaKodesh,* 64c.

49. Nosson Scherman, *Artscroll Siddur Kol Yaakov* (New York: Mesorah Publications, 1987, 1991), p. 288.

50. Macy Nulman, "*Ker'iat Shema al Hamitah,*" in *The Encyclopedia of Jewish Prayer* (Northvale, N.J.: Jason Aronson, 1993), pp. 193–195, fn. 10, citing Nathan Nata Hannover, *Sha'aray Tziyon* (1662).

51. Scherman, *Arscroll Siddur Kol Yaakov,* p. 288.

52. ". . . secrets of the divine realm are presented in the guise of mystical psychology." Scholem, "Hasidism: The Latest Phase," in *Major Trends in Jewish Mysticism*, p. 341. This is Scholem's description of Chabad Hasidism, but he later affirms that it is true for the rest of Hasidism, too.

Chapter 10: Tales of Reincarnation

1. I heard Dr. Brian Weiss tell this story at a lecture that he gave in San Diego in 1997 that was sponsored by the Learning Annex. More recently, it is contained in Weiss's book, *Messages from the Masters: Tapping into the Power of Love* (New York: Warner Books, 2000), p. 174.

2. Rabbi Shneur Zalman (1745–1813) told his son, Rabbi Dov Beir, that he could visualize a Jew as he stood in the primeval thought of

Adam Kadmon as an exercise to focus on the soul's prehistory (Preface of *Poqeah Ivrim,* cited by Schachter-Shalomi, *Spiritual Intimacy: A Study of Counseling in Hasidism* (Northvale, N.J.: Jason Aronson, 1991), p. 90.

3. Isaac the Blind was the son of the famous legal commentator, R. Abraham ben David of Posquieres (the RaBaD, 1120–1198). Isaac the Blind, who wrote a commentary to *Sefer Yetzirah,* is the first Jewish scholar whom we know by name that dedicated all his creative powers to the field of kabbalah.

4. Reading an "aura" in Hebrew is called *hargashat ha'avir,* "feeling the air," and is attributed to Isaac the Blind by Recanti—see Scholem, *Major Trends in Jewish Mysticism,* p. 415, fn. 122.

5. Recanti, *Perush ha-Torah* (Venice, 1545), f. 70a, 209a, cited in Scholem "Gilgul: . . .", p. 207.

6. The Ba'al Shem Tov is quoted as saying about himself that he was a reincarnation of the great Babylonian leader Rabbi Saadiah Gaon. Dan Ben-Amos and Jerome R. Mintz, eds. and trans., *Shivhei ha-Besht: In Praise of the Ba'al Shem Tov* (New York: Schocken, 1984), pp. 106–107.

7. S. Zalmonov, *HaTamim,* Letters, no. 152; cited in Zalman Schachter-Shalomi's *Spiritual Intimacy,* fn. 54. These letters were "discovered" in Russia by Chabad Hasidism in approximately 1914. Today scholars say that the letters are not really by the Ba'al Shem Tov but are forgeries, referred to as the "Kherson Forgeries" (named for the place where found). The critique is based on elements of anachronism and self-serving statements. Yet, the belief among *Hasidim,* particularly Chabad, that the letters are authentic reveals their faith that the early Hasidic rabbis were able to read past lives from a person's presence. See Ada Rapoport-Albert, "Hagiography with Footnotes: Edifying Tales and the Writing of History in Hasidism," *Essays in Jewish Historiography,* ed. Ada Rapoport-Albert (Atlanta: Scholars Press, 1991), pp. 119–159.

8. Jacob Isaac Horowitz (Poland, 1745–1815).

9. Jacob Isaac ben Asher Przysucha (Poland, 1766–1814).

10. Martin Buber, *For the Sake of Heaven* (New York: Harper Torchbooks, 1945, 1953, 1969), p. 66.

11. Issachar Dov Beir ben Aryeh Leib of Zloczow (Germany-Israel, d. 1810).

12. Martin Buber, *Tales of the Hasidim,* vol. 1, (New York: Schocken, 1947, 1975), p. 158, citing Rokotz, *Shiftei Kodesh,* vol. 4 (Lodz, 1929).

13. Zalman Schachter-Shalomi reports that he heard it at a Hasidic *far-brengen* (a festive meal with a *rebbe*), *Spiritual Intimacy,* pp. 155–156.

Chapter 11: Mediums: Judaism's Position

1. Also see Leviticus 19:31.
2. *Moed Katan* 28a.
3. See the article *Doresh el HaMetim* (Hebrew) in *Encyclopedia Talmudit*, vol. 7 (Jerusalem: Talmudic Encyclopedic Institute, 1981), p. 245. A composition that deals with the afterlife and encounters with spirits is Aryeh Cohen's "'Do the Dead Know': The Representation of Death in the Bavli," *AJS Review* 24, no. 1 (1999): pp. 45–71; also see David Kraemer, *The Meaning of Death in Rabbinic Judaism* (London and New York: Rutledge, 2000), pp. 95–116.
4. Mordechai Routenberg (the Maharan), (see Beit Yosef in the Tur, *Yoreh De'ah* 179) and Rabbenu Yerucham (see Rabbi Shabtai Cohen [Sifrei Kohen] on *Shulkhan Arukh, Yoreh De'ah* 179).
5. Meiri, stated with approval by Beit Yosef on the Tur.
6. See Maimonides, *Mishneh Torah, Avodah Zarah,* 11:13; *Sanhedrin* 19:4.
7. *Sefer Yetzirah* in particular presents combinations of letters that are linked with God's names.
8. *Shulkhan Arukh, Yoreh Deah* 179:14. Joseph Karo's work is called *Shulkhan Arukh*, which translates as "The Set Table" and Moses Is-serles' gloss is called *Mappah*, "The Tablecloth."
9. *Sefer HaHizyonot,* pp. 3–4, describes Sonadora, who, imbued by "a zealous spirit," affirmed his attainment in kabbalah and the greatness of his soul; pp. 113–114, 120. Vital describes Mora, who had clair-voyant dreams, and Mazal Tov, who heard "voices." Francis Sarah of Safad, Vital writes, "sees visions while awake and hears a voice speaking to her; most of her pronouncements are true." Vital de-voted seven of the eighty pages of his tightly written diary to de-scribing Rachel Anav, the young daughter of the Rabbi of Damascus, who was initially possessed and then became a medium and even channeled a warning on the need to repent from Elijah the prophet to the leaders of the Damascus Jewish community. Sources cited in Dr. Yosi Chayes' "Women's Mystical Piety" (1998, unpublished paper).

10. R. J. Werblowsky, *Joseph Karo, Lawyer and Mystic* (Philadelphia: Jewish Publication Society, 1977) provides many excerpts in this regard for Karo's diary. Karo identified the *maggid* as both the spirit of the *Mishnah* and as the *Shekhinah*.

11. This claim is buttressed by the Vilna Gaon's condemnation of Maimonides for rejecting the efficacy of charms and amulets, thus denying the possibility of practical kabbalah, which the Vilna Gaon had followed most of his life. *Be'ur ha-Gra to Shulkhan Arukh, Yoreh De'ah* 179:6.

12. Werblowsky's *Joseph Karo*, p. 15.

13. Other great rabbis chose to avoid the aid offered by spirits.

14. Schachter-Shalomi, *Spiritual Intimacy,* p. 99; see also Buber, *For the Sake of Heaven*, p. 64.

15. Schachter-Shalomi, *Spiritual Intimacy,* p. 104.

16. Ibid.

Chapter 12: Psychic Gifts: James Van Praagh

1. James Van Praagh, *Talking to Heaven: A Medium's Message of Life After Death* (New York: Dutton, 1997); *Reaching to Heaven: A Spiritual Journey Through Life and Death* (New York: Dutton, 1999); *Healing Grief: Reclaiming Life After Any Loss* (New York: Dutton, 2000).

2. George Anderson, with Joel Martin and Patricia Romanowski, *We Don't Die* (New York: Berkeley Books, 1988).

Chapter 13: Weighing the Evidence

1. Another kind of past-life memory is called *déjà vu*, the spontaneous sense of familiarity of a place or event. I have not witnessed such remarkable "flashbacks," but I have read about them. For example, there is the story of the American army general who took his Italian guide way off the beaten track to examine an ancient battle site. The American began to describe the battle in great detail and explained to his perplexed tour guide that in a past life he had been a soldier there and remembered the events vividly. Edward Hoffman, *The Way of Splendor: Jewish Mysticism and Modern Psychology* (Northvale, N.J.: Jason Aronson, 1981, 1992).

2. "The Clock" by Bruce Whittier, in Yonassan Gershom, *From Ashes to Healing* (Virginia Beach, Va.: ARE Press, 1996), pp. 12-21.

3. Stevenson, *Children Who Remember Previous Lives,* pp. 55-57.

4. Stevenson, *Children Who Remember Previous Lives,* pp. 64-68.

5. I heard Dr. Brian Weiss relate this story in a presentation that he made in San Diego in 1997.

6. Weiss, *Messages from the Masters,* p. 174.

7. Stevenson, *Unlearned Language: New Studies in Xenoglossy* (Charlottesville, Va.: University Press of Virginia, 1984), pp. 7-71.

8. Stevenson, *Unlearned Language,* pp. 160-164, and Ian Stevenson's fuller treatment in *Xenoglossy: A Review and Report of a Case* (Charlottesville, Va.: University Press of Virginia, 1974).

9. The belief that clairvoyance is the ability to access information from a universal pool of ideas is espoused in Sufi thought. If we were programmed to pick up designated memories that were not necessarily of previous incarnations, there could still be some psychological influence by virtue of incorporating the memory into our lives.

10. Among the most intriguing claims as to the storage of past-life memories is made by Dr. Valerie Hunt, a retired tenured professor of physiology at UCLA. In her decades of research on energy fields surrounding a person, she found that "mind" and "memory" are located in the energy fields or "aura" bands. The brain, she writes, serves as a receiver, not unlike a television drawing from broadcast airwaves. She calls memories of previous lives "life-hoods," because they are not just in the past, but are always with us and profoundly shape our personality and worldview. Valerie V. Hunt, *Infinite Mind: Science of the Human Vibrations of Consciousness* (Malibu, Calif.: Malibu Publishing, 1966, 1989).

11. I. Kant. 1976, *Traume eines Geistersehers, erloutert durch Traume der Metaphsik* (Stuttgart: Philipp Reclam Jun, first published in 1766), p. 52, cited and translated by Stevenson, *Children Who Remember,* p. 20.

Chapter 14: Discrepancies in Afterlife Accounts

1. *Taanit* 11a.

2. *Pesikta Rabbati* 44:8: "Angels are assigned to every human being. And every day they record his deeds, so that everything he does is known to the Holy Blessed One, and everything is put down on his

record and marked with a seal. When a person is righteous, his righteousness is recorded; when a person does wrong, wrongdoing is recorded. Accordingly, when a righteous person arrives at the end of his days, his recording angels precede him into heaven singing his praises. . . . But when a wicked person dies, one who did not bring himself to turn in repentance to God, the Holy Blessed One says:'Let your soul be blasted in despair! How many times did I call upon you to repent and you did not?'"

3. Martin Buber, *Tales of the Hasidim,* vol. 2 (New York: Schocken, 1942, 1972), p. 311; Avram I. Alter, *Meir Einei ha-Golah*, vol. 2 (Warsaw: 1931, 1954), p. 78, quoting R. Yitzhak Meir, the first *rebbe* of Ger; also cited in Buber's *Or Haganuz* (Hebrew).

4. Rabbi Yehuda Patai'ah's *Sefer Minhot Yehudah: HaRuchot Mesaprot* (Jerusalem; 1933, 1995—Hebrew).

5. Moody, *Life After Life,* pp. 65–67.

6. George G. Ritchie, *Return from Tomorrow* (Waco, Tex.: Chosen Books, 1978), pp. 56–57. Moody dedicated *Life After Life* to Ritchie.

7. See Bruce Greyson and Nancy Evans Bush, "Distressing Near-Death Experiences," *Psychiatry* 55 (February 1992): 95–110; P. M. H. Atwater, *Beyond the Light* (New York: Carol, 1994), pp. 27–45.

8. Maurice Rawlings, *Beyond Death's Door* (New York: Bantam, 1979), pp. 4–8. Also see Raymond A. Moody, Jr., with Paul Perry, *The Light Beyond* (New York: Bantam, 1989), pp. 151–152; and Atwater, p. 45.

9. Glynn, *God: The Evidence,* pp. 130–131.

10. Turnus Rufus, a non-Jew at birth later married to Rabbi Akiva, is described as an incarnation of Leah; Rabbi Akiva, himself identified as the son of a Jew-by-choice, is an incarnation of Jacob: Kosbi bat Tzur, the Midianite woman killed while having sex with Zimri, an Israelite prince, was an incarnation of Dinah—see R. Menachem Azarya of Fano, a contemporary of Isaac Luria, *Mei Sheloach* (Israel: *Sifrei Kodesh Mishor,* 1990—Hebrew), *Pinchas,* vol. 1, p. 175.

11. Despite Jewish suffering throughout the ages at the hands of non-Jews, there are some positive remarks about non-Jews in Jewish mystical writings. The *Sefer HaBahir* says that the heads of the seventy nations reflect the seventy members of the Heavenly Court and the seventy (of seventy-two) divine names (also found in *Hechalot DeRebbe Yishmael*). The Ba'al Shem Tov said that Jews and non-Jews were interdependent and in their mutual responsibility to fulfill the

seven laws of Noah (B'aal Shem Tov, *Bereshit*, paragraph 120—*Sefer Reb Yavei*).

12. In most of Stevenson's accounts people reincarnate in the same gender as the previous life. He adds that he has never heard of a Druze man who described memories as a woman in a previous life.

13. Stevenson, *Children Who Remember Previous Lives*, pp. 169-170, 240. This familial return is far less common in reports from India, Lebanon, Sri Lanka, and Turkey.

14. A recent account tells of a boy born in Israel who at the age of three began to say he was from a Druze family in Lebanon. When he was six his family visited a Druze village in Lebanon, where he identified a woman as his wife. When she questioned how he died he told of a car accident including the exact location and description of the car, which proved accurate.

15. Yonassan Gershom writes in *From Ashes to Healing*, p.192, fn. 8: "For example, the soul of the Panchen Lama, who has trained the Dalai Lama for nine incarnations, was believed "lost" after his death in 1989. But in 1995 the Dalai Lama announced that the Panchen Lama had been found—as a six-year-old Tibetan boy, the son of no-mads in Chinese controlled Tibet (Reincarnation International, London, July 1995, pp. 8-11). Note that the Panchen Lama came back immediately after his death and among his own people."

16. In Buddhism only enlightened souls, *rinpoche* ("precious souls"), choose their reincarnation. Yet, there are levels of enlightened souls, too, and the possibility short of enlightenment of a continuum of increasing influence over one's own reincarnation.

17. In the *Tikkunei Zohar* (*Zohar, Bereshit* 25:1) there is the statement that in every generation there are at least 600,000 souls. Chaim Vital in his writings presents a variety of variations as to the number of Jewish soul sparks in the world: $600,000 \times 613$ (*Sha'ar HaGilgulim*, chapter 11); $613 \times 600,000 \times 600,000$ (*Sefer Gilgulim*, chapter 3); $600,000 \times 600,000$ (*Sha'ar HaGilguim*, chapter 17). These numbers have symbolic significance, rather than practical application. In Hasidic writing the idea is presented that each Jew stood at Sinai, as manifest in a spark that was present at revelation.

18. These cultures include the Eskimo, the Igbo of Nigeria, the Tibetans, the Haida of Alaska and British Columbia, and the Gitksan of British Columbia. Stevenson, *Children Who Remember Previous Lives*, pp. 207-208.

19. Stevenson, *Children Who Remember Previous Lives,* p. 124.
20. Van Praagh, *Talking to Heaven,* pp. 41–45.
21. "No time" suggests the possibility of simultaneous, parallel realities.

Chapter 15: The Impact of Affirming the Soul's Survival

1. I owe this imagery of "letting go" to Marielle Fuller of Laguna Beach.

Chapter 16: Cultivating the Soul

1. Rabbi Jack Riemer, Introduction to *So That Your Values Live On: Ethical Wills and How to Prepare Them,* edited by Jack Riemer and Nathanel Stampfer (Woodstock, Vt.: Jewish Lights Publishing, 1991), p. xxvi.
2. Jerusalem Talmud *Kiddushin* 48:2, "Rabbi Hizkiya-Rabbi Cohen in the name of Rav: In the future a person will give a judgment and accounting on all that he saw with his eyes and did not consume."
3. The value of an image is that it allows us to examine what otherwise is invisible, which may lead to positive action. The weakness of an analogy is that it invariably falls short of conveying the full complexity of a dynamic process.
4. Two of my most important teachers are ninety-one-year-old women who are masters of "wakeful dreaming." They are Colette Aboulker-Muscat of Jerusalem and Marielle Fuller of Laguna Beach, California. Although they have different techniques, they each demonstrate how quickly and directly we may access our inner lives through the vehicle of imagination.
5. *Menahot* 43b.
6. The image is taken from Abraham Joshua Heschel, *The Sabbath* (New York: Farrar, Straus, and Giroux, 1951, 1980).
7. Martin Buber, "The Query of Queries," in *Tales of the Hasidim: Early Masters,* vol. 1 (New York: Schocken, 1947; 1975), p. 251.
8. Quoted in Dov Marmur, "The Here and the Hereafter," in Riemer, *Wrestling with the Angel,* p. 335.

Conclusion

1. Jess Byron Hollenback, *Mysticism: Experience, Response, and Empowerment* (University Park, Pa.: The Pennsylvania State University Press, 1996).
2. *Pirkei Avot* 4:17.
3. Quoted by M. M. Schneerson, *HaYom Yom*, p. 51, cited by Schachter-Shalomi, p. 271, fn. 76.
4. Quoted by Schneerson, cited by Schachter-Shalomi, p. 272.
5. Newman, *Hasidic Anthology*, p. 451.

Appendix

1. I wish to thank Rabbi Bradley Shavit Artson for recommending the writing of this appendix.
2. Isaiah 14:15, 24:22; Ezekiel 26:20.
3. Isaiah 38:17; Ezekiel 28:8; Jonah 2:6; Psalm 55:24.
4. Psalm 88:1; Job 26:6, 28:22; Proverbs 15:11.
5. Also see Psalm 6:6—"For there is no praise of you among the dead; in *Sheol*, who can acclaim you";

    Isaiah 38:18—"For it is not *Sheol* that praises You, not Death that extols You; nor do they who descend into the Pit hope for Your grace."
6. The following two etymological possibilities are offered by Raphael, *Jewish Views of the Afterlife*, p. 52.
7. Reprinted over sixty years after its original publication. R. H. Charles, *Eschatology: The Doctrine of a Future Life in Israel, Judaism, and Christianity* (New York: Schocken Books, 1963), pp. 33-36.
8. Herbert Chanan Brichto, "Kin, Cult, Land and Afterlife—A Biblical Complex," HUCA 44 (1973): 2.
9. Johannes Pederson, *Israel: Its Life and Culture*, 2 vols. (London: Oxford University Press, 1926, 1940), discussed in Leonard Greenspoon's "The Origin of the Idea of Resurrection," in Baruch Halpern and Jon D. Levenson, eds., *Traditions in Transformation* (Winona Lake, Ind.: Eisenbrauns, 1981), pp. 249-253.
10. Pederson, *Israel*, vol. 1, p. 104.
11. Ibid., 180.

12. Ibid., 153.

13. Ephram Urbach, *The Sages, Their Concepts and Beliefs*, vol. 1, trans. Israel Abrahams (Jerusalem: Magnes Press, 1975), p. 214.

14. Ibid., p. 215.

15. Ibid., p. 216.

16. Yehezkel Kaufmann, *The Religion of Israel: From Its Beginning to the Babylonian Exile,* trans. Moshe Greenberg (New York: Schocken, 1959, 1972), p. 311.

17. Kaufmann, *The Religion of Israel,* p. 315.

18. Ibid., p. 316.

19. Gillman, *The Death of Death,* p. 22.

20. Ibid., p. 78.

21.   "He [God] will destroy on this mount the shroud
        That is drawn over the faces of all the peoples
        And the covering that is spread
        Over the nations:
        He will destroy death *[mavet]* forever.
        My Lord God will wipe the tears away
        From all faces
        And will put an end to the reproach of His people
        Over all the earth." (Isaiah 25:7–8)

22.   "We were with children, we writhed—
        It is as though we had given birth to wind;
        We have won no victory on earth;
        The inhabitants of the world have not come to life!
        Oh, let your dead revive!
        Let corpses arise!
        Awake and shout for joy,
        You who dwell in the dust!—
        For your dew is like the dew on fresh growth;
        You make the land of the shades come to life."
        (Isaiah 26:18–19)

23. "At that time, the great prince, Michael, who stands beside the sons of your people, will appear. It will be a time of trouble, the like of which has never been since the nation came into being. At that time, your people will be rescued, all who are found inscribed in the book. Many of those who sleep in the dust of the earth will awake,

some to eternal life, others to reproaches, to everlasting abhorrence. And the knowledge will radiant like the bright expanse of sky, and those who lead the many to righteousness will be like the stars forever. . . . But you, go on to the end; you shall rest, and arise to your destiny at the end of days" (Daniel 12:1–3, 9).

24. Biblical scholars are divided on the dating of Isaiah 24–27, with speculation ranging from the seventh to the late second century B.C.E. (see Gillman, *The Death of Death,* p. 91, fn. 9), with Gillman leaning toward the later dating.

25. Gillman, *The Death of Death,* p. 97.

26. Ibid., pp. 96–97.

27. "For much of the past two millennia, the Western world, Jews included, has characterized death as the soul's separation from the body. This view stems originally from Greek philosophy, certainly from Plato and possibly from the earlier mid-sixth Orphic religion" (Ibid., p. 75). "In contrast to the uncertainty regarding the provenance of the idea of bodily resurrection, the notion of the immortality of the soul clearly has it source in Greek philosophy and religion" (Ibid., p. 106).

28. Greenspoon, "The Origin of the Idea of Resurrection," pp. 247–321.

29. Ibid., pp. 248–249.

30. Ibid., pp. 261–281.

31. Ibid., p. 289.

32. Ibid., pp. 287–289.

33. Ibid., p. 294. Greenspoon also says of the Ezekiel passage: "We have no doubt that those scholars are correct who see in Ezekiel's Vision a hope for national restoration addressed to his fellow exiles. We also have no doubt that they are incorrect when they limit Ezekiel's message to only this. In bold and memorable language Ezekiel makes use of imagery drawn from the theme of the Divine Warrior to affirm the "literal" resurrection of God's righteous people. Those who had died trusting in God, yes, even those who were buried outside the Land of Israel, would share in this process" (p. 293).

34. Ibid., p. 255: "a common store of language, motifs, and beliefs was the shared property of the various cultures of the Near East and that authors from each of these cultures drew from the shared store to describe deities and actions that were not identical."

35. Ibid., pp. 255–256.

36. Ibid., p. 260.

37. Ibid., pp. 259–261.
38. Ibid., p. 248.
39. Ibid., pp. 320–321.
40. Brichto, "Kin, Cult, Land and Afterlife," p. 49.
41. Ibid., p. 53.
42. Ibid., p. 2.
43. Ibid., pp. 7–8, citing Kaufman, *The Religion of Israel,* p. 79.
44. Ibid., p. 3.
45. Ibid., quoting Numa Denis Fustel de Coulanges, *The Ancient City* (published as *La Cité Antique*, 1864), trans. Willard Small (Garden City, N.Y.: Doubleday Anchor, 1873), p. 15.
46. Ibid., p. 52.
47. Ibid., p. 53.
48. Hebrew University, Jerusalem, 1925–1965.
49. Scholem, *Major Trends in Jewish Mysticism* (1961), pp. 73–75.
50. Gnosticism distinguishes between a "Supreme Divine Being" and the "Demiurge," a secondary power responsible for creation and involved in the material world. There were Gnostic circles among pagans, Christians, and Jews.
51. Moshe Idel, *Kabbalah: New Perspectives* (New Haven, Conn.: Yale, 1988).
52. Ibid., p. 30.
53. Ibid., pp. 31, 34.
54. Ibid.
55. Ibid., p. 253.
56. Ibid., p. 33.
57. Ibid.
58. Smith, "Afterlife," p. 116: "Despite the variations in conceptions of what the afterlife may entail, a belief that human beings will continue to exist in some form after the experience we term death is a universal phenomenon."
59. Roger Lipsey, "Human Body: The Human Figure as a Religious Sign," in Eliade, *Encyclopedia of Religion,* vol. 6, p. 506.
60. J. Bruce Long, "Reincarnation," in Eliade, *Encyclopedia of Religion*, vol. 12, p. 266.
61. Stevan L. Davies, "Soul—Ancient Near Eastern Concepts," in Eliade, *Encyclopedia of Religion,* vol. 13, pp. 431–434.
62. Smith, "Some form of prayer for the deceased on the part of the liv-

ing continues to be an important responsibility of pious persons in all religious traditions."

63. For a detailed footnoted description of differences between Plato and the rabbis, see Urbach, *The Sages,* pp. 224–248.

64. "The truth is that, as we noted earlier, collective and individual eschatological themes are fused and often confused in rabbinic literature." Raphael, *Jewish Views of the Afterlife,* p. 124.

65. Although there are variations in the Golem story, a popular telling says that the name of God was placed in the Golem's mouth as a kind of battery. On the Golem's forehead was the Hebrew word *EMeT,* which means "truth" and is a name for God and served as an on-and-off switch. When the first letter of *EMeT* was removed, the word that remained was *MeT,* which means dead, and the Golem ceased to function.

66. Ibid., pp. 214–216.

67. See his comment on Genesis 7:22.

68. Bern. Alfrink, "L'Expression, נאסף אל־עמיו," *Oudtestamentische Studien,* vol. 5, 1948.

69. Genesis 25:8–9.

70. Genesis 25:17.

71. Genesis 35:29.

72. Genesis 49:29, 49:33.

73. Numbers 20:24; Deuteronomy 32:50.

74. Numbers 27:13; 31:2; Deuteronomy 32:50.

75. Alfrink, "L'Expression," p. 128.

76. Urbach, *The Sages,* p. 216.

77. Gillman, *The Death of Death,* pp. 69–70.

78. Alfrink, "L'Expression," pp. 126–127.

79. *The JPS Torah Commentary* (Philadelphia: Jewish Publication Society). Nahum M. Sarna, Genesis (1989), Exodus (1991); Baruch A. Levine, Leviticus (1989); Jacob Milgrom, Numbers (1990); Jeffrey H. Tigay, Deuteronomy (1996).

80. Sarna, Genesis (1989), on Genesis 25:8, p. 174.

81. Milgrom, Numbers (1990), on Numbers 20:24 and Excursus 36: "The Penalty of 'Karet,'" p. 407.

82. Tigay, Deuteronomy (1996), on Deuteronomy 32:50, p. 317.

83. Genesis 49:29.

84. Genesis 25:8. Also see Deuteronomy 32:50.

85. Genesis 25:8.
86. Genesis 25:8.
87. Genesis 25:8.
88. Some commentators say that the difference between the two terms is that גוה connotes an "easy death" *(Radak)*, "the sudden departure of the spirit from the body without pain or delay" *(Ra'avah)*— on Genesis 25:8. Ramban (Nahmanides, Spain, 1194–1270) says that when גוה is coupled with ויאסף ("was gathered"), it refers to a quick death without prolonged sickness (Genesis 25:17).
89. Cited in *Bereshis* of *Artscroll Tanakh Series,* vol. 1 (Brooklyn, N.Y.: Mesorah, 1977, 1988), p. 977.
90. Long, "Reincarnation," p. 265.
91. Kaplan, *The Bahir,* p. 46 (section 121) and p. 57 (section 155).
92. Nahmanides, comment on Job 33:30.
93. My gratitude to Dr. Daniel Lang for this adage as well as for our conversation on styles of reading.
94. Abraham Joshua Heschel, *God in Search of Man* (Philadelphia: Jewish Publication Society, 1965), p. 185. Also see Abraham Joshua Heschel, *The Prophets* (New York: Harper and Row, 1962), in which he describes the respective personalities and worldviews of each prophet, along with the shared divine impetus of prophetic ideas.

Glossary

(with translations from the Hebrew)

Adam HaRishon—"The first Adam." In Lurianic kabbalah, a reference to the Adam of the Bible, who suffered a spiritual fall in the Garden of Eden for violating God's command. The process of falling dispersed spiritual sparks in all directions. Adam's descendants possess spiritual sparks generated from different body parts of *Adam HaRishon*. Our task is to elevate the dispersed sparks back to the level of Adam, thereby reconstituting the wholeness of God's original creation.

Adam Kadmon—Primordial man. Used in Lurianic kabbalah to refer to the state of creation when the divine Light was contained in its original vessels, or *sefirot*. As the embodiment of light and wholeness, *Adam Kadmon* existed on a higher spiritual plane than we encounter in our post-shattering-of-vessels world.

Amidah—"Standing," the standing prayer. The centerpiece of Judaism's daily liturgy, recited three times a day. The daily recitation is composed of nineteen blessings. The third is "Praised are You, Adonai . . . who gives life to the dead."

Ashkenazim—"Germans." Jews whose ancestors lived in the Middle Ages in Germany and the surrounding countries. Most Eastern European Jews were *Ashkenazim*. The term *Ashkenazic* may refer to the customs or rabbinic holdings of this community. A common language was Yiddish, a mix of Hebrew and old German.

chakra—Hindu-Sanskrit for energy center; there are seven main *chakras* along the body.

chayah—In Lurianic kabbalah, the fourth level of soul. It is the dimension of the transpersonal and intuitive.

Common Era (C.E.)—the traditional Jewish manner of referring to the

229

secular calendar count of A.D. Likewise, B.C. is referred to by Jews as B.C.E., "before the Common Era."

Gehenna—A form of *Gehinnom*, which in its origin stood for the "Valley of Ben Hinnom," identified as the valley in Jerusalem where human sacrifices were brought during biblical times. The term is synonymous with hell. In the *Zohar*, *Gehenna* is used figuratively to describe the process of soul purification after death.

Hasdei Ashkenaz—"The pious of Germany." A reference to the leading rabbis of the thirteenth century who lived along the Rhine river and emphasized a life of ascetic piety.

Hasidism—Folk-mystical movement founded by Rabbi Israel ben Eliezer, also known as the Ba'al Shem Tov (Master of the Good Name), in the eighteenth century. Members of this movement are known as *Hasidim* (singular—*hasid*). The movement emphasized piety and prayer with *kavannah* as an important path to God. Hasidic worship was often marked by song, including the singing of melodies without words, called a *niggun*. The *rebbe* (the spiritual leader) was at the center of communal life and looked to as a spiritual guide and model of religious living. Based on Jewish mysticism, Hasidism taught that when a simple Jew engaged in a *mitzvah*, the deed helped heal the cosmos and even God.

ibbur—"Impregnation." In Lurianic kabbalah, the term for visiting souls taking up residence in someone's body. An *ibbur* may achieve soul repair through the deeds of the host person and may provide muse-like guidance to the host.

kabbalah—"That which is received." The Jewish mystical tradition, based on a cosmology of ten divine emanations and secret names of God. Although the kabbalistic tradition stretches back two millennia, it received its fullest and most authoritative elaboration in the thirteenth century mystical commentary on the Torah, the *Zohar*, and in the writings of the fifteenth-century Jewish mystics of Safad, Israel.

kavannah—"Directed attention." The act of focusing a person's thoughts and feelings during prayer or during the performance of a commandment. Cultivating *kavannah* was particularly emphasized in Hasidic worship.

kavannot—Kabbalistic meditations that accompany prayer and performing *mitzvot*. The techniques often focus on recombining variations of the four letters of God's tetragrammaton name (YHVH) or the repetition of selected biblical verses. Through *kavannot*, people can participate in bringing the flow of divine lights into the world or elevate divine sparks, thereby aiding in the repair of the world.

maggid—"Teller." An itinerant preacher who teaches Torah through stories. Also used to refer to a spiritual being who offers guidance.

midrash—"Homilies" on the Torah. There are collections of *midrashim* beginning with the early rabbis of Palestine of the first centuries of the Common Era.

Mishnah—"Study by repetition." Earliest code of Jewish oral law, arranged by Judah the Prince in Palestine by 200 C.E.

mitzvah (plural: mitzvot)—"Commandment." One of the 613 divinely ordained commandments articulated in the Torah. In the Lurianic tradition, the *mitzvot* are tools for the repair of the individual's soul and the cosmos.

nefesh—"Animating Spirit." In the realm of levels of soul, *nefesh* is the lowest level, representing the realm of action and physical pleasure. Animals, too, have a body and feelings and thus have soul, but it is a soul that is limited to the lower dimensions of soul's potential development.

neshamah—"Soul." The third level of soul, identified with analytic thought, the quest for meaning, and human transcendence.

rebbe—Yiddish for "Rabbi." The leader of a Hasidic community.

reincarnation—The rebirth of a soul in a new body.

resurrection of the dead—The return of a soul to its original reconstituted body.

ruach—"Affective Spirit." The second level of soul, identified with feelings, which enable personality and the expression of love.

Sefer HaBahir—"The Book of Clarity." The first kabbalistic work to gain widespread circulation. This late-twelfth-century work of unknown authorship from the South of France fully accepted reincarnation.

sefirot—Ten Divine qualities from which the world is composed. The *sefirot* are both divine light and the vessels holding the light. The *sefirot* are usually called Crown, Wisdom, Understanding, Love, Power, Beauty, Eternity, Splendor, Foundation, and Kingdom.

Sephardim—"Spanish [Jews]." The community of Jews that emerged from Spain in the Middle Ages. These Jews largely formed the communities along the Mediterranean. Many spoke Ladino, a Hebrew-Spanish dialect. The term *Sephardic* refers to the customs and rabbinic holdings of the community.

Shabbat—The Jewish Sabbath, which begins at sundown on Friday evening and continues until Saturday night. During this time Jews traditionally refrain from any form of work.

Shekhinah—A term that describes God's "Manifest Presence," also called "God's Majesty," and is identified with God's feminine aspects. In Jewish mysticism it is the tenth and final of the *sefirot*, God's attributes, and is identified with Kingdom and with Israel.

Shema—"Listen." Foundational Jewish prayer of faith known by its first words, *Shema Yisrael, Adonai Elohainu, Adonai Echad* (Hear O Israel, *Adonai* is our God. *Adonai* is One). The *Shema* is traditionally recited three times a day and at the moment before death.

Shulkhan Arukh—"The Set Table." This multivolume work is the most widely accepted Code of Jewish Law. Composed by Joseph Karo in sixteenth-century Safad, Israel, it is the subject of extensive commentary. The most referred-to commentary is the gloss of Moses Isserles ("Ramah," Poland, d. 1572), who provided the *Ashkenazic* holdings (in contrast to Karo's *Sephardic* positions) and whose work is called the *Mappah*, "The Tablecloth."

Talmud—"Teaching." Collection of discussions on the *Mishnah* by generations of scholars in Babylonia and Palestine. The Palestinian discussions were redacted by around the year 400 C.E. and are called the *Jerusalem Talmud*. The *Babylonian Talmud* was compiled by around 500 C.E. The Babylonian Talmud is larger and gained wider study among Jews. When scholars speak of the *Talmud*, they are referring to the Babylonian Talmud.

tikkun—"Repair." Term used to refer to the work of repairing the soul due to previous misdeeds. In the mystical tradition, the doing of *mitzvot* also has cosmic significance, aiding in the repair of the world—*tikkun olam*—which is the process of rescuing divine sparks from darkness *(berur),* thereby strengthening the human and cosmic vessels of divine light.

Torah—"Teaching." The Five Books of Moses, or the Pentateuch, read from a scroll in synagogue. The Torah is the foundation of all Jewish law and practice, as it is seen traditionally as the word of God. The term is elastic, referring sometimes to the Pentateuch, sometimes to the entire body of Jewish law, and occasionally to an individual's teachings based upon traditional text.

Tzaddik (or Zaddik)—"Righteous One." Used both as the term to describe a pious individual (often used in the Hasidic community as a term for their rabbi) and, in Lurianic kabbalah, a person whose soul is complete.

Yechidah—The fifth and highest level of soul. This level is an extension of the Divine and is universal in character.

Zohar—The central work of Jewish mysticism. In format it is a commentary on the Torah. Traditionally attributed to Rabbi Shimon bar Yohai (first century, Palestine), it was first presented and probably composed by Moses de Leon of Guadalajara, Spain, at the end of the thirteenth century.

Selected Bibliography

The following are some of the authors and their books that most impressed me in my study. I have organized this selected bibliography by theme and offer a brief description of the content of the respective books.

Near-Death Experience

Bloom, Harold. *Omen of the Millennia: The Gnosis of Angels, Dreams, and Resurrection* (New York: Riverhead Books, 1996). The erudite author questions the reality of near-death experience accounts, as recorded by a limited review of modern researchers, and asserts that the modern accounts lack a richness of imagination compared to former descriptions of the passion and the demonic in the world to come.

Kübler-Ross, Elisabeth. *Dying Is of Vital Importance: On Life, Death, and Life After Death* (Barryton, N.Y.: Station Hill Press, 1995). A collection of Kübler-Ross's talks, which includes much data on her research on near-death experience. See also Kübler-Ross, *On Life After Death* (Berkeley, Calif.: Celestial Arts, 1991), in which the prominent psychiatrist describes why she has grown to believe in the survival of the soul.

Levine, Stephen. *Who Dies? An Investigation of Conscious Living and Conscious Dying* (New York: Anchor, 1982). An American Buddhist writer looks at survival of the soul through his own experiences as a caregiver at bedside.

Moody, Raymond A., Jr. *Life After Life* (New York: Bantam, 1975, 1981). The groundbreaking study by a physician examining approximately 150 near-death experiences.

Morse, Melvin, Jr., with Paul Perry. *Closer to the Light* (New York: Villard Books, 1990) and *Transformed by the Light* (New York: Ballantine, 1992). Books by a Seattle pediatrician on children with tales of near-death experiences.

Nuland, Sherwin. *How We Die* (New York: Knopf, 1994; Vintage, 1995). A Yale professor of medicine describes the different ways we die. It contains a fine example of the short-shrift treatment of near-death experiences and the identification with the phenomena of oxygen deprivation (anoxia) and endorphins.

Jewish Views of the Afterlife

Raphael, Simcha Paull. *Jewish Views of the Afterlife* (Northvale, N.J.: Jason Aronson, 1994). A comprehensive examination of the layers of Jewish text on the topic of afterlife, plus a look at Tibetan Buddhist parallels, the subject of the author's doctorate dissertation.

Schachter-Shalomi, Zalman. *Spiritual Intimacy: A Study of Counseling in Hasidism* (Northvale, N.J.: Jason Aronson, 1991). A rich repository of materials on the role of the *rebbe* that touches on topics relating to survival of the soul. See also Schachter-Shalomi, "The Fate of the Soul," in Jack Riemer, *Wrestling with the Angel* (New York: Schocken, 1995), pp. 338–348.

Scholem, Gershom. *Major Trends in Jewish Mysticism* (New York: Schocken, 1961, 1973). The master researcher of Jewish mysticism explores Lurianic kabbalah and Hasidism, among other streams of kabbalistic thought. These essays emerge from a series of lectures and, despite new research, remain worthwhile. In describing Luria's imagery, Scholem makes reference to Luria's cosmology and the concept of *partzufim,* which correlates with modern concepts of big bang and holograms (theories that did not exist when the lectures were given). I therefore smiled when the author says of Luria's imagery, "taken as a whole this symbolism is of somewhat a crude texture" (p. 269).

Sonsino, Rifat and Daniel B. Syme. *What Happens After I Die* (New York: UAHC Press, 1990). Outstanding Reform movement educators provide a concise survey of Jewish opinions on what happens upon death.

Resurrection

Gillman, Neil. *The Death of Death: Resurrection and Immortality in Jewish Thought* (Woodstock, Vt.: Jewish Lights Publishing, 1997). A contemporary theologian reclaims the traditional faith in resurrection.

Maimonides. "Epistle on Resurrection of the Dead," translated and with commentary by Fred Rosner (New York: Ktav, 1982). The master of Jewish law explains his position on resurrection of the dead and how it meshes with his emphasis on a nonphysical reward for a well-lived life.

Nahmanides. "The Gate of Reward." In *Ramban (Nahmanides): Writings and Discourses,* translated and annotated by Charles B. Chavel. (New York: Shilo, 1978, 1995), vol. 2. The mystic and important commentator to the Torah challenges Maimonides and describes resurrection into a perfected body.

Past-Life Regression

Fiore, Edith. *You Have Been Here Before* (New York: Ballantine, 1979). A psychologist records her sessions using past-life regressions that are very similar in technique and result to that of Brian Weiss.

McClain, Florence Wagner. *A Practical Guide to Past Life Regression* (St. Paul, Minn.: Llewellyn Publications, 1985, 1994). More commonly found in the "New Age" section of bookstores, the book offers some helpful tips for doing past-life regression mixed with personal philosophy.

Weiss, Brian. *Many Lives, Many Masters* (New York: Fireside Books, 1978). Now translated into more than thirty languages, this is Brian Weiss's first book, in which he recounts his experience with Catherine and how that led him to affirm both the usefulness of past-life regression and why he believes that past-life memories are real. *Through Time into Healing* (New York: Fireside Books, 1992) describes a variety of psychological ailments Dr. Weiss has addressed with past-life regression. *Only Love Is Real* (New York: Time Warner, 1996) is Weiss's account of how two of his patients independently described the same scenes in a previous life, suggesting that we travel through this life with people we may have known in a previous incarnation. *Messages from the Masters* (New

York: Warner Books, 2000) offers Weiss's insight, gleaned from his work with past-life regression, into how to live more lovingly.

Mediums and Psychic Gifts

Anderson, George, with Joel Martin and Patricia Romanowski. *We Don't Die* (New York: Berkeley Books, 1988). A leading New York talk show radio host relates how he moved from skeptic to believer in the mediumship of Anderson.

Crichton, Michael. *Travels* (New York: Ballantine, 1988). Written by a Harvard-trained physician, the popular writer of such novels as *The Andromeda Strain* and *Jurassic Park*. He tells of his exotic treks up tall mountains and his dives into the depths of the sea. Toward the end of the book he recounts his inner explorations and experiences with energy fields and psychic phenomena. The closing chapter is a well-written essay on why science needs to take into account that which can't be "scientifically tested."

Hoffman, Edward. *The Way of Splendor: Jewish Mysticism and Modern Psychology* (Northvale, N.J.: Jason Aronson, 1992). An integration of psychological insights and kabbalah, including accounts of the place of the psychic in Jewish mysticism.

Orloff, Judith. *Second Sight* (New York: Warner Books, 1997). UCLA-trained psychiatrist shares how she squelched her psychic gifts while in medical school. While sitting at the bedside of a patient of whom she had an earlier hunch that the patient would try and commit suicide, Dr. Orloff decided not to ignore her psychic intuitions again. The book tells her personal journey and describes how others can develop their psychic gifts.

Van Praagh, James. *Talking to Heaven: A Medium's Message of Life After Death* (New York: Dutton, 1997) and *Reaching to Heaven* (New York: Dutton, 1999). The author describes how he came to discover and develop his psychic gifts and provides many examples of his work as a medium; he also tells how to develop your own psychic gifts.

Werblowsky, R. J. *Joseph Karo, Lawyer and Mystic* (Philadelphia: Jewish Publication Society, 1977). A biography of the premier codifier of Jewish law, who kept a diary recording the aid he received throughout his adult years from a *maggid* (spirit).

Reincarnation and Past-Life Memory

Gershom, Yonassan. *Beyond the Ashes: Cases of Reincarnation from the Holocaust* (Virginia Beach: ARE Press, 1992) and *From Ashes to Healing: Mystical Encounters with the Holocaust* (Virginia Beach: ARE Press, 1996) provide short accounts of people who have previous-life memories of being a Jew in the Holocaust.

Head, Joseph, and S. L. Cranston, eds. *Reincarnation: The Phoenix Fire Mystery* (New York: Warner Books, 1977). An anthology of cross-cultural accounts and literature on reincarnation.

Stevenson, Ian. *Children Who Remember Previous Lives: A Question of Reincarnation* (Charlottesville, Va.: University Press of Virginia, 1987, 1992) and *Twenty Cases Suggestive of Reincarnation* (Charlottesville, Va.: University Press of Virginia, 1974, 1995). These offer detailed accounts of spontaneously generated memories of previous lives that the author examines with alternative sources of information. In *Unlearned Language: New Studies in Xenoglossy* (Charlottesville, Va.: University Press of Virginia, 1984), Stevenson provided two detailed case studies of the ability to the two subjects to speak a language they seemingly never learned in this lifetime. In *Where Reincarnation and Biology Intersect* (Charlottesville, Va.: University Press of Virginia, 1997), Stevenson correlates birthmarks and other physical qualities between living people and deceased, with whom there is a claim of a link through a past life.

A Post-Modern Sensibility

Friedman, Richard. *The Disappearance of God: A Divine Mystery* (New York: Little, Brown, 1995) The Bible scholar looks at the unfolding of God's relationship to creation in Judaism and Christianity and through the prism of nineteenth-century literature identifies the need of a God to overcome moral chaos.

Glynn, Patrick. *God the Evidence: The Reconciliation of Faith and Reason in a Postsecular World* (Rocklin, Calif.: Forum, 1997). A professor of communications and political science examines his initial skepticism of religion and finds that modern science, including physics and the research on NDEs, reinforces traditional religious faith.

Hunt, Valerie V. *Infinite Mind: Science of the Human Vibrations of Consciousness* (Malibu, Calif.: Malibu Publishing, 1989, 1996). A description by a UCLA professor of physiology of her studies on energy fields surrounding the body, which she describes as concentric circles of energy bands containing information of "mind," including past lives (which she calls "lifehoods").

Matt, Daniel. *God and the Big Bang: Discovering Harmony Between Science & Spirituality* (Woodstock, Vt.: Jewish Lights Publishing, 1996) looks at the overlap between modern cosmology and kabbalah.

Peck, M. Scott. *In Heaven as on Earth: A Vision of the Afterlife* (New York: Hyperion, 1996). A novel that is apparently inspired by near-death experience accounts. The book's description of "hell" as self-generated psychological torment was particularly insight-giving.

Remen, Rachel Naomi. *Kitchen Table Wisdom* (New York: Riverhead Books, 1996). An oncology counselor elegantly describes the intrinsic link of body, emotion, and spirit she learned from her patients.

Index

About JEWISH LIGHTS Publishing

People of all faiths and backgrounds yearn for books that attract, engage, educate and spiritually inspire.

Our principal goal is to stimulate thought and help all people learn about who the Jewish People are, where they come from, and what the future can be made to hold. While people of our diverse Jewish heritage are the primary audience, our books speak to people in the Christian world as well and will broaden their understanding of Judaism and the roots of their own faith.

We bring to you authors who are at the forefront of spiritual thought and experience. While each has something different to say, they all say it in a voice that you can hear.

Our books are designed to welcome you and then to engage, stimulate and inspire. We judge our success not only by whether or not our books are beautiful and commercially successful, but by whether or not they make a difference in your life.

We at Jewish Lights take great care to produce beautiful books that present meaningful spiritual content in a form that reflects the art of making high quality books. Therefore, we want to acknowledge those who contributed to the production of this book.

Stuart M. Matlins

Stuart M. Matlins, Publisher

PRODUCTION
Marian B. Wallace, Tim Holtz & Bridgett Taylor

EDITORIAL
Sandra Korinchak, Emily Wichland
Martha McKinney & Amanda Dupuis

COVER DESIGN
Stacey Hood, Big Eyedea Visual Design,
Waitsfield, Vermont

TYPESETTING
Sans Serif, Inc., Saline, Michigan

PRINTING AND BINDING
Lake Book, Melrose Park, Illinois

  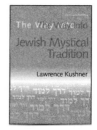

Theology/Philosophy

Love and Terror in the God Encounter: *The Theological Legacy of Rabbi Joseph B. Soloveitchik, Vol. 1* by *Dr. David Hartman*

Renowned scholar David Hartman explores the sometimes surprising intersection of Soloveitchik's rootedness in halakhic tradition with his genuine responsiveness to modern Western theology. An engaging look at one of the most important Jewish thinkers of the twentieth century. 6 x 9, 240 pp, HC, ISBN 1-58023-112-8 **$25.00**

These Are the Words: *A Vocabulary of Jewish Spiritual Life*

by *Arthur Green*

What are the most essential ideas, concepts and terms that an educated person needs to know about Judaism? From *Adonai* (My Lord) to *zekhut* (merit), this enlightening and entertaining journey through Judaism teaches us the 149 core Hebrew words that constitute the basic vocabulary of Jewish spiritual life. 6 x 9, 304 pp, Quality PB, ISBN 1-58023-107-1 **$18.95**

Broken Tablets: *Restoring the Ten Commandments and Ourselves*

Ed. by *Rabbi Rachel S. Mikva*; Intro. by *Rabbi Lawrence Kushner* AWARD WINNER!

Twelve outstanding spiritual leaders each share profound and personal thoughts about these biblical commands and why they have such a special hold on us.
6 x 9, 192 pp, Quality PB, ISBN 1-58023-158-6 **$16.95**; HC, ISBN 1-58023-066-0 **$21.95**

A Heart of Many Rooms: *Celebrating the Many Voices within Judaism* AWARD WINNER!
by Dr. David Hartman 6 x 9, 352 pp, Quality PB, ISBN 1-58023-156-X **$19.95**; HC, ISBN 1-58023-048-2 **$24.95**

A Living Covenant: *The Innovative Spirit in Traditional Judaism* AWARD WINNER!
by Dr. David Hartman 6 x 9, 368 pp, Quality PB, ISBN 1-58023-011-3 **$18.95**

Evolving Halakhah: *A Progressive Approach to Traditional Jewish Law*
by Rabbi Dr. Moshe Zemer 6 x 9, 480 pp, HC, ISBN 1-58023-002-4 **$40.00**

The Death of Death: *Resurrection and Immortality in Jewish Thought* AWARD WINNER!
by Dr. Neil Gillman 6 x 9, 336 pp, Quality PB, ISBN 1-58023-081-4 **$18.95**

The Last Trial: *On the Legends and Lore of the Command to Abraham to Offer Isaac as a Sacrifice* by Shalom Spiegel 6 x 9, 208 pp, Quality PB, ISBN 1-879045-29-X **$17.95**

Tormented Master: *The Life and Spiritual Quest of Rabbi Nahman of Bratslav*
by Dr. Arthur Green 6 x 9, 416 pp, Quality PB, ISBN 1-879045-11-7 **$18.95**

The Earth Is the Lord's: *The Inner World of the Jew in Eastern Europe*
by Abraham Joshua Heschel 5½ x 8, 128 pp, Quality PB, ISBN 1-879045-42-7 **$14.95**

A Passion for Truth: *Despair and Hope in Hasidism* by Abraham Joshua Heschel
5½ x 8, 352 pp, Quality PB, ISBN 1-879045-41-9 **$18.95**

Your Word Is Fire: *The Hasidic Masters on Contemplative Prayer* Ed. by Dr. Arthur Green and Dr. Barry W. Holtz 6 x 9, 160 pp, Quality PB, ISBN 1-879045-25-7 **$14.95**

Spirituality

My People's Prayer Book: *Traditional Prayers, Modern Commentaries*
Ed. by *Dr. Lawrence A. Hoffman*

Provides a diverse and exciting commentary to the traditional liturgy, helping modern men and women find new wisdom in Jewish prayer, and bring liturgy into their lives. Each book includes Hebrew text, modern translation, and commentaries *from all perspectives* of the Jewish world.

Vol. 1—*The Sh'ma and Its Blessings,* 7 x 10, 168 pp, HC, ISBN 1-879045-79-6 **$23.95**
Vol. 2—*The Amidah,* 7 x 10, 240 pp, HC, ISBN 1-879045-80-X **$23.95**
Vol. 3—*P'sukei D'zimrah* (Morning Psalms), 7 x 10, 240 pp, HC, ISBN 1-879045-81-8 **$24.95**
Vol. 4—*Seder K'riat Hatorah* (The Torah Service), 7 x 10, 264 pp, HC, ISBN 1-879045-82-6 **$23.95**
Vol. 5—*Birkhot Hashachar* (Morning Blessings), 7 x 10, 240 pp, HC, ISBN 1-879045-83-4 **$24.95**

Becoming a Congregation of Learners
Learning as a Key to Revitalizing Congregational Life by Isa Aron, Ph.D.;
Foreword by Rabbi Lawrence A. Hoffman, Co-Developer, Synagogue 2000
6 x 9, 304 pp, Quality PB, ISBN 1-58023-089-X **$19.95**

Self, Struggle & Change
Family Conflict Stories in Genesis and Their Healing Insights for Our Lives
by Dr. Norman J. Cohen 6 x 9, 224 pp, Quality PB, ISBN 1-879045-66-4 **$16.95**;
HC, ISBN 1-879045-19-2 **$21.95**

Voices from Genesis: *Guiding Us through the Stages of Life*
by Dr. Norman J. Cohen 6 x 9, 192 pp, Quality PB, ISBN 1-58023-118-7 **$16.95**;
HC, ISBN 1-879045-75-3 **$21.95**

God Whispers: *Stories of the Soul, Lessons of the Heart*
by Rabbi Karyn D. Kedar 6 x 9, 176 pp, Quality PB, ISBN 1-58023-088-1 **$15.95**

The Business Bible: *10 New Commandments for Bringing Spirituality & Ethical Values into the Workplace*
by Rabbi Wayne Dosick 5½ x 8½, 208 pp, Quality PB, ISBN 1-58023-101-2 **$14.95**

Being God's Partner: *How to Find the Hidden Link Between Spirituality and Your Work*
by Rabbi Jeffrey K. Salkin; Intro. by Norman Lear **AWARD WINNER!**
6 x 9, 192 pp, Quality PB, ISBN 1-879045-65-6 **$16.95**; HC, ISBN 1-879045-37-0 **$19.95**

God & the Big Bang
Discovering Harmony Between Science & Spirituality **AWARD WINNER!**
by Daniel C. Matt 6 x 9, 224 pp, Quality PB, ISBN 1-879045-89-3 **$16.95**

Soul Judaism: *Dancing with God into a New Era*
by Rabbi Wayne Dosick 5½ x 8½, 304 pp, Quality PB, ISBN 1-58023-053-9 **$16.95**

Finding Joy: *A Practical Spiritual Guide to Happiness* **AWARD WINNER!**
by Rabbi Dannel I. Schwartz with Mark Hass
6 x 9, 192 pp, Quality PB, ISBN 1-58023-009-1 **$14.95**; HC, ISBN 1-879045-53-2 **$19.95**

Life Cycle & Holidays

How to Be a Perfect Stranger, 2nd Ed. In 2 Volumes
A Guide to Etiquette in Other People's Religious Ceremonies

Ed. by *Stuart M. Matlins* & *Arthur J. Magida* **AWARD WINNER!**

What will happen? What do I do? What do I wear? What do I say? What are their basic beliefs? Should I bring a gift? Explains the rituals and celebrations of North America's major religions/denominations, helping an interested guest to feel comfortable. Not presented from the perspective of any particular faith. SKYLIGHT PATHS Books

Vol. 1: *North America's Largest Faiths,* 6 x 9, 432 pp, Quality PB, ISBN 1-893361-01-2 **$19.95**
Vol. 2: *Other Faiths in North America,* 6 x 9, 416 pp, Quality PB, ISBN 1-893361-02-0 **$19.95**

Celebrating Your New Jewish Daughter
Creating Jewish Ways to Welcome Baby Girls into the Covenant— New and Traditional Ceremonies

by *Debra Nussbaum Cohen;* Foreword by *Rabbi Sandy Eisenberg Sasso*

Features everything families need to plan a celebration that reflects Jewish tradition, including a how-to guide to new and traditional ceremonies, and practical guidelines for planning the joyous event. 6 x 9, 272 pp, Quality PB, ISBN 1-58023-090-3 **$18.95**

The New Jewish Baby Book **AWARD WINNER!**
Names, Ceremonies & Customs—A Guide for Today's Families
by Anita Diamant 6 x 9, 336 pp, Quality PB, ISBN 1-879045-28-1 **$18.95**

Parenting As a Spiritual Journey
Deepening Ordinary & Extraordinary Events into Sacred Occasions
by Rabbi Nancy Fuchs-Kreimer 6 x 9, 224 pp, Quality PB, ISBN 1-58023-016-4 **$16.95**

Putting God on the Guest List, 2nd Ed. **AWARD WINNER!**
How to Reclaim the Spiritual Meaning of Your Child's Bar or Bat Mitzvah
by Rabbi Jeffrey K. Salkin 6 x 9, 224 pp, Quality PB, ISBN 1-879045-59-1 **$16.95**

For Kids—Putting God on Your Guest List
How to Claim the Spiritual Meaning of Your Bar or Bat Mitzvah
by Rabbi Jeffrey K. Salkin 6 x 9, 144 pp, Quality PB, ISBN 1-58023-015-6 **$14.95**

Bar/Bat Mitzvah Basics, 2nd Ed.: *A Practical Family Guide to Coming of Age Together*
Ed. by Cantor Helen Leneman 6 x 9, 240 pp, Quality PB, ISBN 1-58023-151-9 **$18.95**

Hanukkah, 2nd Ed.: The Family Guide to Spiritual Celebration—The Art of Jewish Living
by Dr. Ron Wolfson 7 x 9, 240 pp, Quality PB, Illus., ISBN 1-58023-122-5 **$18.95**

The Shabbat Seder—The Art of Jewish Living
by Dr. Ron Wolfson 7 x 9, 272 pp, Quality PB, Illus., ISBN 1-879045-90-7 **$16.95**

The Passover Seder—The Art of Jewish Living
by Dr. Ron Wolfson 7 x 9, 352 pp, Quality PB, Illus., ISBN 1-879045-93-1 **$16.95**

Children's Spirituality

God Said Amen

For ages 4 & up

by *Sandy Eisenberg Sasso*
Full-color illus. by *Avi Katz*

A warm and inspiring tale of two kingdoms: one overflowing with water but without oil to light its lamps; the other blessed with oil but no water to grow its gardens. The kingdoms' rulers ask God for help but are too stubborn to ask each other. It takes a minstrel, a pair of royal riding-birds and their young keepers, and a simple act of kindness to show that they need only reach out to each other to find God's answer to their prayers.

9 x 12, 32 pp, HC, Full-color illus., ISBN 1-58023-080-6 **$16.95**

For Heaven's Sake

For ages 4 & up

by *Sandy Eisenberg Sasso*; Full-color illus. by *Kathryn Kunz Finney*

Everyone talked about heaven: "Thank heavens." "Heaven forbid." "For heaven's sake, Isaiah." But no one would say what heaven was or how to find it. So Isaiah decides to find out, by seeking answers from many different people.
9 x 12, 32 pp, HC, Full-color illus., ISBN 1-58023-054-7 **$16.95**

But God Remembered

For ages 8 & up

Stories of Women from Creation to the Promised Land

by *Sandy Eisenberg Sasso*; Full-color illus. by *Bethanne Andersen*

A fascinating collection of four different stories of women only briefly mentioned in biblical tradition and religious texts. Vibrantly brings to life courageous and strong women from ancient tradition; all teach important values through their actions and faith.
9 x 12, 32 pp, HC, Full-color illus., ISBN 1-879045-43-5 **$16.95**

God in Between

For ages 4 & up

by *Sandy Eisenberg Sasso*; Full-color illus. by *Sally Sweetland*

If you wanted to find God, where would you look? A magical, mythical tale that teaches that God can be found where we are: within all of us and the relationships between us.
9 x 12, 32 pp, HC, Full-color illus., ISBN 1-879045-86-9 **$16.95**

A Prayer for the Earth: The Story of Naamah, Noah's Wife

For ages 4 & up

by *Sandy Eisenberg Sasso*; Full-color illus. by *Bethanne Andersen*

This new story, based on an ancient text, opens readers' religious imaginations to new ideas about the well-known story of the Flood. When God tells Noah to bring the animals of the world onto the ark, God also calls on Naamah, Noah's wife, to save each plant on Earth.
9 x 12, 32 pp, HC, Full-color illus., ISBN 1-879045-60-5 **$16.95**

Children's Spirituality

In Our Image
God's First Creatures

For ages
4 & up

by *Nancy Sohn Swartz*

Full-color illus. by *Melanie Hall*

A playful new twist on the Creation story—from the perspective of the animals. Celebrates the interconnectedness of nature and the harmony of all living things. "The vibrantly colored illustrations nearly leap off the page in this delightful interpretation." —*School Library Journal*

9 x 12, 32 pp, HC, Full-color illus., ISBN 1-879045-99-0 **$16.95**

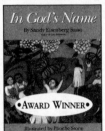

God's Paintbrush

For ages
4 & up

by *Sandy Eisenberg Sasso*; Full-color illus. by *Annette Compton*

Invites children of all faiths and backgrounds to encounter God openly in their own lives. Wonderfully interactive; provides questions adult and child can explore together at the end of each episode.

11 x 8½, 32 pp, HC, Full-color illus., ISBN 1-879045-22-2 **$16.95**

*Also available: **A Teacher's Guide:** A Guide for Jewish & Christian Educators and Parents*
8½ x 11, 32 pp, PB, ISBN 1-879045-57-5 **$8.95**

God's Paintbrush Celebration Kit 9½ x 12, HC, Includes 5 sessions/40 full-color Activity Sheets and Teacher Folder with complete instructions, ISBN 1-58023-050-4 **$21.95**

In God's Name

For ages
4 & up

by *Sandy Eisenberg Sasso*; Full-color illus. by *Phoebe Stone*

Like an ancient myth in its poetic text and vibrant illustrations, this award-winning modern fable about the search for God's name celebrates the diversity and, at the same time, the unity of all the people of the world.

9 x 12, 32 pp, HC, Full-color illus., ISBN 1-879045-26-5 **$16.95**

What Is God's Name? (A Board Book)

For ages
0–4

An abridged board book version of the award-winning *In God's Name*.

5 x 5, 24 pp, Board, Full-color illus., ISBN 1-893361-10-1 **$7.95** A SKYLIGHT PATHS Book

The 11th Commandment: Wisdom from Our Children

For
all ages

by *The Children of America*

"If there were an Eleventh Commandment, what would it be?" Children of many religious denominations across America answer this question—in their own drawings and words. "A rare book of spiritual celebration for all people, of all ages, for all time."—*Bookviews*
8 x 10, 48 pp, HC, Full-color illus., ISBN 1-879045-46-X **$16.95**

Children's Spirituality

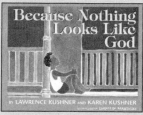

Because Nothing Looks Like God
by *Lawrence and Karen Kushner*
Full-color illus. by *Dawn W. Majewski*

For ages 4 & up

MULTICULTURAL, NONDENOMINATIONAL, NONSECTARIAN

What is God like? The first collaborative work by husband-and-wife team Lawrence and Karen Kushner introduces children to the possibilities of spiritual life. Real-life examples of happiness and sadness—from goodnight stories, to the hope and fear felt the first time at bat, to the closing moments of life—invite us to explore, together with our children, the questions we all have about God, no matter what our age.

11 x 8½, 32 pp, HC, Full-color illus., ISBN 1-58023-092-X **$16.95**

Where Is God?
What Does God Look Like?
How Does God Make Things Happen? (Board Books)

For ages 0–4

by *Lawrence and Karen Kushner*; Full-color illus. by *Dawn W. Majewski*

Gently invites children to become aware of God's presence all around them. Three board books abridged from *Because Nothing Looks Like God* by Lawrence and Karen Kushner.
Each 5 x 5, 24 pp, Board, Full-color illus. **$7.95** SKYLIGHT PATHS Books

Sharing Blessings

Children's Stories for Exploring the Spirit of the Jewish Holidays
by *Rahel Musleah* and *Rabbi Michael Klayman*
Full-color illus. by *Mary O'Keefe Young*

For ages 6 & up

What is the spiritual message of each of the Jewish holidays? How do we teach it to our children? Many books tell children about the historical significance and customs of the holidays. Through stories about one family's preparation, *Sharing Blessings* explores ways to get into the *spirit* of 13 different holidays.
8½ x 11, 64 pp, HC, Full-color illus., ISBN 1-879045-71-0 **$18.95**

The Book of Miracles

A Young Person's Guide to Jewish Spiritual Awareness
by *Lawrence Kushner*

For ages 9 & up

Introduces kids to a way of everyday spiritual thinking to last a lifetime. Kushner, whose award-winning books have brought spirituality to life for countless adults, now shows young people how to use Judaism as a foundation on which to build their lives.
6 x 9, 96 pp, HC, 2-color illus., ISBN 1-879045-78-8 **$16.95**

Life Cycle/Grief

Against the Dying of the Light
A Parent's Story of Love, Loss and Hope
by *Leonard Fein*

The sudden death of a child. A personal tragedy beyond description. Rage and despair deeper than sorrow. What can come from it? Raw wisdom and defiant hope. In this unusual exploration of heartbreak and healing, Fein chronicles the sudden death of his 30-year-old daughter and reveals what the progression of grief can teach each one of us.
5½ x 8½, 176 pp, HC, ISBN 1-58023-110-1 **$19.95**

Mourning & Mitzvah, 2nd Ed.: *A Guided Journal for Walking the Mourner's Path through Grief to Healing* with *Over 60 Guided Exercises*
by *Anne Brener, L.C.S.W.*

For those who mourn a death, for those who would help them, for those who face a loss of any kind, Brener teaches us the power and strength available to us in the fully experienced mourning process. Revised and expanded. 7½ x 9, 304 pp, Quality PB, ISBN 1-58023-113-6 **$19.95**

Grief in Our Seasons: *A Mourner's Kaddish Companion*
by *Rabbi Kerry M. Olitzky*

A wise and inspiring selection of sacred Jewish writings and a simple, powerful ancient ritual for mourners to read each day, to help hold the memory of their loved ones in their hearts. Offers a comforting, step-by-step daily link to saying Kaddish.
4½ x 6½, 448 pp, Quality PB, ISBN 1-879045-55-9 **$15.95**

Tears of Sorrow, Seeds of Hope
A Jewish Spiritual Companion for Infertility and Pregnancy Loss
by Rabbi Nina Beth Cardin   6 x 9, 192 pp, HC, ISBN 1-58023-017-2 **$19.95**

A Time to Mourn, A Time to Comfort
A Guide to Jewish Bereavement and Comfort
by Dr. Ron Wolfson   7 x 9, 336 pp, Quality PB, ISBN 1-879045-96-6 **$18.95**

When a Grandparent Dies
A Kid's Own Remembering Workbook for Dealing with Shiva and the Year Beyond
by Nechama Liss-Levinson, Ph.D.
8 x 10, 48 pp, HC, Illus., 2-color text, ISBN 1-879045-44-3 **$15.95**

Healing/Wellness/Recovery

Jewish Paths toward Healing and Wholeness
A Personal Guide to Dealing with Suffering
by *Rabbi Kerry M. Olitzky*; Foreword by *Debbie Friedman*

Why me? Why do we suffer? How can we heal? Grounded in personal experience with illness and Jewish spiritual traditions, this book provides healing rituals, psalms and prayers that help readers initiate a dialogue with God, to guide them along the complicated path of healing and wholeness. 6 x 9, 192 pp, Quality PB, ISBN 1-58023-068-7 **$15.95**

Healing of Soul, Healing of Body
Spiritual Leaders Unfold the Strength & Solace in Psalms
Ed. by *Rabbi Simkha Y. Weintraub*, CSW, for The National Center for Jewish Healing

A source of solace for those who are facing illness, as well as those who care for them. Provides a wellspring of strength with inspiring introductions and commentaries by eminent spiritual leaders reflecting all Jewish movements.
6 x 9, 128 pp, Quality PB, Illus., 2-color text, ISBN 1-879045-31-1 **$14.95**

Jewish Pastoral Care
A Practical Handbook from Traditional and Contemporary Sources
Ed. by *Rabbi Dayle A. Friedman*

Gives today's Jewish pastoral counselors practical guidelines based in the Jewish tradition.
6 x 9, 464 pp, HC, ISBN 1-58023-078-4 **$35.00**

Twelve Jewish Steps to Recovery: *A Personal Guide to Turning from Alcoholism &* *Other Addictions . . . Drugs, Food, Gambling, Sex . . .* by Rabbi Kerry M. Olitzky & Stuart A. Copans, M.D. Preface by Abraham J. Twerski, M.D.; Intro. by Rabbi Sheldon Zimmerman; "Getting Help" by JACS Foundation 6 x 9, 144 pp, Quality PB, ISBN 1-879045-09-5 **$13.95**

One Hundred Blessings Every Day: *Daily Twelve Step Recovery Affirmations,* *Exercises for Personal Growth & Renewal Reflecting Seasons of the Jewish Year* by Rabbi Kerry M. Olitzky 4½ x 6½, 432 pp, Quality PB, ISBN 1-879045-30-3 **$14.95**

Recovery from Codependence: *A Jewish Twelve Steps Guide to Healing Your Soul* by Rabbi Kerry M. Olitzky 6 x 9, 160 pp, Quality PB, ISBN 1-879045-32-X **$13.95**; HC, ISBN 1-879045-27-3 **$21.95**

Renewed Each Day: *Daily Twelve Step Recovery Meditations Based on the Bible* by Rabbi Kerry M. Olitzky & Aaron Z. Vol. I: *Genesis & Exodus*; Vol. II: *Leviticus, Numbers and Deuteronomy*
Vol. I: 6 x 9, 224 pp, Quality PB, ISBN 1-879045-12-5 **$14.95**
Vol. II: 6 x 9, 280 pp, Quality PB, ISBN 1-879045-13-3 **$14.95**

Spirituality—The Kushner Series
Books by Lawrence Kushner

The Way Into Jewish Mystical Tradition

Explains the principles of Jewish mystical thinking, their religious and spiritual significance, and how they relate to our lives. A book that allows us to experience and understand the Jewish mystical approach to our place in the world. 6 x 9, 224 pp, HC, ISBN 1-58023-029-6 **$21.95**

Eyes Remade for Wonder
The Way of Jewish Mysticism and Sacred Living

A Lawrence Kushner Reader Intro. by *Thomas Moore*

Whether you are new to Kushner or a devoted fan, you'll find inspiration here. With samplings from each of Kushner's works, and a generous amount of new material, this book is to be read and reread, each time discovering deeper layers of meaning in our lives.
6 x 9, 240 pp, Quality PB, ISBN 1-58023-042-3 **$16.95**; HC, ISBN 1-58023-014-8 **$23.95**

Because Nothing Looks Like God

by *Lawrence and Karen Kushner*; Full-color illus. by *Dawn W. Majewski*

What is God like? The first collaborative work by husband-and-wife team Lawrence and Karen Kushner introduces children to the possibilities of spiritual life with three poetic spiritual stories. Real-life examples of happiness and sadness—from goodnight stories, to the hope and fear felt the first time at bat, to the closing moments of life—invite us to explore, together with our children, the questions we all have about God, no matter what our age. **For ages 4 & up**
11 x 8½, 32 pp, HC, Full-color illus., ISBN 1-58023-092-X **$16.95**

Invisible Lines of Connection: *Sacred Stories of the Ordinary* AWARD WINNER!
6 x 9, 160 pp, Quality PB, ISBN 1-879045-98-2 **$15.95**; HC, ISBN 1-879045-52-4 **$21.95**

Honey from the Rock: *An Introduction to Jewish Mysticism* SPECIAL ANNIVERSARY EDITION
6 x 9, 176 pp, Quality PB, ISBN 1-58023-073-3 **$15.95**

The Book of Letters: *A Mystical Hebrew Alphabet* AWARD WINNER!
Popular HC Edition, 6 x 9, 80 pp, 2-color text, ISBN 1-879045-00-1 **$24.95**; *Deluxe Gift Edition,* 9 x 12, 80 pp, HC, 2-color text, ornamentation, slipcase, ISBN 1-879045-01-X **$79.95**; *Collector's Limited Edition,* 9 x 12, 80 pp, HC, gold-embossed pages, hand-assembled slipcase. With silkscreened print. Limited to 500 signed and numbered copies, ISBN 1-879045-04-4 **$349.00**

The Book of Words: *Talking Spiritual Life, Living Spiritual Talk* AWARD WINNER!
6 x 9, 160 pp, 2-color text, ISBN 1-58023-020-2 **$16.95**;
152 pp, HC, ISBN 1-879045-35-4 **$21.95**

God Was in This Place & I, i Did Not Know
Finding Self, Spirituality and Ultimate Meaning
6 x 9, 192 pp, Quality PB, ISBN 1-879045-33-8 **$16.95**

The River of Light: *Jewish Mystical Awareness* SPECIAL ANNIVERSARY EDITION
6 x 9, 192 pp, Quality PB, ISBN 1-58023-096-2 **$16.95**

Spirituality/Jewish Meditation

Discovering Jewish Meditation
Instruction & Guidance for Learning an Ancient Spiritual Practice
by *Nan Fink Gefen*

Gives readers of any level of understanding the tools to learn the practice of Jewish meditation on your own, starting you on the path to a deep spiritual and personal connection to God and to greater insight about your life. 6 x 9, 208 pp, Quality PB, ISBN 1-58023-067-9 **$16.95**

Entering the Temple of Dreams: *Jewish Prayers, Movements, and*
Meditations for the End of the Day by *Tamar Frankiel* and *Judy Greenfeld*

Nighttime spirituality is much more than bedtime prayers! Here, you'll uncover deeper meaning to familiar nighttime prayers—and learn to combine the prayers with movements and meditations to enhance your physical and psychological well-being.
7 x 10, 192 pp, Quality PB, Illus., ISBN 1-58023-079-2 **$16.95**

One God Clapping: *The Spiritual Path of a Zen Rabbi* AWARD WINNER!
by *Alan Lew* with *Sherril Jaffe*

A fascinating personal story of a Jewish meditation expert's roundabout spiritual journey from Zen Buddhist practitioner to rabbi. 5½ x 8½, 336 pp, Quality PB, ISBN 1-58023-115-2 **$16.95**

The Handbook of Jewish Meditation Practices
A Guide for Enriching the Sabbath and Other Days of Your Life
by *Rabbi David A. Cooper*

Gives us ancient and modern Jewish tools—Jewish practices and traditions, easy-to-use meditation exercises, and contemplative study of Jewish sacred texts.
6 x 9, 208 pp, Quality PB, ISBN 1-58023-102-0 **$16.95**

Stepping Stones to Jewish Spiritual Living: *Walking the Path Morning, Noon, and Night*
by Rabbi James L. Mirel & Karen Bonnell Werth
6 x 9, 240 pp, Quality PB, ISBN 1-58023-074-1 **$16.95**

Meditation from the Heart of Judaism
Today's Teachers Share Their Practices, Techniques, and Faith
Ed. by Avram Davis 6 x 9, 256 pp, Quality PB, ISBN 1-58023-049-0 **$16.95**;
HC, ISBN 1-879045-77-X **$21.95**

The Way of Flame: *A Guide to the Forgotten Mystical Tradition of Jewish Meditation*
by Avram Davis 4½ x 8, 176 pp, Quality PB, ISBN 1-58023-060-1 **$15.95**

Minding the Temple of the Soul: *Balancing Body, Mind, and Spirit*
through Traditional Jewish Prayer, Movement, and Meditation
by Tamar Frankiel and Judy Greenfeld 7 x 10, 184 pp, Quality PB, Illus.,
ISBN 1-879045-64-8 **$16.95**; Audiotape of the Blessings and Meditations (60-min. cassette), JN01
$9.95; Videotape of the Movements and Meditations (46-min.), S507 **$20.00**

Women's Spirituality / Ecology

Torah of the Earth: *Exploring 4,000 Years of Ecology in Jewish Thought*
In 2 Volumes Ed. by *Rabbi Arthur Waskow*

Major new resource offering us an invaluable key to understanding the intersection of ecology and Judaism. Leading scholars provide us with a guided tour of ecological thought from four major Jewish viewpoints.
Vol. 1: *Biblical Israel & Rabbinic Judaism,* 6 x 9, 272 pp, Quality PB, ISBN 1-58023-086-5 **$19.95**
Vol. 2: *Zionism & Eco-Judaism,* 6 x 9, 336 pp, Quality PB, ISBN 1-58023-087-3 **$19.95**

Ecology & the Jewish Spirit: *Where Nature & the Sacred Meet* Ed. and with Intros.
by Ellen Bernstein 6 x 9, 288 pp, Quality PB, ISBN 1-58023-082-2 **$16.95**;
HC, ISBN 1-879045-88-5 **$23.95**

The Jewish Gardening Cookbook: *Growing Plants & Cooking for Holidays & Festivals*
by Michael Brown 6 x 9, 224 pp, Illus., Quality PB, ISBN 1-58023-116-0 **$16.95**;
HC, ISBN 1-58023-004-0 **$21.95**

Moonbeams: *A Hadassah Rosh Hodesh Guide*
Ed. by *Carol Diament, Ph.D.*
This hands-on "idea book" focuses on *Rosh Hodesh,* the festival of the new moon, as a source of spiritual growth for Jewish women. A complete sourcebook that will initiate or rejuvenate women's study groups, it is also perfect for women preparing for *bat mitzvah*, or for anyone interested in learning more about *Rosh Hodesh* observance and what it has to offer. 8½ x 11, 240 pp, Quality PB, ISBN 1-58023-099-7 **$20.00**

The Women's Torah Commentary: *New Insights from Women Rabbis on the 54 Weekly Torah Portions* Ed. by *Rabbi Elyse Goldstein*
For the first time, women rabbis provide a commentary on the entire Five Books of Moses. More than 25 years after the first woman was ordained a rabbi in America, these inspiring teachers bring their rich perspectives to bear on the biblical text. In a week-by-week format; a perfect gift for others, or for yourself. 6 x 9, 496 pp, HC, ISBN 1-58023-076-8 **$34.95**

Lifecycles, in Two Volumes AWARD WINNERS!
V. 1: *Jewish Women on Life Passages & Personal Milestones*
Ed. and with Intros. by Rabbi Debra Orenstein
V. 2: *Jewish Women on Biblical Themes in Contemporary Life*
Ed. and with Intros. by Rabbi Debra Orenstein and Rabbi Jane Rachel Litman
V. 1: 6 x 9, 480 pp, Quality PB, ISBN 1-58023-018-0 **$19.95**; HC, ISBN 1-879045-14-1 **$24.95**
V. 2: 6 x 9, 464 pp, Quality PB, ISBN 1-58023-019-9 **$19.95**

ReVisions: *Seeing Torah through a Feminist Lens* AWARD WINNER!
by Rabbi Elyse Goldstein 5½ x 8½, 224 pp, Quality PB, ISBN 1-58023-117-9 **$16.95**;
208 pp, HC, ISBN 1-58023-047-4 **$19.95**

The Year Mom Got Religion: *One Woman's Midlife Journey into Judaism*
by Lee Meyerhoff Hendler 6 x 9, 208 pp, Quality PB, ISBN 1-58023-070-9 **$15.95**

Spirituality & More

The Jewish Lights Spirituality Handbook
A Guide to Understanding, Exploring & Living a Spiritual Life
Ed. by *Stuart M. Matlins, Editor-in-Chief, Jewish Lights Publishing*

Rich, creative material from over 50 spiritual leaders on every aspect of Jewish spirituality today: prayer, meditation, mysticism, study, rituals, special days, the everyday, and more.
6 x 9, 456 pp, Quality PB, ISBN 1-58023-093-8 **$18.95**; HC, ISBN 1-58023-100-4 **$24.95**

Six Jewish Spiritual Paths: *A Rationalist Looks at Spirituality*
by *Rabbi Rifat Sonsino*

The quest for spirituality is universal, but which path to spirituality is right *for you?* A straight-forward, objective discussion of the many ways—each valid and authentic—for seekers to gain a richer spiritual life within Judaism. 6 x 9, 208 pp, HC, ISBN 1-58023-095-4 **$21.95**

Criminal Kabbalah
An Intriguing Anthology of Jewish Mystery & Detective Fiction
Edited by *Lawrence W. Raphael*; Foreword by *Laurie R. King*

Twelve of today's best known mystery authors provide an intriguing collection of new stories sure to enlighten at the same time they entertain.
6 x 9, 256 pp, Quality PB, ISBN 1-58023-109-8 **$16.95**

Mystery Midrash: *An Anthology of Jewish Mystery & Detective Fiction* AWARD WINNER!
Ed. by Lawrence W. Raphael 6 x 9, 304 pp, Quality PB, ISBN 1-58023-055-5 **$16.95**

Sacred Intentions: *Daily Inspiration to Strengthen the Spirit, Based on Jewish Wisdom*
by Rabbi Kerry M. Olitzky & Rabbi Lori Forman
4½ x 6½, 448 pp, Quality PB, ISBN 1-58023-061-X **$15.95**

Restful Reflections: *Nighttime Inspiration to Calm the Soul, Based on Jewish Wisdom*
by Rabbi Kerry M. Olitzky & Rabbi Lori Forman
4½ x 6½, 448 pp, Quality PB, ISBN 1-58023-091-1 **$15.95**

The Enneagram and Kabbalah: *Reading Your Soul*
by Rabbi Howard A. Addison 6 x 9, 176 pp, Quality PB, ISBN 1-58023-001-6 **$15.95**

Embracing the Covenant: *Converts to Judaism Talk About Why & How*
Ed. and with Intros. by Rabbi Allan L. Berkowitz and Patti Moskovitz
6 x 9, 192 pp, Quality PB, ISBN 1-879045-50-8 **$16.95**

Wandering Stars: *An Anthology of Jewish Fantasy & Science Fiction* Ed. by Jack Dann;
Intro. by Isaac Asimov 6 x 9, 272 pp, Quality PB, ISBN 1-58023-005-9 **$16.95**

Israel—A Spiritual Travel Guide AWARD WINNER!
A Companion for the Modern Jewish Pilgrim
by Rabbi Lawrence A. Hoffman 4¾ x 10, 256 pp, Quality PB, ISBN 1-879045-56-7 **$18.95**

Spirituality

Does the Soul Survive?
A Jewish Journey to Belief in Afterlife, Past Lives & Living with Purpose
by *Rabbi Elie Kaplan Spitz*; Foreword by *Brian L. Weiss, M.D.*

Spitz relates his own experiences and those shared with him by people he has worked with as a rabbi, and shows us that belief in afterlife and past lives, so often approached with reluctance, is in fact true to Jewish tradition.

6 x 9, 288 pp, Quality PB, ISBN 1-58023-165-9 **$16.95**; HC, ISBN 1-58023-094-6 **$21.95**

The Women's Torah Commentary: *New Insights from Women Rabbis on the 54 Weekly Torah Portions* Ed. by *Rabbi Elyse Goldstein*

For the first time, women rabbis provide a commentary on the entire Torah. In a week-by-week format; a perfect gift for others, or for yourself.

6 x 9, 496 pp, HC, ISBN 1-58023-076-8 **$34.95**

The Gift of Kabbalah
Discovering the Secrets of Heaven, Renewing Your Life on Earth
by *Tamar Frankiel, Ph.D.*

Makes accessible the mysteries of Kabbalah. Traces Kabbalah's evolution in Judaism and shows us its most important gift: a way of revealing the connection between our "everyday" life and the spiritual oneness of the universe. 6 x 9, 256 pp, HC, ISBN 1-58023-108-X **$21.95**

Bringing the Psalms to Life: *How to Understand and Use the Book of Psalms*
by Rabbi Daniel F. Polish 6 x 9, 208 pp, Quality PB, ISBN 1-58023-157-8 **$16.95**;
HC, ISBN 1-58023-077-6 **$21.95**

The Empty Chair: *Finding Hope and Joy—*
Timeless Wisdom from a Hasidic Master, Rebbe Nachman of Breslov **AWARD WINNER!**
4 x 6, 128 pp, Deluxe PB, 2-color text, ISBN 1-879045-67-2 **$9.95**

The Gentle Weapon: *Prayers for Everyday and Not-So-Everyday Moments*
Adapted from the Wisdom of Rebbe Nachman of Breslov
4 x 6, 144 pp, Deluxe PB, 2-color text, ISBN 1-58023-022-9 **$9.95**

Ancient Secrets: *Using the Stories of the Bible to Improve Our Everyday Lives*
by Rabbi Levi Meier, Ph.D. 5½ x 8½, 288 pp, Quality PB, ISBN 1-58023-064-4 **$16.95**